Gregory Peck

By the same author

Gene Hackman

GREGORY PECK

MICHAEL MUNN

ROBERT HALE · LONDON

© Michael Munn 1998
First published in Great Britain 1998

ISBN 0 7090 6265 6

Robert Hale Limited
Clerkenwell House
Clerkenwell Green
London EC1R 0HT

2 4 6 8 10 9 7 5 3 1

Typeset in North Wales by
Derek Doyle & Associates, Mold, Flintshire.
Printed in Great Britain by
St Edmundsbury Press Limited, Bury St Edmunds.
Bound by WBC Book Manufacturers Limited, Bridgend.

This book is for Tina who's a huge fan of
Gregory Peck – and for Mervyn who's a
huge fan of Tina.

Contents

Illustrations

the filming of *Moby Dick* (1956)

14 In between takes on the Shepperton Studios set of *The Guns of Navarone* (1961) with director J. Lee Thompson

15 Anthony Quinn, Gregory Peck and Tony Quayle in *The Guns of Navarone* (1961)

16 Greg and Veronique go to the races with their close friends, the Nivens

17 In Martin Scorsese's 1991 remake of Peck's own 1962 production *Cape Fear*

18 Professional gambler Peck in a clinch with river boat singer Debbie Reynolds in the all-star Cinerama epic *How the West Was Won* (1962)

19 As the small-town lawyer defending a black man (played by Brock Peters) charged with rape in *To Kill a Mockingbird* (1962)

20 With Sophia Loren running from the bad guys in *Arabesque* (1966)

21 On the set of the western adventure *Mackenna's Gold* (1968) with producer Carl Foreman and director J. Lee Thompson

22 Peck with satanic screen son, Damien, in *The Omen* (1976)

23 Peck fulfilling his long-held wish to portray General Douglas MacArthur in *MacArthur* (1977)

24 Peck playing the evil, real-life Nazi, Dr Josef Mengele, in the fictitious *The Boys from Brazil* (1979)

25 Peck with Jane Fonda and Jimmy Smits in *Old Gringos* (1989)

Illustration Credits

British Film Institute: 1–6, 9–13, 16 & 17, 19–20, 22–25.

1
Life on the Beach

I FIRST MET GREGORY PECK in 1973 at EMI's Elstree Studios, where he was in the process of producing – but not acting in – *The Dove*. I was then a young Wardour Street press officer at Cinerama who was at the studio to meet Peter Cushing, but when I heard that Gregory Peck was in residence, I took the opportunity to ask him for some advice about the business we were in. He was, at that time of his phenomenal career, rather down on acting and wanted to concentrate only on producing films; he didn't think it was likely he would act again in the foreseeable future. I asked him why he wanted to be an actor in the first place, and he told me, very gently, very charmingly,

I didn't want to be an actor. I wanted to be a sailor. Or a boat maker. Then a doctor. Then a priest. Then a writer. Then the dice fell in a totally unexpected way and I became an actor. But when I was a young boy I never so much as thought about being an actor. I just liked to play in boats. And I hated my Christian name. It was Eldred – Eldred Gregory Peck. My mother wanted to give me a name that was out of the ordinary – and she did, thumbing through the telephone book. My middle name was from my father, who was the first Gregory Peck. So eventually I dropped 'Eldred' and called myself simply 'Gregory Peck', which made my father very proud. He was an Irishman who delighted in telling everyone he was also called Gregory Peck and that his son was the 'famous *film* star'. My father was known as 'Doc Peck' because he was a pharmacist. So I was Greg and he was Doc.

Two years later Peck had returned to acting, and on the set of *The*

Omen told me, 'I got rather bored not acting. Once acting is in your blood, it becomes your life.'

'Doc' Gregory Peck never was a real doctor, but he wanted to be one. So he became the next best thing – a pharmacist. He was set up in business in La Jolla, California, by his mother, Catherine Ashe, an immigrant from Ireland, who in 1880, at the age of 24 met and married Samuel Peck, and gave birth to their only son, Gregory. Shortly after, Samuel died from diphtheria, so Catherine returned to Ireland with eleven-month-old Gregory to raise him on the Ashe family farm. He was ten when Catherine decided to go back to America, and there he was educated at a Catholic school, while she became one of the original travelling saleswomen, going from state to state and city to city.

By the time Gregory graduated from the University of Michigan, she had saved a considerable amount of money and was living in comfortable retirement in San Diego. Down the coast was the southern Californian village of La Jolla, which, she discovered, had no drug store. So in 1910 she gave Gregory $10,000 to open one. He not only dispensed drugs but also treatment for minor ailments and the locals began calling him Doc Peck.

He was twenty-nine when he met and fell for twenty-year-old Bernice Ayres who had come up from St Louis, Missouri, to see her sister get married. Their whirlwind romance resulted in Bernice – or Bunny as everyone called her – staying on in La Jolla. But because Doc was a Catholic, there was to be no living in sin, so Bunny converted to Catholicism and married him back home in the St Louis Cathedral. Then they returned to La Jolla to live in a house they called the Dewdrop Inn, and two months later Bunny became pregnant.

Their son, Eldred Gregory Peck, was born on 5 April 1916. Much of his babyhood was spent on the sandy beach, and almost as soon as he was walking he was also paddling in the shallows of the Pacific and playing about in small boats. He began elementary education at the village's Little Red Schoolhouse.

'It was a small town where I came from,' Peck recalled, 'where we ran around in bare feet in the summertime and lived in trees half the time and rolled down the street curled up in an old rubber tire.' At weekends the local children gathered at the cove with their packed lunches. It seemed to be an idyllic childhood.

His father's drugstore was a favourite haunt.

> My father could perform some remarkable treatments – the best of which was being able to get rid of a drunken patient's black eye without the patient's wife ever knowing about it! He had a jar of leeches from which he would pull the hungriest specimen and attach it to the black eye. An enamel basin would rest on the patient's knee, into which the blood-filled leech would finally fall, leaving the patient's eye looking remarkably unblackened.

Greg was blissfully unaware of his father's financial troubles, caused partly because Doc tended to spend more than he could afford. He also had an accountant who was creaming off his profits. And he hated asking customers to repay the debts they tended to run up at the pharmacy, so when Bunny took it upon herself to go debt collecting, furious arguments broke out. The business and the marriage went from bad to worse until, finally, he had to give up the shop and move the family to San Diego, where he was employed as a druggist on the late shift. The marital rows, the loss of the business and the late hours he worked drove the marriage deeper into strife, and not long after the move from La Jolla, Doc and Bunny separated and thereafter divorced. Young Greg was just six.

He lived with his mother in St Louis in a rambling boarding house where Bunny went to work as a telephone operator. 'It was straight out of a Tennessee Williams play,' Peck recalled.

> There was the sound of jazz music on the phonograph, bootleg booze and most of the guests were waiters, travelling salesmen and store clerks. There were poker games in the dining room where I earned a nickel or two by selling my own lemonade which I made in the kitchen. The landlady, who had red hair, a finely developed bust and could have been Tallulah Bankhead, would spike the lemonade with the gin she made in her own bathtub.

Greg earned extra cash by shining the shoes of the poker players and selling newspapers where the trolley cars stopped. Bunny took Greg to the movies on Saturday afternoons; the first film he could remember seeing was *The Scarlet Letter*, starring Lilian Gish. He said, 'Movies had no great impact on my life at that time. They

13

were just a form of recreation, and I certainly enjoyed them, but I was just eight or nine then and had no real perception of what acting was all about.'

Greg's young life was uprooted yet again when his mother gave up her job and moved to Los Angeles to work as a telephone operator, sending Greg back to La Jolla to live with her mother, Kate Ayres, who had recently moved there from St Louis. Although downcast at being separated from his mother, Greg was delighted to be back in his home village, to be beside the sea once more, and especially to be in close proximity to his father again. Peck Senior still lived in San Diego, but he took every Thursday afternoon off and drove to La Jolla to be with Greg until bedtime. 'That was a wonderful thing for me, to be with my father on those Thursday afternoons,' Peck recalled. 'But I didn't see so much of my mother, who was over a hundred miles away in Los Angeles, although she did visit when she could. Sometimes she was able to stay over for a weekend, but for three years my grandmother was the one who raised me.'

Greg's constant companion was his black and brown mongrel, Bud. 'I swear that dog had a bit of Airedale and a bit of greyhound in him,' Peck recalled. 'The greyhound part was most important to me because he could run at thirty miles an hour, and I could boast to my pals that Bud could run as fast as my father's Nash car. And my father would let me prove it by taking me and my pals for a ride while Bud ran alongside.' His neighbours were less impressed by Bud, and they complained about his constant barking.

Doc spent all of his vacation time with him, often taking him off to Santa Catalina Island by steamship, living for a week in a tent, fishing, swimming and playing golf. During some of these vacations Bunny joined them for the weekend, and for a couple of days Greg could enjoy the company of both parents, who set aside their differences. When Greg came home from Santa Catalina, Bud was always waiting for him.

One day down in the cove Greg was surprised and delighted to find it had been taken over by a film company. Peck recalled,

The leading actor was Lew Cody, who specialized in playing playboys and wicked charmers. I remember watching from behind a rope with all the other kids, watching Lew Cody, dressed for yachting, sitting under an umbrella, smoking a cigarette from a long holder in a very sophisticated manner, and playfully picking up the skirt of one of several beautiful young women in swimsuits. These girls were, to this young, innocent boy, rather strange creatures with orange make-up and black eye-shadow – and I noticed that even Lew Cody had orange make-up on his face. It never occurred to me that I would one day wear make-up! And when I film in small towns, I remember that time, and now I *am* one of the strange creatures with orange paint on my face!

He built his first boat, a twelve-foot sailboat called *The Daisy*, when he was nine. His single-handed efforts left him with blistered hands, which he neglected to have treated as he wanted to launch his boat into the Pacific immediately. After just two days *The Daisy* sank and Greg had to swim to shore. The kindly local doctor treated him for exposure and blisters, and so taken was Greg with the doctor that he decided to abandon his dreams of a life at sea for a life of doctoring.

He did have one more attempt at boat-building, but this time in partnership with his friend Johnny Buchanan. They acquired an authentic blueprint for a boat which they proceeded to build at Grandmother Ayres' bungalow. They named it *The Tar Baby* and moored it on the beach. That night a sudden storm blew up and destroyed it.

In the summer of 1924 he returned from a holiday with his father and was dismayed when Bud, for the first time ever, wasn't there to greet him. Greg searched high and low but his beloved mongrel was nowhere to be found. Finally his father confessed that after an argument with disgruntled neighbours, he'd agreed that Bud could 'disappear' while they were on holiday.

Greg never found out if Bud was simply removed or done away with. But he did discover, he said, that grown-ups were not always honest and reliable. It was a bitter lesson to learn at this stage of his dysfunctional life, as he approached early adolescence. Fortunately he didn't go off the rails, but he did become increasingly introverted and shy. His boat-building career had been scuttled on the rocks, and his dreams of doctoring were shattered when he was sent to Los Angeles to attend St John's Military Academy.

His parents had discussed his future upbringing and education and had decided that St John's Military School was the solution. It didn't have any actual connection with the army, but it was run with military precision, its purpose being to give its students strict discipline in order to instil decency, maturity and Catholic doctrine. The three-storey building on Washington Boulevard reeked of wax polish, a smell that stayed with Peck for years.

He liked the blue grey uniform he was given, but it was a tough place for any ten-year-old boy. His spiritual teaching was in the hands of Father Timothy Crowley, from the convent adjoining the school. Greg liked him because he was Irish and reminded him of his father. He enjoyed the spiritual side of school and took readily to his job as an altar boy. By the age of twelve he could recite the two-hour Latin Mass in its entirety, and he gave up the idea of doctoring for the priesthood. He was given a small, cheap crucifix, which became a talisman he took with him everywhere – and still does.

'It was at St John's Military School where my Catholicism was installed for life,' he said, 'although some of what I was taught was rather narrow. I couldn't see the point of having to polish our boots like madmen for twenty minutes each and every evening, then our brass buttons and belt buckles until we could see our faces in them. It was more like West Point than high school.'

He was allowed the whole last weekend of the month away, so on those Friday evenings he caught the Sante Fe train from Los Angeles and was met at the San Diego depot by his father, with whom he spent most of the weekend. But he always made the effort to go to La Jolla to be with Grandmother Ayres, who was now suffering from stomach cancer. His weekends away would end on Sunday at twelve noon, when he'd catch the train to Los Angeles and be back at St John's by six p.m. for inspection.

Each time he visited his grandmother he saw how she was fading away. When she became bedridden he sat and read to her. As months past, she became increasingly racked by pain. Though only in her fifties, her illness aged her. He was aware that when he visited, she made every attempt to hide her pain, but when he was outside of her room he could hear her cry in agony.

'Seeing my grandmother dying was my first experience of cancer,' he told me. 'The feelings I had of helplessness never left me and I suppose in some subconscious way it made me feel that at some time in the future I would do all I could to try to find a way to beat the disease that took the grandmother who had raised me.'

He was away at school when she died.

By the time he turned thirteen, Greg was tall, slim and athletic. He was promoted to Cadet Captain Peck and was given the responsibility of whipping sixty of the youngest students, aged from eight to ten, into shape. 'I shouted at them like Erich von Stroheim,' he recalled. 'God knows what I did to the psyches of those poor little kids. But having put the fear of God, the Pope and the school chaplain into them, we won the gold medal for drill.'

He loved reading everything from Zane Grey to Walter Scott, and as the editor of the school's monthly newspaper, *The Bugle Call*, he developed a keen writing skill. He also developed a competitiveness that went with him when he graduated from St John's at the age of fourteen and started San Diego High School. There he rediscovered his ambition to become a doctor.

He lived with his father, who still worked the night shift, and most days they had breakfast and evening dinner together. Much of Greg's spare time was spent at an athletic club, but his happiest days were during the summer holidays when his father would take him camping to Yosemite or Yellowstone Park in California. He saw little of his mother, who had married an Italian salesman, Joseph Maysuch – he had Americanized his surname from Masucci – and travelled the country with him.

At the age of fifteen, he was awkward and shy in the company of girls; he'd hardly ever known any. He had become something of a loner, getting used to being on his own – even at Christmas.

On the morning of 25 December 1931, Doc Peck came home from his night shift and he and his son had breakfast together and exchanged Christmas gifts. Then, exhausted, Doc fell into bed. Greg went out for a walk and made his way into the deserted city centre of San Diego. He went to the athletic club and found it eerily quiet. He felt completely alone. He took himself to see a movie, then went home in time for his father to wake up and take him for Christmas dinner at a local café. That day remained one of the bleakest of his teenage days.

By the age of sixteen, he stood 6 feet 2 inches. He renewed his love of boats when he joined the San Diego Rowing Club, and in an attempt to help him overcome his shyness with girls he took dancing lessons. He summoned up the courage to ask a girl on whom he had a crush to the school prom. She went with him, but the fact she had twelve brothers discouraged him from asking her on a second date.

When he turned eighteen he decided it was time to discover what else life had to offer, find some fun that had been lacking, and simply assert himself. He announced to his father that he was leaving full-time education to get a job. Doc tried to persuade him to go on to higher education and become a doctor, but nothing he could say changed Greg's mind.

He found himself a job as night-watchman at the Union Oil Company, where the manager was so impressed with his ability to learn quickly that he promoted Greg to driving red Union lorries, which carried 5,000 gallons of oil. It was a highly responsible job, which involved loading the barrels of highly flammable oil himself, packing them safely and then unloading them at the destination. With his salary he was able to buy his first car, a Model 'A' Ford with wire wheels, a white canvas top and a rumble seat.

He had two good friends, the Moore brothers, who came complete with a pretty sister called Kathie. The Moore brothers gave him their wholehearted backing when he found the courage to ask her to a dance. Like him, she was an Irish American, but unlike him, she came from a close-knit family. Before long he had become integrated into her family, eating supper with them most evenings and generally making himself at home. The Moores were not surprised when Greg drove his Union lorry up to their house in the daytime and stopped off for a snack. The once shy, awkward teenager had turned into a self-assured, intelligent, handsome and exceptionally amiable young man.

Doc Peck was also spreading his romantic wings and had a ladyfriend of his own, Harriet, a very conservative Protestant from Denver, Colorado. She and Greg clashed; he thought she was too 'straight-laced', and she found it difficult to communicate with him. Doc wanted to marry her, but she was simply overwhelmed at the prospect of suddenly acquiring a tall, confident and hostile teenage stepson, and so the marriage was put on hold.

At weekends Greg and Kathie drove off to the beach for picnics, met with friends to play touch football and just hung out in typical teenage fashion. But he was becoming restless, wondering whether he actually wanted to spend his whole life working for the Union

Oil Company and living in San Diego. He made up his mind to aim once more for a medical career and applied to go to University of California at Berkeley. To qualify, he needed to spend a year attending the San Diego State College to study mathematics, literature, history and science. Most evenings he was at Kathie's house, where she helped him study. He ended his year at college with top grades that gained him a place at Berkeley.

Just before he started at university, Doc Peck married Harriet. Relations between stepmother and stepson were still strained, and the situation was not helped when Harriet's mother, who was even more straight-laced than Harriet, came to live with them. Greg was escaping to Berkeley just at the right time.

He started university full of enthusiasm, even though he had to leave Kathie behind. Before long, he was dating other girls. And he got to see more of his mother, who now lived in nearby San Francisco with husband Joseph. Both Bunny and Doc sent him a little money to contribute to his rent, but to make up the rest he took on the job as janitor in the block where he lived with two roommates. He also waited on tables and washed dishes at the student café for an hour each day, which was repaid in as much food as he could eat.

He became a member of the university's rowing team, and would row between twelve and sixteen miles a day. He recalled that after one particularly gruelling session he went straight to his job at the student café and ate three steaks, a pile of mashed potatoes, three pieces of pie and a quart of milk. He quickly earned the right to wear a gold 'C' on his sweater on campus – a symbol of his excellence in rowing.

He hated physics and was floundering in his courses after a year, but as he developed an interest in literature, he switched his major from medicine to English, having decided now to become a writer. He was also expressing his political convictions, leaning to the liberal Left. There was much talk about the civil war raging in Spain, and driven by dreams of adventure and political expression he decided to join the Abraham Lincoln Division of the International Brigade, which was fighting on the side of government troops. But first he had to finish university.

2

Broadway

THE UNIVERSITY HAD its own theatre, although the Wheeler Auditorium was not so much a real theatre as a lecture hall that seated 1,200 people. Greg thoroughly enjoyed lectures and spent many hours there, but the idea of being in one of the plays put on by Edwin Duerr, the theatre's director, never even occurred to him until the day Duerr caught up with him as he was walking across campus.

Duerr was in the process of staging Melville's *Moby Dick* and asked him if he would like to get involved in the next production. 'Why ask me?' asked Greg who'd never acted before and certainly had no idea whether or not he could even do it.

Duerr told him, 'Because all my actors are short and I need someone tall to play Starbuck.'

Greg decided to do it on a whim, but when he appeared on stage with as many as a thousand eyes upon him, he began to regret his decision. 'My acting debut was not a smash,' he recalled. 'I simply was not very good. I seriously thought of burrowing a hole in the floor backstage and digging my way to Mexico. But I didn't give up. I did more plays, and there were moments for me on the stage when I felt the power of acting, when I felt the audience watching only *me*, listening only to *me*. I think that had to be the reason I enjoyed being an altar boy so much.'

He quickly grew to enjoy acting but was slow to rid himself of the nerves that dogged him during his first few plays. A rehearsal of *Rain from Heaven* was interrupted by a clattering sound. The director demanded to know what was causing the noise, and Greg owned up. 'I'm afraid it's me. It's this tea cup and saucer I have to

21

hold. I can't stop shaking.' The director solved the problem by taping the cup and saucer together.

Greg knew he was not a particularly bad actor because he was asked to do more, but Kenneth Tobey, one of the campus's most popular actors, was heard to say after watching Greg in a Greek tragedy, 'I don't know why we have to watch people who don't know how to speak or act. I refer, of course, to Mr. Peck.'

Greg persevered and felt that with each successive play he got better. But sometimes the learning process was confusing. Playing an Irish sailor in Eugene O'Neill's *Anna Christie*, he was required to deliver a line of dialogue which was preceded by the stage direction, '*Turning purple with rage*'. He practised his rage alone in his room and discovered a way of turning purple by closing his mouth and blowing.

During rehearsal he turned upstage and turned purple, at which point the director yelled, 'What the hell do you think you're doing, Peck? How can you turn your back on the audience in this big scene?'

Greg explained, 'The stage directions say "turning purple with rage".'

'Forget the stage directions,' the director told him. 'Just do it the way you think it should be done. Pay no attention to stage directions.'

A San Francisco critic praised *Anna Christie* as being 'all well and good,' noting that the actress who played Anna and the actor who played the captain were fine, 'but Eldred Peck's overacting dangerously marred the production.'

Not all in the audience for *Anna Christie* felt the same way. Professional actor George Marion, who had played Anna's father in the original 1922 New York production, was there, and after the final curtain fell, he went backstage to meet Peck and encouraged him to head for New York and set his sights on Broadway.

Greg felt that, while he still had much to learn, some aspects of his acting were right. 'It had to be,' he said, 'because they kept asking me to do more plays.'

His mother and stepfather always came to watch him, and Bunny clearly saw how dramatically he had evolved from a shy, awkward adolescent to a self-assured and assertive young man. And, of course, she thought he was a marvellous actor.

In 1938 the University boat crew, including Peck, was invited to take part in the Poughkeepsie Regatta in New York. They won all their races, and after it was all over, Greg and a few friends decided to stay on in New York, selling their train tickets so they could afford beds at the YMCA. Peck was mesmerized by the big city, visiting the Brooklyn Bridge, listening to jazz in the Harlem clubs and seeing his first Broadway play, *I Married an Angel* (by playwright, Vaszary Janos), at the Sam S. Shubert Theater. That was the moment he made up his mind once and for all to become an actor. He and his friends made the long return trip by bus with only bananas to eat.

By the time he gained his degree at Berkeley, the Spanish Civil War was over, and besides, he had a new goal in life. In 1939, at the age of twenty-three, he told his parents that he was going to New York to be an actor. His father warned him that he would find himself among people he wouldn't know, that he would be ridiculed and that he would be broke at the age of thirty-five and having to borrow money to live on. 'Don't do it!' Doc begged.

Greg replied bluntly, 'I will do it.'

Bunny and Joseph were more encouraging and told him, 'You can do it if you really want to.'

He left in early summer of 1939 to become an actor. He arrived in New York with a letter written by his stepfather introducing him to a business colleague who ran one of the thrilling rides at the New York World's Fair. Peck was given the job of a 'barker', at $25 a week, persuading fairgoers to take the Auto Ride, a small bus with a powerful engine that roared around the walls of a giant bowl. Peck recalled:

> It was an easy script. Something like, 'Step this way, folks, to the Auto Ride. For just half a dollar you can speed like a bullet around the rim of a giant bowl, defying the laws of gravity. Step this way, folks! Step this way!' And I did that for half an hour at a time, alternating with another fellow. We did some eight hours a day each. It was a painful but excellent voice exercise. When I started I had, you could say, a rather high voice, but a month later, crying 'Step this way, folks' for eight hours a day above the din of the crowd, I had developed what I like to think are rather mellow tones! But I became concerned I would end up damaging my vocal cords, so I had to seek employment elsewhere.

After four weeks of 'barking', Peck got a job as a tour guide at Radio City in Rockefeller Center. The average weekly wage was $40, but he earned more if he could fit in extra tours, so some weeks he managed to make as much as $54. It was easier on his voice but murder on his feet, which hurt from so much standing and walking. He was acutely aware that any damage to his body could affect his hopes of treading the boards.

His arches were saved when he passed an audition for a two-year scholarship to the Neighborhood Playhouse School of Dramatics, one of the city's most noted drama schools. His tuition was free, but he still needed money to buy food and rent lodging, so he did modelling jobs that ranged from posing in top hat and tails to promote Palmolive soap, to climbing a telephone pole for the New Jersey Lighting Corporation.

When there was no work and no money to pay his rent, he simply moved out, put his luggage in a locker at Grand Central Station and slept in Central Park. When further modelling jobs came his way, he was able to rent another room, usually without a bath or a shower and with only running cold water.

Another Berkeley graduate, Kenneth Tobey, once one of Peck's most vehement critics, had arrived in New York to study at the Neighborhood Playhouse. But Greg held no grudge and, since they found themselves in generally the same financial predicament, they became firm friends, sharing both good and bad times. With Tobey's equally broke roommate, they pooled their funds for food. One time they had between them a mere eleven cents, with which they purchased milk, flour and eggs, and proceeded to make piles of pancakes to see them through the next few days.

During this time of co-operative poverty Gregory Peck moved further to the left and considered that Communism could be the means to solving global poverty, and the roommates attended Communist rallies in Madison Square. 'I moved about as far Left as you can go without becoming a Communist,' recalled Peck.

I never had a card, but I read the Communist newspaper, *New Masses*, which many thought was as good as having a card. I was certainly in sympathy with a lot they had to say, but I was saved by my ambition to be an actor, which meant I didn't have time to help create a better society. I was obviously naive then, and when they had the McCarthy witch hunt in the 1950s, I could think *there but for the grace of God*. But that was the time, when I was in New York, that I first got interested in politics.

He described himself as a liberal Democrat, but despite his rejection of Communism, his liberal views would eventually land him in trouble.

During one of the Neighborhood Playhouse dance classes, he had trouble with a particularly difficult stretching exercise and was assisted by his dance coach, Martha Graham, who pushed her knee into his back, allowing him to reach further back. He felt something pop in his back and carried on exercising in some pain.

The following morning he was in such agony he couldn't move. A doctor's examination revealed that he had a slipped disc. The next several weeks were spent undergoing various forms of therapy and treatment by osteopaths and other spinal specialists until he was back on his feet. But he was never able to reach his previous peak of physical fitness.

During the summer recess of 1940, Peck was one of the small handful of actors from the Neighborhood Playhouse selected to work through the season at the Barter Theater, owned and run by Robert Porterfield in Abingdon, Virginia. This was a prestigious honour for any drama student, but his excitement was quickly dampened when he was told his first job would be to drive the theatre lorry, loaded with the sets, props and lighting equipment for a comedy called *Button, Button*, to a school hall in Big Stone Gap, Virginia.

However, just a day before setting off, he was told that the leading actor had fallen ill and, with a script thrust into his hands, he was told to do the part. He had only twenty-four hours to learn the whole play. And there was no time for rehearsal. He still had to drive the truck, and on the way down he did his best to remember the lines he had tried to commit to memory. By the time the play was ready to start he had only managed to learn a portion of the play, and as he prepared to make his first entrance, he forgot every line but his first, which was, 'Hello, Mollie, I hope your hot biscuits are as good as they used to be.' He was overwhelmed by a serious bout of stage fright.

Luckily for him, Kenneth Tobey was on hand, and he told Greg he would sit in the wings and feed him the lines. Peck stepped on to the stage, delivered his first line, took one of Mollie's biscuits, and slowly munching, he ambled over to the wings where Tobey whispered the second line. The entire play seemed to feature Greg constantly on the move as time and again he walked towards the wings, trying to catch the lines that Tobey whispered as loud as he dare. Peck recalled, 'It wasn't a complete disaster. I got the second and third acts mixed up, and gave the wrong cues to the other actors, but we got through to the end and the audience hadn't noticed the difference.'

Unable to afford to buy food, Peck took advantage of the supply of cottage cheese and spinach made available by the theater. Already thin, he began to lose weight. He didn't think much of the second play he was in, *On Earth As It Is*, but he enjoyed *Family Portrait*, a modern version of the Mary and Jesus story set in Virginia. Then, to close the eight-week season, he assumed the title role in Christopher Marlowe's *Edward II*. By then the lack of decent food had left him considerably run-down and wan, but his part was a firm success.

When it came time to return to New York, Peck, Tobey, a young lady and another young actor climbed into a lorry for the long trip. They stopped off in Washington DC and decided to join the long queue leading to the chamber of the Senate, where the question of whether America should aid Britain in World War II was being debated inside. The young actors queued for four hours and were very near the front when nature called Greg to the men's room. When he returned to his place, a burly policeman tapped him on the shoulder and said, 'Back of the line, buddy.'

'But I've been here for four hours,' Peck protested. 'I only went to the rest room.'

'I said *get to the back of the line*!'

'That's not fair,' said Peck. 'My friends here held my place.'

Peck next felt the policeman's truncheon poking him in the chest as the officer growled, 'Get out of here!'

Peck then displayed what was one of his rare but quite explosive bursts of temper, shoving the policeman hard. The officer blew his whistle and in moments Peck was grabbed by six other policemen who proceeded to frogmarch him away. Tobey and the others loudly protested Greg's innocence, and they were all arrested and thrown into a cell beneath the Capitol.

They spent two hours behind bars before the police chief came to question them. He asked if they were there to agitate in the gallery. Peck told him, 'We've never been here before and we just wanted to see what was going on.' The police chief told them he'd let them all go if they basically 'got out of town'. They accepted the terms of release.

Greg began his second term that autumn at the Neighborhood Playhouse, and was spotted by Kay Brown, the eastern representative of David O. Selznick, then one of the most powerful independent Hollywood producers with his own studio. Brown thought he saw in Peck potential as a film actor, and she arranged his first screen test. He had to perform a scene from *This Above All* (which was filmed a year later with Tyrone Power). Then he acted in a short scene from *The Young in Heart*, which Douglas Fairbanks Jnr had made the year before.

Selznick failed to see the same qualities in Peck that Miss Brown had observed. In a memo to her, he said, 'I am sorry to have to say that I don't see what we could do with Gregory Peck. He photographs like Abe Lincoln, but if he has a great personality, I don't think it comes through in these tests.' Peck's first screen test was a flop, and he went back to his drama training.

In the spring of 1941 the New York theatre establishment was invited to see the Neighborhood Playhouse's final exercise for its graduating students. Broadway producer Guthrie McClintic came looking for a new, young actor for a tour production of George Bernard Shaw's *The Doctor's Dilemma*, which starred McClintic's wife, the fabulous Katharine Cornell. It had played successfully on Broadway at the Sam S. Shubert Theater, but one of the supporting actors, David Orrick, was unable – or unwilling, with just eight lines – to go on tour in September.

McClintic saw Gregory Peck on stage and was impressed. One source has it that McClintic saw him in a Russian play, *The Chief Thing*, another says Peck was simply reading both the prologue and epilogue from *Promenade*. Whatever the actual performance, McClintic thought he was perfect. Peck remembers the time:

> The next day, I happened to be hanging around the school reception when a call came through for the school director from Guthrie McClintic, and the receptionist, who managed to catch some of the conversation, said to me, 'They're discussing you, Greg. He wants

you for a part.' Well, I didn't need to hear anymore. I didn't even wait for the Playhouse director to call me in. I knew McClintic's office was in the RKO building and I just took off. I leapt down four flights of stairs, ran half a block across 46th Street to Sixth Avenue, ran four blocks up to 50th Street, charged into the RKO building, into the elevator, up to the eighth floor, and strode right into his office and stood before his desk. He was still on the phone to the director. And when he saw me he said into the phone, 'My God, he's here,' then he dropped the phone and told me, 'You've got yourself a job.'

There was still the rest of summer to go before Peck could join Katherine Cornell on tour, but the news of his casting was enough to get him a part in the comedy *Rebound* at the Cape Playhouse, Cape Cod, opposite Ruth Chatterton, the great actress who had just retired from the screen to resume her stage career. Peck credited the director, Arthur Sircom, as one of those who were of invaluable help to him in learning the craft of acting. One Boston critic who came to see him play the young man who woos the older woman wrote, 'There is a young actor called Gregory Peck playing with Miss Chatterton who strikes us as the complete actor. Inside and out he gives an electrifying performance.'

After *Rebound*, Peck was relegated to a supporting part opposite the Viennese light opera star Fritzi Scheff in Somerset Maugham's *The Circle*. He was also the call boy on that production, and as such he knocked on Miss Scheff's dressing-room door on the opening night and said, 'Half an hour please.' There was no reply. He knew she was in there because he had seen her enter with her manager. After she failed to materialize close to curtain up, he explained the predicament to the stage manager, who told him to try again. Peck gave her door an exceptionally loud rap and shouted, 'Curtain going up, Miss Scheff.'

Miss Scheff opened the door and bluntly told him, 'Young man, I'll tell *you* when the curtain's going up.'

The summer over, Greg made his first appearance opposite Katherine Cornell in *The Doctor's Dilemma* on 22 September 1941 at the Walnut Street Theater in Philadelphia. The date also happened to be the twenty-fifth wedding anniversary of Miss Cornell and Guthrie McClintic, so many Broadway stars attended to help celebrate. Peck noted how their presence in the audience made Miss Cornell nervous, and she calmed herself by drinking champagne. The curtain went up and all went well until the fifth act when she suddenly dried. Greg, standing right next to her, whispered her line in her ear, and the play continued without further problem. After the curtain went down, she said, 'Gregory, you saved my life. I didn't have a clue what I was supposed to say.' She told the Lunts and Helen Hayes about how Peck saved her from disaster on the stage, and McClintic was so impressed he saw to it that Greg had a permanent job with his company.

During the play's tour Greg became attracted to Greta Rice, a pretty young Finnish divorcee who was Miss Cornell's hairdresser. Her real name had been Greta Kukkonen, but her parents changed the family name to Konen when they came to America. Greta had wed an American called Charles Rice, but it had been a short-lived marriage. She and Greg were the youngest members of the company and were naturally thrown together in their free time during their four months on the road. She was a fun-loving girl, and Greg found her sense of humour infectious.

The tour ended when the very final curtain came down at the Curan Theater, San Francisco, in December. Greg's mother and stepfather attended, as did the local newspapers, which boasted that Gregory Peck had been a student at Berkeley.

San Francisco became the company's base for a while, and Katharine Cornell rehearsed her next play, *Rose Burke*, there. Although he had no role in the play, Peck was assistant stage manager and understudy to not one but two of the male leads, one of whom was Jean-Pierre Aumont, the 33-year-old French film star. Peck was twenty-five and certainly not French, and he dreaded the thought that he might have to go on should Aumont become indisposed. Nevertheless, Peck got to rehearse both parts, which kept his acting muscles toned, and he was also still in close proximity to Greta, who stayed on to do Miss Cornell's hair each night.

During one performance in Detroit in early 1942, Peck knocked on Aumont's dressing-room door, and when the star failed to respond to his call, Greg discovered the room was empty. It was 8.10 and there were only twenty minutes to go to curtain-up. He panicked and ran out of the theatre, racing through a blizzard to the hotel where the actors were staying. There he roused Aumont from a deep sleep. With just ten minutes to go, Peck dressed him and virtually dragged him through the snow to the theatre, packed

him into his costume, and breathed a heavy sigh of relief as
Aumont went on stage at exactly 8.30.

In the spring of 1942 Greg was the company's male juvenile lead in
McClintic's next play, *Punch and Julia*, a comedy featuring Jane
Cowl, who had been a triumph on Broadway in *Romeo and Juliet*.
The ingenue was Fran Heflin, young sister of Van Heflin, and the
leading man was Arthur Margetson. It opened in Cape Cod
Playhouse in Dennis, Massachusetts, to disastrous reviews and a
less-than-enthusiastic audience response. As the company moved
on to Wilmington in Washington DC and then Baltimore,
Maryland, the play flagged. When Arthur Margetson saw that little
more than twenty people sat in the 1,600-seat auditorium in
Baltimore, he said, 'I am not going on.'

Jane Cowl told him in no uncertain terms, 'Arthur, we are going
to give them the show of their lives.' They certainly went on, but
nothing the cast injected into it could make the two score people
laugh or applaud.

With America now at war, Greg received his call-up papers and
went for his medical examination, but was rejected for service
because of the back injury he had sustained at the Neighborhood
Playhouse. With mixed feelings about his exemption, he began
rehearsing the role of a dance-school owner in the hit comedy *You
Can't Take It With You*. He was a huge success and he made up his
mind that he would concentrate on comedy acting. When he next
did the restoration comedy *The Duenna*, in which he had to dance,
he felt sure that comedy would be his forte.

One day McClintic called him and told him to come to his
house on Martha's Vineyard to discuss a new play. Greg didn't
replicate the urgency of his first visit to Guthrie's office, but he
nevertheless wasted no time in heading for Martha's Vineyard,
where McClintic handed him a copy of *The Morning Star* by British
playwright Emlyn Williams. McClintic was going to direct the play
on Broadway and he wanted Greg to play the male lead opposite
Jill Esmond, former wife of Laurence Olivier and mother of
Tarquin Olivier. The role didn't fit into Peck's plan of establishing
himself as a comedy actor, but he could not turn down such an
exciting proposition.

He rented an apartment on East 39th Street for $14 a week, not
knowing how long he would be living there: the success of *The*

Morning Star would dictate that. He knew he'd be there for at least three weeks while rehearsals proceeded under McClintic's own unique style of directing. Peck recalled, 'McClintic was a taskmaster who used to listen to rehearsals from the rear of the balcony and wouldn't let an actor finish a sentence if he couldn't hear every syllable of every word. "Can't understand it! Do it again! They pay to sit up here, too!" McClintic would shout down to his actors on stage.'

The play met with a mixed critical response when it opened at the Morosco Theater, but Peck received good personal notices. During its run, an enterprising press agent decided it would be a good idea to have the Broadway's new acting sensation pose for a photograph with the new singing sensation, Frank Sinatra. Miller took Peck to the nearby Riobama where Sinatra was appearing; Peck remembered listening to Sinatra sing 'That Old Black Magic'. They didn't hit it off immediately, but years later they would enjoy a close friendship.

Audiences for *The Morning Star* were sparse, and the play folded after just twenty-four performances. Despite its commercial failure, Peck was put on the books of a leading agent, Leland Hayward, whose company dealt with many of the big stars of Broadway and Hollywood. Hayward was married to actress Margaret Sullivan, who hated agents and was continually trying to persuade him to change his profession. But he was exceptional at his job and had a reputation for being able to charm the most powerful studio heads around to his way of thinking.

He didn't deal directly with Peck, leaving the career of the rising star in the hands of one of his associates. Greg got the lead in a Broadway play, *The Willow and I*, with his name up in lights and a salary of $250 a week. Once more he received good personal notices while the critical fraternity was largely unimpressed by the play itself.

In October 1942 Peck asked Greta to marry him, and she agreed. He had missed the stability of family life, even though his own had hardly been stable by conventional standards, but he nevertheless craved the sense of belonging. He wanted what passed for a sense of normality, and he felt marriage to Greta would bring him just that. His method of inviting his friends to the wedding was certainly not conventional; he simply called several of them and said that he had tickets for them all to see the Yankees

in a World Series game one Saturday afternoon. He then added
that he had also acquired a marriage licence, which would be put
to use after the game.

Greg, Greta and their friends stopped at the Lutheran Church
on Fifth Avenue on their way back from the Yankee Stadium, and
there the marriage vows were exchanged in a simple ceremony.
Greta returned with Greg to his $14-a-week apartment to begin
their new life. Before long they vacated their modest dwelling and
moved into a lavish $200-a-month apartment on Lexington
Avenue.

Greg could have done with a good long run to help pay for their
new home and clear some small debts he'd managed to run up,
but *The Willow and I* closed after twenty-eight performances.

3

Hollywood

GREGORY PECK'S BROADWAY reputation had reached the West Coast, where another of the great independent studio-owning producers, Samuel Goldwyn, decided he had to have Peck under contract, even though he had never seen him perform. The fact was, many of Hollywood's biggest stars were signing up to serve in the forces and Hollywood found itself short of leading men. New stars were being actively sought to replace the likes of Clark Gable, Tyrone Power and James Stewart, who were donning uniforms and, in some cases, putting their lives on the line. Peck's exemption from military service as well as his Broadway career made him an ideal prospect for film stardom.

Goldwyn phoned Leland Hayward and asked, 'How much do you want for Gregory Peck? I'm willing to pay him a thousand dollars a week.'

Leland, who was not actually sure Peck was on his books, replied, 'Make it $3,000.' Goldwyn agreed, and after hanging up the phone, Hayward turned to an associate and said, 'Do we have Gregory Peck?'

When he learned they did, he called Peck and said he was taking him to Hollywood. It was a three-day journey by train to California, and it would be reasonable to assume Peck was eager to accept a lucrative movie contract after going all that way and with financial troubles piling up back on the East Coast. But when Goldwyn said he wanted Peck to sign an exclusive seven-year contract, Greg told him he wanted a contract that allowed him to work for other studios and allowed him to do plays in New York. Goldwyn told him that was out of the question, and the meeting ended.

When Louis B. Mayer, head of Metro-Goldwyn-Mayer, the biggest of the Hollywood studios, heard that the new Broadway star was in town and being wooed by Goldwyn, he invited Peck to his office at the Culver Studios. Mayer also insisted that Peck sign a seven-year exclusive contract, and Peck made his position clear to him, as he had to Goldwyn. Peck recalled,

> This did not particularly appeal to Mayer. But signing to a long term contract would have meant I belonged to the studio and committed me exclusively to films. L.B. Mayer used the fatherly approach first, which he was famous for. He pointed out how he had personally sired the careers of many great stars. When he saw that didn't work with me, he changed his campaign by launching an attack on the theatre and so demean my career in it. Well, that certainly didn't work. Then he pulled out a handkerchief and began to cry into it, so deeply saddened was he by my ingratitude, which wouldn't allow him to make me the biggest movie star of all time. His final ploy was to depict my refusal to sign his contract as an offence to motherhood, the American flag and decency. I half expected he should go on and claim it was also atheistic!

Jack Warner also offered him a seven-year contract at Warner Brothers; Peck's response was the same, and he returned to New York. Leland Hayward could hardly believe Peck had turned down so many lucrative offers, and he was even more alarmed when Peck said he was accepting the lead role in Irwin Shaw's *Sons and Soldiers* at the Morosco Theater for $400 a week. Hayward tried to dissuade him, saying the play needed cutting, and the playwright was 5,000 miles away in North Africa driving an ambulance: no one could cut any of his words without his express permission. He also told Peck he should be earning more than $400 a week. But Peck was attracted by the prospect of being directed by Germany's Max Reinhardt. Although Reinhardt had turned to directing a handful of films, he was still considered a legend of the theatre.

Reinhardt directed rehearsals by sitting at the very back of the auditorium and, being rather old and unwell, gave his instruction to the actors via his assistant, Lili Darvas, who spent her time walking back and forth trying to relay the director's comments. Greg, playing a small-town American boy, had a highly emotional scene that involved him telling his parents he is going to join the airforce. He had to switch from laughing to crying, but he felt too self-conscious to do this with any conviction. The more he failed at it, the more nervous he became, until the tense and frustrated state he was getting into was affecting the rest of the cast. Finally Reinhardt got up and slowly made his way to the stage, where he looked up at Peck and said, 'We do not stop being children when we grow up. Play-act! Play-act! You must put part of your grown-up self in one corner off the stage and send on the child part to play-act. It is nothing to be afraid of. It is only *playing*.'

That, said Peck, was his 'breakthrough' in acting. 'I discovered acting's all about being willing to make a damn fool of yourself and be lousy and even embarrassing before you get it right. I really began to enjoy the play and that scene after that. I learned so much from Max Reinhardt. He died shortly after the play opened.'

One thing Peck also learned, and that was that Hayward had been right in saying the play needed some judicious cutting. The critics slated it and closure came early in 1943, after just twenty-two performances.

Peck was in the peculiar position of being a highly praised actor who starred in flop after flop. He was in danger of sliding down the ladder of success before having reached the very top. Fortunately, Hollywood was still interested.

Among those who did see *Sons and Soldiers* was film producer Casey Robinson, who went backstage to meet the actor who had had the audacity to turn down Goldwyn, Mayer and Warner. Robinson wanted him for the male lead in *Days of Glory*, the story of Russian people resisting the Nazis who invaded their land in 1941; now that America was well and truly into the war against Germany, Italy and Japan, Hollywood was bold in its depiction of the evil enemy, whereas before it had been careful not to offend the Germans.

Peck reiterated his refusal to accept a seven-year contract, to which Robinson responded by offering him four pictures over four years, each film taking ten weeks to make, with a salary of $10,000 per picture. 'What you do during the other forty-two weeks of the year is up to you,' Robinson told him.

Peck remembered, 'I thought that was a *hell* of a lot of money.' He still had some debts to pay off, which the money from his films would certainly cover, and with the Broadway season coming to a close, he and Greta decided that ten weeks in Hollywood was just what they needed.

'I hadn't any great ambition to become a movie star,' Peck told me, 'but I can't deny that it wasn't entirely an unappealing prospect either, but I made up my mind that after this one film I would go back to New York and leave movies behind.'

Hollywood proved to be not quite all they expected. They arrived in spring 1943 to find a wartime housing shortage, and the cost of hotels prohibitive. So they camped out on the Monterey Auto Court for several days, until they were able to rent a pink and white stucco house on a Hollywood hilltop. Now they were introduced to top Hollywood society, and Greta in particular enjoyed the parties they found themselves attending.

Casey Robinson was both producer and screenwriter of *Days of Glory*, and decided to cast several new names, including Peck, to achieve the realistic approach for which he was aiming; unknowns, rather than a procession of well-known stars, would give it gritty European realism. Gregory Peck was actually the second new face to be cast, the first belonging to ballerina Tamara Toumanova, who happened to be Robinson's fiancée. She had to take leave from the Ballet Russe de Monte Carlo to play the role of Nina, a dancer from Moscow who finds herself stranded behind Nazi lines. Peck was to play Vladimir, the valiant partisan with whom Nina falls in love. Tamara, by accounts, was more reluctant than Peck to do the film, and had to be persuaded by Robinson.

Jacques Tourneur, the director assigned to the task, had made a number of high-quality, low-budget films at RKO where *Days of Glory* was to be produced; RKO rarely tried to compete with the big-budget productions of the top studios, such as MGM and Warner Brothers, and specialized in low-budget, black-and-white thrillers.

When filming began that summer, Peck quickly discovered the great difference between screen acting and stage acting, when he stood before the cameras and delivered his lines as though he half expected Guthrie McClintic to be standing at the very rear of the sound stage, telling him to speak up.

Tourneur told him, 'Greg, the microphone's right above your nose. It's two and a half feet from you, just off camera range. Why are you shouting so? Common it up! Don't project! Common it up.'

It took a few days for Peck to settle into this new style of acting, but he credits Tourneur as having been a positive influence on him. 'He was a good teacher,' he said. The director had a very different problem with his leading lady. Toumanova was not used to speaking at all on stage, and her voice was barely a whisper, so Tourneur had to coax her into speaking up.

There were other distractions in the first week of shooting that threatened to hold up the tight schedule. Toumanova had a miniature French poodle, Bella, who came to the set every day. The little dog behaved impeccably at first, and the film crew adopted her as their mascot. But when she watched Greg and Toumanova enact their first love scene, the normally docile and amiable poodle became overwrought and began yapping and howling. Filming was halted while Toumanova soothed Bella, and after that Tourneur banned the tiny dog from the set. After those ripples of disruption were smoothed out, filming proceeded at a much more cost-effective rate and it was completed on schedule.

Peck was disappointed with *Days of Glory* and seemed convinced that it could spell the end of his sudden but brief Hollywood career. 'I saw the rough cut and I knew enough to know that the picture was bad.' When the critics eventually saw it a considerable time later, they would generally agree with his estimate.

Kate Cameron of the *New York Daily News* called the film 'a bit of theatrical tripe that bears scant resemblance to the Russian films which have shown the Soviet's partisans in action'. Bosley Crowther of *The New York Times* wrote that Casey Robinson 'has tried something artful but daring. But less credit to him for loading his characters with dialogue rather than stirring deeds. Tourneur failed to make the best of what he had. As consequence, *Days of Glory* is more heroic in conception than effect.'

Some favour was shown by Howard Barnes, who, writing in the *New York Herald Tribune*, thought, 'The picture has heart and artistry. Tourneur has staged both the talk and the doings with imagination and considerable force.' The same critic gave Peck a good personal notice – 'Gregory Peck is excellent' – but was generally dismissed as another matinee idol by Bosley Crowther who wrote, 'Gregory Peck comes recommended with a Gary Cooper angularity and a face somewhat like that modest gentleman's, but his acting is equally stiff.'

Knowing the film would get panned, Peck said, 'I was reluctant to go back to New York with one bad picture on the record, so I stayed on in the hope I'd make a good second film. But I figured that once *Days of Glory* was out, no one would want me for another picture'. He was given a second chance by Darryl F. Zanuck, the head of production at Twentieth Century-Fox, who wanted him to play Father Chisholm in *The Keys of the Kingdom*. No screen test was needed. Word leaked out around town during filming of *Days of Glory* that a new star was on the horizon, or perhaps just below it, and so Zanuck had decided to take a look at this new boy Peck. He had, in fact, seen Peck on Broadway and apparently found him an interesting type, but now that Peck was in Hollywood making a picture at someone else's expense, Zanuck took advantage of the opportunity to get a look at some of the rushes from *Days of Glory*. He decided Peck was perfect for the star part of the nineteenth-century Scottish priest who finds himself in the line of fire during the Chinese Civil War.

Peck knew the A.J. Cronin novel and wanted to do it, but when he found out that Zanuck wanted to put him under contract he gave him the same response he gave to Goldwyn, Mayer and Warner. However, Zanuck was quite open to Hayward's suggestion that he simply sign Peck to a four-picture deal with a salary of $750 a week.

When word got round Hollywood that Darryl F. Zanuck wanted Peck for a key role in an important film, other studios began virtually falling over themselves to sign Peck on Hayward's terms. Louis B. Mayer agreed to a non-exclusive contract for Peck to make four films for MGM over the next five years, starting with a salary of $750 a week on the first film, called *The Valley of Decision*, with a flat salary of $45,000 for the second, then $55,000 for the third and $65,000 for the fourth.

David O. Selznick now kicked himself for not signing Peck when he had the chance, and he managed to buy half the contract Greg had with Casey Robinson and cast him in *Spellbound*. And all this before *Days of Glory* had been seen. Peck's head swam in the confusion of all these contractual complications, but Leland Hayward told him to let the agency worry about all that.

Peck still had to be convinced about accepting the Fox offer. He recalled, 'After a lot of soul-searching, I decided to do it. The part in *The Keys of the Kingdom* and the story appealed to me more than anything that was being offered on the stage.' In essence Leland

Hayward had succeeded in getting Zanuck, Selznick and Louis B. Mayer to agree to signing Peck for four films at each studio and his first had not been released.

Hayward advised Peck that if he were to appear opposite three or four of the screens' greatest leading ladies, by the time he would have made half a dozen films, he would be known all around the world. 'That made sense from his point of view,' said Peck, 'and I was getting more and more intrigued with movies. So it ended up with my being signed for *sixteen* pictures. I just worked my way through them, one after the other. And I was with Ingrid Bergman, Greer Garson, Ava Gardner, Jennifer Jones – all the top ladies of the Forties'. Thus he became the first actor to embark on a successful movie career without the usual exclusive studio contract, a trend that was followed by Burt Lancaster, Kirk Douglas and Charlton Heston, eventually leading to the complete breakdown of the studio star system.

Greta was delighted that they were to remain in Hollywood; she had come to enjoy the high life there, and the differences between the generally quiet Greg and the fun-loving Greta were beginning to show. Not that Greg was a dull man, as has sometimes been claimed. He liked to drink, but not when he was working. And work was foremost on his mind. Greta thrived on the parties and the socializing. Peck had little time to devote to anything but work. The couple were, by this time, probably already beginning to sense that their marriage was not a match made in heaven. But they seemed determined to try and give it a go, especially since Greta fell pregnant late in 1943.

On finishing *Days of Glory* Peck went virtually straight from the RKO studios over to Fox to make *The Keys of the Kingdom*. It was David O. Selznick who in 1941 first purchased the screen rights to A.J. Cronin's bestseller, which the *New Republic* had described as 'an adventure and travel story packed with melodramatic action'. But he lost interest in it and sold it to Zanuck. In his view the film would not only repeat the 1943 success of *The Song of Bernadette* for the studio but also be as great a personal triumph for Peck as *Bernadette* had been for Jennifer Jones.

Zanuck assigned Joseph L. Mankiewicz to produce the film and Nunnally Johnson to script it, although Mankiewicz, as usual, did much rewriting. Zanuck made clear to Mankiewicz that in view of the public's unfamiliarity with Peck, he wanted Ingrid Bergman to play the mother superior as box-office insurance. But this was a role Mankiewicz had promised to his wife, Rosa Stradner. He was relieved when Bergman turned it down. According to Nunnally Johnson, 'Ingrid Bergman heard that Joe practically got down on his knees to get Rosa Stradner into *The Keys of the Kingdom* with the appeal "this will save or doom my marriage". The studio wanted Ingrid but Stradner was accepted mainly for Joe's sake and because they knew she wouldn't harm the picture.'

Peck was concerned that changes and omissions from Cronin's original work might offend the novelist and he was eager himself to do justice to Cronin's work. He was also keen to perform the part, in which he would age to seventy, as accurately as possible and he relied heavily on a Catholic missionary, Father O'Hara, to advise him on set. Greg recalled:

> We had tremendous assistance from Father O'Hara, who was a Catholic missionary who spoke Chinese and had lived for eight years in China. There was a scene in which I had to preach in Chinese. I had trouble with the scene; I somehow couldn't catch the feeling of it, I didn't feel natural. So Father O'Hara was asked to play the scene to demonstrate to me how he would do it – he took some persuading, too. But he did it, walking through the crowd of Chinese extras, ringing a little silver bell and bowing to each one and talking to each in Chinese. He did it the way he might have done it a thousand times in his own life, and he made me realize what it was that I was missing in my performance which was that grave courtesy and respect for each person as an individual. He was able to give me something no director ever could.

The question of why Peck was not in the military came up during filming, and Zanuck issued a statement to the effect that he had been excluded because of a back injury sustained when he was a rowing star for Berkeley; this propped up the actor's masculine image while bending the truth. Years later Peck put the record straight.

The film was shot over three months entirely on the studio lot where art directors James Basevi and Bill Darling designed and constructed some remarkably convincing sets. The film cost $3 million, making it one of the most expensive films of that year. It failed to live up to all Peck's hopes, although, as the critics would later agree, he was quite outstanding in an otherwise uneven film. Bosley Crowther wrote in *The New York Times* that Peck 'gives a quiet and forceful performance [and] carries a fine impression of godly devotion and dignity'.

'Peck is remarkably good as the good father,' wrote Howard Barnes in the *New York Herald Tribune*. Alton Cook, in the *New York World-Telegram*, wrote that Peck gave 'the soundest and most intelligently presented performances of a year that has abounded in those merits. He has added to the picture a rich life and vitality that the novel did not have for a good many of its readers.'

'Gregory Peck does a magnificent job,' wrote Lee Mortimer in the *New York Daily Mirror*. Irene Thirer in the *New York Post* described it as 'a personal triumph for Gregory Peck, whose ingratiating performance expresses dignity, warmth and on occasion, a wryly humorous controversial streak'.

Perhaps most approving of all the critics was Kate Cameron of the *New York Daily News*, who said the film was 'a must on any moviegoer's list'. Peck's performance, she said, was 'one of this year's outstanding character portraits. Peck carried the burden of the story with competence and artistry. A fine spirited quality shined through his acting.'

However, all the critical plaudits for Peck awaited the film's opening. Prior to that A.J. Cronin watched it, and to Peck's relief he not only approved of the film, with all its changes, but also praised Peck's performance. With this resounding screen success Peck was now rubbing shoulders with the biggest movie stars in the world.

I met everybody but I don't recall being bowled over by them. I remember meeting Gary Cooper, who said to me, 'How many movies have you made?'

I told him, 'Two.'

'How'd they turn out?' he asked.

'One good, one bad,' I answered.

'You're ahead of the game,' he replied. Then he said, 'Don't worry if you get a few flops. You'll be lucky if you have two good movies out of every five.'

I certainly admired the big stars. They were not stars for no reason, you know. They were stars because they were so damn interesting.

Around this time, Leland Hayward gave in to his wife's demands to quit, selling his interests to MCA. Though delighted to have Peck as one of their clients, the agents found themselves with the headache of trying to unravel his tangled contracts. This unenviable task was handed to George Chasin by MCA boss Lew Wasserman, who told him, 'If you do nothing else for the next six months, make yourself Gregory Peck's agent because he's going to be a very, very big and important star. Just devote yourself to him.'

Chasin took a look at the various contracts and was horrified to discover that each studio had pre-emptory rights. This meant in effect that each of them had precedence over the other – a contradictory legal minefield. Chasin decided the best way to deal with the situation was to meet with Mayer, Selznick, Robinson and Zanuck in turn, and just come clean and explain that none of them actually had pre-emptory rights in practice, and that they should agree among themselves how to schedule Peck's films without them overlapping. The moguls realized none of them would benefit by holding out, and they agreed to co-operate.

While filming *The Valley of Decision* at Culver City Studios, Peck often met Louis B. Mayer, the man he had made cry, and whom he had offended in so many ways. Mayer was arguably the most powerful of all the studio heads in Hollywood and he could most likely have hurt Peck's career had he chosen to do so. But, as Peck noted, 'I think Mayer gained a great respect for me as a result of my haggling with him, because in the years to come he never once held it against me. And it wasn't beneath Mayer to join everyone at lunch at the commissary, where he usually had chicken soup for lunch.'

The outcome of *Days of Glory* now seemed superfluous as its opening grew nearer. On 26 May 1944 RKO's publicity department put out a press release: 'It has always been considered daring to cast an important picture with newcomers to the screen, but *Days of Glory* will introduce no fewer then eleven new faces.'

The publicity department pulled out the stops to present this as a classy, neo-realistic drama, and the posters emphasized the fact that the two leads were great stars of the stage; they figured that no one would really know that Gregory Peck had not exactly achieved greatness on Broadway, but the fact that he emerged unscathed from the New York stage was, in 1944, reason enough to elevate him. He was billed as 'Mr. Gregory Peck' and his leading lady as 'Miss Tamara Toumanova'.

Peck recalled, 'It was embarrassing to be given the reverence due to a great stage star – which I was not. But you couldn't tell them that. Mind you, it was the one and only time I ever got that particular billing.'

Days of Glory opened on 16 June 1944. But if anyone thought that his debut film was hardly enough to turn him into a major star, he was nevertheless treated like one at MGM, where he was treated to a salute from the guards at the gate when he arrived each morning. He admitted that he felt somewhat out of place being treated almost like a king at a studio where the biggest stars were indeed America's royalty.

4

Spellbinding Star

A T MGM EVERYTHING WAS BIG, and the sets for *The Valley of Decision* designed by Cedric Gibbons and Paul Groesse were no exception: the shanty town, the steel mill, and the Pittsburgh streets, complete with mansions were entirely on the Culver City back lot.

Peck was to star opposite his first great leading lady, Greer Garson, in this adaptation of Marcia Davenport's bestselling 1942 novel about an 1870 Pittsburgh steel family. Peck was playing Paul Scott, head of a steel dynasty, who is determined to carry on the family business built up by his father. Garson played Mary Rafferty, the Irish lass who loves Paul but whose father (played by Lionel Barrymore) hates the Scotts; she tries against all the odds to bridge the gulf between the families.

Peck discovered the price an actor has to pay for appearing opposite one of the screen's true beauties. 'When I viewed the rushes I saw how every time I was in a scene with Greer, her face was the only thing you saw. It shone like a luminous moon floating in the centre of the screen, and I was just a rather dim figure next to her. I didn't mind. I thought it was funny, and so did she when I called her Big Red.'

On 20 July 1944, while Peck was filming at Culver City, Greta went into labour. He was called to the hospital and spent several hours pacing in an outer room. When he finally heard the nurse say over the loudspeaker, 'Mr Peck, your son wants to speak to you,' he shouted, 'Yippee!' When the nurse came into the room to take him to see his baby boy, he told her, 'The Yankees have found themselves another pitcher.' The Pecks already had a boy's name chosen: Jonathan.

Greg had little time to enjoy the company of his baby son

straight away as he still had a film to finish. The fact that he was working so much and spending so little time off the set, added tension into the marital home, especially now that the baby had come along.

One evening, after *The Valley of Decision* had been completed, MGM sent a Cadillac to collect Greg and Greta and drive them to Pasadena for a sneak preview of the film. Greer Garson was also present, along with the film's producer Edwin H. Knopf and director Tay Garnett, and together they waited for the audience response. Cards filled out by the audience were hastily brought out and handed to an MGM executive who picked up the first card and read it. With a look of despair, he passed it to Peck. It said, 'Junk it.'

MGM, of course, did no such thing, and just as well. Most of the other preview cards were favourable, as were the reviews when the film was seen by the critics. Bosley Crowther noted in *The New York Times*, 'Gregory Peck is quietly commanding,' and the *New York Herald Tribune*'s reviewer wrote that 'Garson is sheerly brilliant. Gregory Peck rarely fails her.' The *New York Herald Tribune* announced, 'A tale of an American dynasty has come to the screen with great feeling and some sense. Tay Garnett's acute direction holds a tender romance in the shifty outlines of a politico-social period piece. It deserves to be a hit.'

As soon as he had finished on *Valley of Decision*, Peck went to work for David O. Selznick, the man who had first screen-tested and rejected him in quick succession. After Peck signed his four-picture deal with Selznick, Kay Brown, who had first brought Peck to Selznick's attention, recalled, 'It cost David about four times what he would have had to pay originally.'

Spellbound had its roots in Selznick's own experience of psycho-analysis. After his counselling experiences, he became a champion of psychiatry and its remarkable healing powers, and in wanting to share this with the world, he bought the screen rights to *The House of Dr. Edwardes*, by Francis Beeding, which was set in an insane asylum.

Selznick wanted Alfred Hitchcock, the much acclaimed master of suspense, to direct. He was under contract to Selznick and had an interest in psychiatry, so the project held an immediate appeal for him. He had to return to Britain in 1944 to direct some short films for the war effort, and while there he met an old friend, Angus MacPhail, who had been a writer at Gaumont-British and was now head of Gaumont's script department. Together they began work on a screenplay based on Beeding's book, but Selznick, when he read it, found it too meandering and awkward to translate to the screen, so he assigned Ben Hecht to turn out a filmable script.

Peck played John Ballentine, who arrives at a mental hospital and is immediately assumed to be the new director. But then he is found to be an amnesiac who suspects himself of having murdered the new director. The plot centres on the therapy he receives which both reveals his true identity and unravels the murder mystery. Selznick had originally wanted his contract star Joseph Cotten to play that part, and Dorothy McGuire to play the doctor who treats him and then falls in love with him. But having acquired Peck, as well as Ingrid Bergman, Selznick fashioned the film as a joint star vehicle for them. Bergman, however, was reluctant. 'I won't do this movie,' she told him, 'because I don't believe the love story.' Contractually, she was not, however, in a position to say no.

Selznick treated his stars with considerable respect. Joseph Cotten told me, 'I was never so happy being a slave.' Peck said, 'Selznick believed in treating his actors like little tin gods. But he was a little hard on directors. Hitchcock, I think, learned to take it all in his stride.'

Hitchcock, as masterful as he was, knew that even he might not be able to make a success of the sequences that needed to symbolize Peck's confused amnesiac mind. So he asked Selznick to bring in Surrealist artist Salvador Dalí, who had had experience of film before, working with Luis Buñuel on two Spanish films, *Un Chien Andalou* (1928) and *L'Age d'Or* (1930), that both became *avant-garde* classics. The imagery conjured up by Buñuel and Dalí to reflect the fears and taboos they claimed were buried deep within the collective unconscious of their audience was too disturbing for some countries, which banned it. Hitchcock knew Dalí was the man to do something remarkable with *Spellbound.*

One of his sequences, which featured Peck and Bergman having their first kiss, was designed so that as their lips move towards each other, the camera sweeps past them and through seven opening doors, one after the other, going on towards infinity.

Hitchcock displayed much of his own exceptional cinematic

inventiveness, creating a remarkable moment towards the end of the film when the real murderer (played by Leo G. Carroll) aims a gun at Ingrid Bergman. To prevent the audience discovering the killer's identity, Hitchcock shot the scene from the murderer's point of view, with just his hand holding the gun on Bergman in shot. When she calls his bluff, turns and walks out of the room, his hand turns the gun on the camera and fires. The film was shot in black and white but Hitchcock had a single solid red frame inserted to produce a sudden red flash as the gun fired, jolting the audience. Unfortunately, subsequent prints made for reissues did not include the red flash and the effect is rarely seen by modern audiences. Ingrid Bergman told me:

> That shot with the hand and the gun with me in the background was all a clever trick. It was impossible with the lenses then in use to have the hand and gun in the foreground in focus and me in the background also in focus. They tried all sorts of ways to achieve the effect, including filming me without the hand and gun in shot and then putting the scene on rear projection while they filmed the hand and gun 'live'. But it didn't look realistic. Then they came up with the clever device of building a giant hand and gun which could be placed away from the camera while the perspective would make it look closer to the camera, keeping it and me in sharp focus.

Hitchcock managed to acquire over his many years a reputation for being hard on actors, and he coined a well-known phrase – 'Actors are like cattle' – that appeared to justify his reputation. Peck, however, refuted this notion and explained Hitchcock's method:

> Hitchcock is like an architect in his manner; he never starts to erect the building until he has drawn up the perfect plan so that when he begins there is very little that can go wrong. His preparation is meticulous. He needs to be able to place his actors into this plan, and he is always at his best with 'technical' actors – that is, actors like Cary Grant who have an accomplished technique of producing effects. Grant worked very hard on his technique and it's very facile, something he can just turn on. Hitch likes this because he can then control the actor's expression and emotion just as he controls the sets and the script and the camera. He will always eliminate the

intangibles if possible, so he is always at his best when working with technical actors. Then there are the actors who have to delve around and find an emotional reality in a situation before they can produce the right effect, and those are the actors he can get impatient with. He can't control them. They can't just give him what he wants. I don't think I was his kind of actor at the time. I was so inexperienced. I felt I need a good deal of direction. In answer to my questions about mood or expression, he would simply say that I was to drain my face of all expression and he would photograph me. But later I could produce any kind of effect he, or any director, wanted.

As for his reputation of treating actors like cattle, I never saw him browbeat or humiliate any actor.

Peck conceded, however, that Hitchcock didn't give actors much in the way of direction, a fact not lost on Bergman who complained that she didn't know how to play a particular scene and was finally told by Hitchcock: 'Fake it.'

Curiously, Hitchcock was more interested in Peck's lack of experience in regard to wine than acting. 'He gave me a case of wine and was more willing to improve my education in that regard,' recalled Greg. He also remembered being puzzled by what appeared to be a rare and barely perceptible lack of enthusiasm displayed by Hitchcock during this particular production. 'But I had the feeling that something ailed him, and I could never understand what it might be.'

Something ailed Peck too – at home. Despite the arrival of Jonathan, Greg and Greta were not finding much happiness together. They had discovered they had very different attitudes to life and fulfilment, and as a consequence their marriage was going downhill. There were rumours that Peck and Bergman were having an affair, and it was said that on one occasion the two stars appeared on the set adjusting their dishevelled clothing.

Ingrid Bergman told me, 'Greg was a very handsome man – very sexy. It was difficult not to be attracted to him.'

Peck admitted, 'I fell a little bit in love with her.'

Neither star admitted more than that. During filming Gregory Peck was interviewed by Hedda Hopper, and he told her how much he admired actors Edmund Gwenn, Barry Fitzgerald, James Cagney and Humphrey Bogart. He also said how much he admired Miss Bergman for her professionalism and lack of temperament on the set. 'She just goes into a scene and does a wonderful job without any fuss,' he said.

Hitchcock and Selznick had a unique partnership. Peck recalled, 'Selznick was usually on the set of his films all the time, certainly more times than most other producers. He liked to make suggestions and often he would get to the point of interference and annoy his directors. But he didn't do that with Hitchcock. I only saw him on the set of *Spellbound* maybe a couple of times.'

Selznick ensured that each and every one of his pictures came up to a certain standard of excellence, in both entertainment and production values. He was an independent producer who made far fewer films than any of the major studios, but he tried to ensure each one was a prestigious event. This often led to problems with directors who resented his interference on the set. Even on his biggest and most enduring success, *Gone with the Wind*, he directed some of the scenes himself. But he left Hitchcock alone, involving himself purely in the pre-production and post-production stages. Yet by controlling the editing and scoring, he essentially took the picture out of Hitchcock's hands, deviating from Hitchcock's rough cut and removing two reels entirely.

He also wanted Miklos Rozsa to write highly romantic music for the kiss-and-seven-doors sequence, which Hitchcock felt ruined the visual effect he and Dalí had achieved. Nevertheless, Selznick felt so indebted to the director that he allowed the film to be advertised as 'Alfred Hitchcock's *Spellbound*.'

Today it is certainly remembered more as a Hitchcock film than a Selznick picture. Its impact is still as striking today as it was to 1945's film critics. 'The secret recesses of the mind are explored with brilliant and terrifying effect,' wrote Howard Barnes in the *New York Herald Tribune*. 'The work is a masterful psychiatric thriller. Peck's portrait of the mentally ill ex-army doctor is ably modulated and utterly convincing.' Bosley Crowther also had praise for it in *The New York Times*, saying that 'the manner and quality of its telling is extraordinarily fine. Peck's performance, restrained and refined, is precisely the proper counter to Miss Bergman's exquisite role.' 'Peck handles the suspense scenes with great skill and has one of the finest screen roles to date,' declared *Variety*.

At this time, neither *The Keys of the Kingdom* nor *The Valley of Decision* had been released, and *Spellbound* was still in production. All audiences knew of him was what they had seen in *Days of Glory*.

But Hedda Hopper seemed to be in no doubts as to Peck's star quality. She wrote in October 1944, 'Gregory Peck is the hottest thing in town. Some say he is a second Gary Cooper. Actually he's the first Gregory Peck.'

His popularity was confirmed when Selznick held a sneak preview of *Spellbound* and reported to one of his vice-presidents, Neil Agnew, 'We could not keep the audience quiet from the time his name appeared on the screen until we had shushed them through three or four sequences and stopped all the dames from "ohing" and "ahing" and gurgling.'

Greg went to New York for the premiere of *The Keys of the Kingdom* on 28 December 1944, and was confronted by a fifty-foot high billboard featuring his portrait. 'It stretched for half a block,' he recalled, 'and the impact on me was not lost, let alone on the people it was meant to attract.'

To Peck's surprise and delight, he was nominated for an Academy Award as Best Actor for *The Keys of the Kingdom* and attended his first Oscar ceremony in April 1945. In the event, he lost to Bing Crosby for his performance as Father O'Malley in *Going My Way*. He won financially, though, because Zanuck gave him a $25,000 bonus, doubling his original fee for the film.

The Pecks were now able to afford a home of their own, and they bought Boris Karloff's house on Mulholland Drive. Before long, Kenneth Tobey came to Hollywood to try his luck in movies, and he rented a room from Peck above the garage.

On 3 May 1945 *The Valley of Decision* was premiered, and went on to become a huge hit. The sneak previewer who'd told them to 'junk it' clearly had no taste for the kind of opulent films MGM produced.

By the time *Spellbound* was ready to hit the screens, Selznick was concerned that mystery thrillers were losing their appeal, so he decided that the film's publicity should stress the love aspect of the picture. One advertisement featured Peck and Bergman embracing, and was headlined, 'Irresistible their love! Inescapable their fears!' Another proclaimed, 'The magnificence of its cast – the intensity of its emotions – will hold you SPELLBOUND!'

The film opened on 1 November 1945 at New York's Astor Theater and became an immediate critical and commercial hit. It had cost $2 million to make, quite a considerable sum for 1944, and it recouped $7.9 million on its first release. It brought Ingrid

Bergman a 'Best Actress Performance' from the New York Film Critics' Circle, although it was for *The Bells of St. Mary*'s that she won an Oscar nomination that year. *Spellbound*'s Oscar nominations were for Michael Chekhov as Best Supporting Actor, for Hitchcock's direction, for Miklos Rozsa's superb music, and for the film itself; of them only Rozsa won.

Peck's next film for David Selznick – *Duel in the Sun* – gave him a complete change of image, that of a rogue, a killer and a rapist.

5

Duel in the Sun and Snow

DUEL IN THE SUN was based on Niven Busch's novel, which had, in fact, been a commercial failure. Busch had written a handful of screenplays, including *In Old California* and *The Westerner*, and was married to actress Teresa Wright; somehow he managed to persuade RKO to buy the rights to it and appoint him as producer. He hired Oliver H.P. Garrett to write the screenplay, and cast John Wayne in the principal role of outlaw Lewt McCanles.

He was looking around for an actress to play the sensual Pearl when he heard that David Selznick was looking to loan out his favourite star – and mistress – Jennifer Jones. Selznick felt the script wasn't good enough for Jennifer to do, so Busch rewrote it. Selznick objected to the casting of Wayne, whom he pointed out 'represented the exact opposite of what this script requires; and if this doesn't come off as a powerful sex story, it is going to misfire'.

Selznick began to interfere more and more in Busch's production, changing the ending so that instead of Pearl killing Lewt and riding off into the sunset with his brother Jesse, Lewt and Pearl shoot each other and die in each other's arms. When Selznick announced that he wanted to cast Gregory Peck in Wayne's role, RKO decided they would do better just to sell the rights to him.

At this time Selznick saw the film as 'an artistic little western,' and thought it a great coup to cast the normally nice Gregory Peck as Lewt McCanles; Jennifer Jones was also a hot property, having shot to fame in *The Song of Bernadette*, as a French peasant girl who saw a holy vision at Lourdes. One newspaper noted, before *Duel in the Sun* was released, 'It will be quite a sight to see the erstwhile Father Chisholm leering at the onetime Saint Bernadette'.

Selznick wanted Walter Huston to play 'The Sin Killer', a revivalist preacher. The role originally required Huston for only a few days' shooting, so when his agent pointed out that his minimum fee was $40,000, Selznick protested at such a high sum for so little work. Finally the producer agreed to the agent's concession that Huston would work for $4,000 a week for up to ten weeks. Selznick was sure he could dispense with Huston in one week. In the end, Huston worked the full ten weeks – and more.

Selznick regular Joseph Cotten was cast as Lewt's better-behaved brother, Jesse. Selznick wanted a great supporting cast, and he got one: Lilian Gish, Charles Bickford, Lionel Barrymore and Herbert Marshall. 'It was a dream to work with all those wonderful actors,' Peck told me. 'They weren't always easy to work with because many of them had their own stylish temperaments, but I was in awe of them.'

Filming began near Tucson, Arizona, on 1 March 1945, with snow still lying on the ground after an unusually extended winter. 'There was Greg Peck and me wearing warm underclothes under our Western costume trying to look hot in freezing conditions,' Joseph Cotten told me. 'They had to spray our faces with water to make us look as though we were sweating. The sweat just turned to ice. Vidor had to shoot only close-ups when we started because he couldn't show the supposedly burning desert white with snow.'

The hold-ups caused by the wintry weather gave Selznick ample opportunity to work on rewrites. The screenplay had run to 170 pages when they began filming. Only fifty-two of those had actually been shot by 7 April.

Peck had never made a western before and was unfamiliar with guns. When he came to film the scene in which he shot and killed Charles Bickford, Bickford drew and fired first in each take. Vidor told Peck, 'Draw faster.' Peck tried, but each time he was beaten to the draw. So Vidor told Bickford to slow down his draw.

The cantankerous Bickford replied, 'It won't look right. Peck has to go and practise.'

'But we don't have time, Charlie,' Vidor pleaded. 'Let's finish the shot.'

Again Bickford outdrew Peck, and the director begged Peck to draw faster. Finally, Vidor called a halt and told Peck to go off and practise. He later returned to tell Vidor he thought he'd got the hang of it, and they had another go at the scene.

Peck was considerably faster but for the first six or seven takes Bickford still outdrew him. And no amount of pleading from Vidor could persuade Bickford to slow down. On take 9, Peck outdrew him. Peck recalled, 'When Vidor called, "Print that!" I could hear the relief in his voice.'

Selznick personally chose a magnificent show horse for Peck to ride in the film. But Selznick had failed to take into consideration that the horse was not used to riding over rocky terrain. As the cameras turned, Peck had to ride close to boulders that looked far too dangerous to the horse, and it panicked, taking off with Peck still in the saddle but out of control. It ran straight into a barbed-wire fence, throwing Peck through the air. Vidor watched in horror, convinced his star was about to be maimed or killed. Peck landed hard and was thoroughly shaken and bruised but not seriously hurt. The poor horse, however, lay tangled in the barbed wire. Peck rushed over to it and tried desperately to calm it as it struggled to get up again, blood pouring from its lacerations. He had to hold its head down with his foot to keep it as still as possible while members of the crew cut the wire. Its cuts were treated by a vet, but it remained scarred for life, making it useless as a show horse.

A black and white pinto was chosen next for Peck. It was a good cow horse that not only looked splendid but performed impeccably. Peck was also giving an excellent performance as Lewt, and he thoroughly enjoyed being so bad for once. He said:

I played it for fun. I had virtually started my film career playing a saintly priest, and then Selznick cast me as a rapist, a forger, a killer, a liar, but the part also had a certain likeability. I just kind of imitated a cousin of mine who was a bit of a rascal, a black sheep in the family, but likeable. His name was Warren Rannell, but the girls called him Stretch. He took pride in being the town's Lothario; he went from job to job, and he was married four times. I borrowed his arrogance; he could seduce women and then leave them flat, all with a clear conscience. He was a likeable rogue. Apart from that, I didn't really have to do much acting. I just rode horses, necked a lot with Jennifer and shot poor old Charlie Bickford.

As the weeks turned into months and spring turned into summer and then early autumn, Selznick kept revising the script, which meant certain scenes had to be reshot. The rewrites, the late winter, a strike in Hollywood and the death of President Roosevelt saw the film running 75 days behind schedule by June. The budget had risen to $3.5 million and the script had reached 200 pages.

As the script continued to evolve and inflate, sets were redesigned to keep pace with the changing aspects and proportions of the screenplay. A small cantina developed into a dance hall and casino, and humble ranch houses became haciendas. On top of all this, Selznick demanded nothing less than authenticity; every prop, costume and piece of furniture created and gathered had to be checked and double-checked by experts and consultants. This was a David O. Selznick production, and that meant total quality.

The numbers of livestock increased, and 2,500 extras were hired. As the production grew, so did the budget to $6 million, a million more than *Gone with the Wind* had cost. Selznick was determined that this film would be bigger and better than his perennial Civil War epic of 1939. What had begun as his 'artistic little western' was growing into the biggest western since movies began talking. 'David would spare neither expense nor effort if he felt a scene could be improved by redoing it, no matter how infinitesimal the changes might be,' Vidor recalled.

While most of *Duel in the Sun* was directed by King Vidor, some of the more spectacular scenes were shot by second-unit directors Reeves Eason and Otto Bower. Josef von Sternberg was brought in to supervise some of Jennifer Jones's more sensual scenes; Selznick wanted von Sternberg to give Jones the sort of glamorous look he'd given Marlene Dietrich in *The Blue Angel* and *Morocco*. Von Sternberg later said that none of his contributions was evident in the final version.

There were further delays when Selznick decided Jones wasn't sexy enough in a scene where she dances for Lewt. The problem was partly to do with Jones's own modesty, but she seemed unable to move her hips the way Selznick wanted. He halted filming while she was coached until she could perform the dance perfectly.

Peck was leaning against a tree, guitar in hand, pretending to strum it while Jennifer went through her paces beautifully but painfully; her own physical limitations made the requisite hip movements agony for her. Take after take was shot at Selznick's demand, but somehow it failed to work and the scene was eventually cut.

One of the most difficult scenes to shoot was the one when Lewt ravishes Pearl. It was known as the 'rape scene' and was intended to be both savage and arousing. There were many sceptics who were convinced it would never work, and a considerable crowd gathered to watch it, including Anita Colby, a former model whom Selznick hired to coach Jennifer. Colby watched as Jennifer knelt, washing the floor, wiggling her bottom and looking over her shoulder at Peck. Colby said, 'She looked up; it was a very sexy look to begin with, then Peck took the hat off and went after her.' She said that as Jennifer tried to fight him off, 'he just put his head down and got right on her mouth. I'll never forget it.' The scene proved to be one of the most effective and successful in the picture.

Each script revision made the violence more graphic and the sexual content ever more lusty. The Breen Office, Hollywood's censor, was consulted more than twenty-five times by Selznick, and changes, costing an extra $200,000 were suggested by production code chief Joseph I. Breen.

'Vidor never knew what surprise Selznick would pull when he arrived on the set,' said Joseph Cotten.

One day Vidor walked onto the saloon set to see a man he'd never seen before. He asked him who he was, and the man explained he was a real bartender who'd met Selznick at a party the previous evening, and Selznick had decided to hire the bartender to super-vise the saloon scenes to make sure that everything, including the pouring of liquor, was done correctly. Vidor did not appreciate Selznick's impulsive interference and told the man to leave the set.

On and on the production went with delay after delay. Vidor's patience was stretched to the limits with Selznick's constant pres-ence on the set. Matters between them came to a head on 10 August while they were shooting the final scene; Peck and Jones, having mortally wounded each other, crawl towards each other in the dust for one last blood-soaked embrace. Selznick wanted this scene to be everything he had envisaged, full of searing emotional impact. He had written the scene himself, shot for shot, and he insisted that Vidor shoot it his way. Joseph Cotten recalled:

Greg and Jennifer lay on the ground, waiting for Vidor to start the cameras rolling. Then Selznick decided that Peck and Jones needed more blood on them, so he reached for the make-up blood and began to splash it over them. Vidor just sat in his director's chair, silently looking at his script. Then he stood up, handed the script to Selznick and said, 'You can take this picture and shove it!'

Everyone was aghast as Vidor walked to his limousine, got in and drove away, up the dusty road, into the distance, disappearing into the far mountains.

Selznick looked at the script Vidor had shoved in his hand, looked up at everybody looking at him, and said, 'Well, that's all for today.'

Selznick thought he could placate Vidor and that all would be well the next day. He was wrong. Vidor quit the picture for good. Selznick prevailed upon William Dieterle to wind up the remaining scenes, while further second-unit sequences were shot by William Cameron Menzies. Earlier scenes began to be rewritten and reshot all over again. 'It was like starting from the beginning in some ways,' said Joseph Cotten.

Selznick, a showman of extreme and flamboyant flair, put advertisements in the Hollywood trade papers, quoting diverse people as having proclaimed *Duel in the Sun* the greatest film ever, even though it was not finished. Billy Wilder consequently ran a similar piece for the picture he was directing, *Double Indemnity*, which read, '*Double Indemnity* is the greatest picture I have ever seen – George Oblath.' Oblath was the owner of a small restaurant in Hollywood! Most thought it funny, but not Selznick; he threatened to cancel his ongoing advertisements if the papers accepted further copy which ridiculed his film.

While his methods and approach may seem excessive and even obsessive, the truth was that Selznick's studio stood or fell on the success of virtually every film. Unlike the big studios, he could not afford to have a failure. Even after principal photography had finished, he kept adding and enlarging scenes, including the spectacular train wreck which Reeves Eason directed. Peck was called back to work on the film, and in line with the new version of the scene as written by Selznick, sang 'I've Been Workin' on the Railroad' as he rode away from the terrible devastation he had just caused.

When Vidor saw that scene during a preview of the picture, he felt that it destroyed what little sympathy the audience had for

Peck's Lewt McCanles. He went to see Selznick at his home; although he had quit the film, he and Selznick were still on relatively friendly terms and he begged the producer, who was shaving in his bathroom, to take the rail wreck scene out. Selznick turned to Vidor and said, 'I want to make Lewt the worst sonofabitch that's ever been seen on a motion picture screen, and I believe the train wreck will prove my point.' The scene stayed. Peck thought the sequence was hilarious when he saw it.

When the critics finally saw the film, they were often as merciless as Lewt. It was, said Bosley Crowther of *The New York Times*, 'a spectacularly disappointing job. Selznick seems to have been more anxious to emphasize the clash of love and lust than to seek some illumination of a complex of arrogance and greed. The best and the most consistent [performance] is that of Mr. Peck, who makes of the renegade brother a credibly vicious and lawless character.'

Howard Barnes of the *New York Herald Tribune* thought the film was 'a more or less conventional horse opera, extravagant in treatment, performance, color and exploitation.' He found it had 'interludes of arresting cinematic action' as well as 'passages of straight pictorial composition which are sometimes stunning ... but it is more ponderous and tasteless than cumulatively entertaining. The acting is as hamstrung by the script as the direction. Jennifer Jones overacts at every turn. Peck is not much better.'

Said *Variety*, 'Rarely has a film made such frank use of lust and still been cleared for showings. Miss Jones proves herself extremely capable in quieter sequences but is overly meller [melodramatic] in others. Same is true of Peck. The role has no audience sympathy but will cast a great fascination for the femmes.'

Life called it 'the costliest, most lushly Technicolored, the most lavishly cast, the loudest ballyhooed, and the sexiest horse opera ever made. A knowing blend of oats and aphrodisiac with rip-roaring gunplay, over heated histrionics. The audience eventually learns that Illicit Love doesn't really pay in the long run, but for about 134 minutes it has appeared to be loads of fun.'

Peck probably hit the nail on the head as to why the film went so awry when he said, 'You began to feel the picture would never end. Maybe this was because David was in love with Jennifer, and this film was his way of showing how much he loved her. He was in love with the film, and he spoiled it the way he tried to spoil her. He just couldn't leave it alone.'

Selznick continued to cut and re-edit it and shoot new scenes while Peck went on to his next assignment, in MGM's *The Yearling*.

Peck came into *The Yearling* towards the end of a five-year troubled history. Marjorie Kinnan Rawlings's novel, published in 1938, was hailed as an instant classic of American literature for its depiction of a Florida backwoods lad who raises an orphan fawn. Even before Rawlings had received the Pulitzer Prize for fiction in 1939, MGM had bought the screen rights, and the film went into production in 1941.

It was to be an important film project, produced by Sidney Franklin, written by Pulitzer Prize-winning playwright Marc Connelly and filmed on location in the forests of central Florida. A farm in Ocala National Forest was found and leased by MGM, where crops were planted and the area was carefully reshaped. A large assortment of animals – fawns, pigs, chickens, racoons, squirrels, buzzards, doves, snakes, foxes and even a bobcat were rounded up and transported to Hollywood for training at considerable cost.

Even while the animals were being given their own brand of drama lessons, MGM was looking for a young actor to play Jody Baxter, the boy around whom the story revolves. The studio launched a huge and much publicized search in February 1940, and out of thousands of boys from all over the southern states, a young lad from Atlanta, Georgia, by the name of Gene Eckman, was given the part. Marjorie Kinnan Rawlings declared to him, 'You *are* Jody.'

In May 1941 the film began shooting in Ocala. Spencer Tracy played Jody's father, and Victor Fleming was directing. They ran into immediate problems. Gene Eckman's authentic southern accent contrasted with Tracy's drawl. Fleming worried that the boy's voice would not be understood in the northern states. Creative differences arose, the early summer heat became unbearable, tempers became frayed, and just three weeks after filming started, it ground to a halt, with the entire unit being returned to Hollywood.

On 28 May, MGM announced that King Vidor would take over direction from Fleming. Then Vidor announced that he could not go to work straight away as he had to familiarize himself with the script, story and characters as well as the logistics of the production itself. Louis B. Mayer began to worry; more than $500,000 had already been spent, and as the delay grew, so too did their performing fawns – into full grown deer. The studio announced that the project was being shelved 'in the best interests of the company'.

Sidney Franklin fought to salvage the film and early in 1942 MGM announced that it was being revived; this time it was to be filmed entirely in Hollywood with Roddy McDowall, then fourteen years old, playing Jody. No sooner had this happened than it was shelved again when America entered the war; the public, it was decided, wanted war pictures.

In 1944 Franklin revived the film yet again, this time with Clarence Brown directing, Gregory Peck playing the father and Jane Wyman the mother. Some 12,000 more boys were interviewed for the role of Jody, until Brown discovered ten-year-old Claude Jarman Jr., at the Eakin Grammar School in Nashville, Tennessee. Franklin convinced the studio to allow them to film on location in Florida. It wasn't a particularly good time for Peck to be away from home as Greta was pregnant again. They seemed to have concluded that having more children would strengthen their marriage.

The cast and crew were transported to Florida once more in January 1946. It was thought that shooting in winter would avoid the heat and humidity that plagued the first attempt in the early summer of 1941. But the winter conditions in Florida were not much cooler and still managed to produce a plague of insects and unpredictable weather.

'It was a most difficult film to make,' said Peck, adding that the pressure and tension were eased by Jane Wyman's 'plucky humor'.

It took seventy-two takes to film a scene featuring the pet fawn, because the creature, which hadn't been trained, kept disappearing from shot while the actors delivered their dialogue. Over the two days it took to get the single scene, Clarence Brown paid more attention to the fawn than he did the actors. After the film was finished, he said, 'Never again. You have to direct a deer or a stalk of corn to understand my problems.'

Peck is fond of the film but said he found it too 'saccharin', and that the many moments when Claude Jarman had tears running down his cheeks were 'too much! *Too much!*' But he received some of his best personal notices to date. 'Gregory Peck is excellent,' said the *New Yorker*. 'Peck is particularly appealing,' said Howard Barnes in the *New York Herald Tribune*, adding, 'He gives a superb portrayal.' As for the film, Barnes thought it, 'ranked among the fine achievements of the cinema. A piece of universal experience has been spread across the screen.'

John Mason Brown of the *Saturday Review* wrote, 'In Gregory Peck's and young Claude Jarman's admirable playing of father and son, it comes through with dignity.' Bosley Crowther of *The New York Times* raved about the way Peck performed 'with simple dignity and strength'. He felt that despite the moments 'when the Aurora Borealis is turned on and the heavenly choir starts singing' as well as the overlong hysterics of Jody towards the end of the film, it was 'a cheerful and inspiring film'.

Life thought that 'although *The Yearling* tends to become tediously sentimental toward its conclusion and its beautiful scenery sometimes dares to improve on reality, it is nevertheless a stunning production'.

The location was wrapped in February 1946 and the rest of the film shot in the luxury of MGM's Culver City studio. At the same time, David O. Selznick was doing retakes for *Duel in the Sun,* and Peck found himself going from one studio to the other. 'I'd get out of my Southern cracker overalls and my Southern accent and put on a cowboy suit and climb into my Texas drawl. I really enjoyed it, actually. It was frantic and fun.'

6

A Hitch at Selznick

WHEN HE HAD FINISHED work on both *The Yearling* and *Duel in the Sun*, Peck returned, albeit briefly, to the stage, playing Christy Mahon in J.M. Synge's sardonic play *Playboy of the Western World* at the Cape Playhouse. He was welcomed back there as a special guest star, but as well as wanting to tread the boards again, he wanted to express his gratitude to Arthur Sircom for the training he'd given him as director of *Rebound* with Ruth Chatterton.

Peck had chosen *Playboy of the Western World* because, as well as his admiration of the play, he was attracted to the challenge of achieving a convincing Irish brogue. Some of the critics who came to see him in the play were not convinced he had completely conquered the accent, but Peck was undaunted by bad reviews. 'I stuck my neck out and that's what happened,' he said at the time. 'I don't really care, though. I got what I came for. I wanted to try something I hadn't done before. I did. And I feel better for it, and I think I'll go back to Hollywood and do better work because of it. I think it's good to do things the hard way once in a while.'

When, in 1946, he was reminded that he needed to do one more film for Casey Robinson to fulfil his commitment to the man who brought him to Hollywood in the first place, Peck suggested they make a film based on a short story by Ernest Hemingway he liked called *The Short Happy Life of Francis Macomber*. Robinson asked him who he thought should direct it, and Peck replied, 'How about Zoltan Korda?' Hungarian-born Korda was the brother of ace producer Alex and had made several good jungle-based films such as *Sanders of the River* and *The Jungle Book*.

Robinson had a co-producer, Benedict Bogeaus, whom Korda disliked. 'Zoltan could be very bad-tempered,' said Peck, 'though not with me; he liked me and I liked him. He was one of my very favourite directors. But he was short tempered with certain types – phoneys and hypocrites – and he didn't like the producer, Benedict Bogeaus. Bogeaus was a nice enough fellow, but he wore too much cologne and too much gold jewellery and was too elegant in his attire for Korda's liking. Korda was a really tough guy, but he was also sensitive and we had a good working partnership.'

While Peck played rugged British hunter Robert Wilson, the story actually pivots around Robert Preston as Francis Macomber, a wealthy hunter whose courage is in question; Wilson is hired by Macomber to guide him on a hunt, during which Macomber has to overcome his cowardice to establish his true manhood. Providing the romantic interest was Joan Bennett as Margaret, Macomber's wife.

During the initial stage of production the film had no formal title and for weeks, Peck recalled, he, Korda, Robinson and Bogeaus racked their brains to find a suitable title – Hemingway's original was far too long.

Much of the film was shot on the sound stages of General Service Studio. Since the film required scenes of the African landscape and real animals alongside the rubber buffalo, three cameramen were dispatched to Africa to shoot backgrounds and wildlife. But Korda insisted they not shoot exterior scenes on the back lot, and he took his cast and crew to the Mexican border in the northern part of Baja. Peck recalled, 'We were there for about six weeks; eighty men and only two women – Joan Bennett and the hairdresser. We were all going kinda stir crazy.'

Every evening on location Bennett went to bed at eight-thirty, as did her hairdresser, who shared her bungalow. The men, said Peck, had 'one big stag party every night. Zoltan Korda sensibly avoided these parties we had – he went to bed at ten. Sometimes some of the crew drove eighty miles to Tijuana to take advantage of the bars and brothels. The road to Tijuana was so terrible that they called it "Dead Man's Highway". All the curves were graded the wrong way and ran along cliffs above the sea.' There was, he said, a local marimba band 'who looked more like pirates; they all had gold teeth and looked really rough. We'd all sing along with them and drink beer and tequila with them, play poker.'

One night Peck, Preston and the whole crew, minus Zoltan

Korda, who was tucked up in bed, stayed up through to sunrise, drinking and singing with the marimba band. Around 6 a.m., someone said, 'The cars are leaving for the location in twenty minutes.' They were all drunk and faced with an hour-and-a-half drive ahead of them. 'To sober up, we all stripped off and swam in the sea,' said Peck. 'We got back into our clothes, drank as much black coffee as possible and climbed into the cars for the long trek over the worst terrain. But we were sober and ready to shoot at eight-thirty.'

When they wound up the location, Peck, Preston and the unit could barely bring themselves to part from their Mexican musician friends who'd helped them to endure the nights with much music, tequila and general carousing. 'We all got along so well that when we had to go back to Hollywood we tried to import this band for a party,' said Peck. 'Unfortunately the band leader and two of his musicians were wanted for murder in San Bernardino after they'd been involved in some shoot-out, so we couldn't import them after all.'

They still had no title, Peck recalled:

One day at lunch at the General Service Studios, which was a little old-fashioned Hollywood studio, Aldous Huxley, who was doing some writing in an office there, overheard us discussing our title problem. We were also discussing a mechanical buffalo that was to charge down a track at Robert Preston while he stood his ground and fired away at it. Finally it falls at his feet with him standing over it. This buffalo was under construction and its hide was made of rubber and hair, and it had pistons to make its legs go, and it looked very lifelike at a cost of some $30,000. All this amused Aldous Huxley who put the problem of the buffalo and the problem of the title together and said, 'Why don't you call it *The – ah – Rubber Buffalo?*'

By this time Korda was under tremendous pressure because there was a problem with how to end the film. In Hemingway's original story, Margaret Macomber deliberately shoots her husband dead, and Wilson tells her that he'll report the shooting as an accident, even though he has no affection for her at all. The two go their separate ways while she literally gets away with murder. The script had to have a love story so a romance was concocted between Wilson and Margaret, giving Peck and Joan Bennett the requisite screen kiss. The Breen Office had a strict rule that criminals could never get away with the crime (a code which remained in force until broken by Sam Peckinpah's *The Getaway* in 1972.) There was also the problem of giving the film the requisite feel-good ending demanded by United Artists, which was paying for the privilege of distributing it.

Peck, although not a producer of the film, sat in on every script conference as they tried to come up with alternative endings. 'We all had a go at rewriting the ending,' he said. 'Finally we cabled Hemingway and told him our problem, but he never answered our cables. He had been paid $80,000 for his story, but when we tried to let him know we didn't want to corrupt his story, he wouldn't help. Not a single reply. So in the end we did the best we could.'

The film ended with a coroner's inquest into the death of Macomber. Waiting to go in and face the jury, Margaret tells Wilson that her husband's death should be blamed on the bad treatment she had suffered at his hands. She tells Wilson she will accept a degree of guilt and pay for it with a term in jail. The picture ends leaving the audience to wonder if Wilson will wait for her.

'We tried to preserve the hard unsentimental nature of Hemingway's story while maintaining the production code,' said Peck. 'But it just screwed up the entire picture. We spent the last ten minutes of screen time trying to wrap up those loose ends, and it killed it.'

The compromise was not lost on *The New York Times*'s Bosley Crowther, who noted, 'It is not a romantic story, and the producers have not improved it by trying to make it so.' But it was, he said, 'a quite credible screen telling [and] a tight and absorbing study of character. The measured performance of Gregory Peck implies the distrust and cynicism of the latter toward the unsporting dame.'

It was, said Otis L. Guernsey in the *New York Herald Tribune*, 'a confused and shapeless screen translation, as though they were hiding their meanings from the censors, so the whole thing ends up in the air in a muddle of motives and excuses. Except for some difficulty with English slang phrases, Peck does a good job of mirroring a sort of masculine independence of manner toward both women and wealthy cowards.'

Along with the story pressures, Korda and Robinson still had to contend with the issue of a title. Peck said that one day, towards the end of shooting, Bogeaus burst on to the set in the middle of a tense rehearsal, and said, 'Zolly, listen to this! I've got a title! It's great!'

Korda called a halt to the rehearsal and said to Bogeaus, 'OK, Benedict, what the hell is it?'

Bogeaus opened wide his arms and shouted '*Congo! ... Congo!*'

Said Peck, 'Korda just stared at him for a few moments, then he took out his pocket knife which he always carried, and opened it. He walked up to Bogeaus, stuck the knife against his upper-abdominal region and said, "You stupid son-of-a-beetch! You get off my set and if you ever come back here again, I cut your leever out!"

By the time the film wrapped someone had come up with the idea of calling it *The Macomber Affair*.

On 16 August 1946, Greta gave birth to their second son, Stephen. It was a time Peck might have wanted to devote to domestic life, but there was still too much work to allow him that luxury.

In November 1946, post-production work on *Duel in the Sun* was finally concluded and the release was planned for May 1947. As for *The Yearling*, MGM felt they had a special picture of great quality on their hands, and hoping to garner some Oscar nominations they opened it in Los Angeles in December 1946 so that it might qualify for the Academy Awards. Their ads announced 'This is the year of THE YEARLING – and it's worth waiting for!'

The New York premiere at the Radio City Hall in January 1947 was nearly delayed when Guy Eyssell, managing director of the hall, saw the film and complained to MGM that blood in a scene in which a bear mauls a pig looked far too vivid in Technicolor for his theatre; he insisted that the scene be cut from the film. The MGM labs were in the process of preparing the 200 prints to be sent countrywide for the film's general release, and had already printed ninety with the scene intact. The remaining 110 were produced minus the scene.

Peck, meanwhile, was back with Selznick for *The Paradine Case*. In the end Selznick wrote the screenplay himself; it was based on the novel by Robert Hitchens in which Mrs Ingrid Paradine is accused of poisoning her husband. Her defence lawyer, seemingly happily married, falls in love with her. In the book, Mrs Paradine kills herself after she is acquitted.

Selznick had wanted to film the book since he first read it in 1933 when he was working at MGM. He persuaded the studio to buy the screen rights as a vehicle for Greta Garbo, but despite a script having been written, neither the studio nor Garbo showed much interest in taking it further. Selznick bought it from the studio for $60,000 in 1945 for Alfred Hitchcock to direct.

Hitchcock and his wife, Alma Reville, proceeded to adapt the book for the screen and then persuaded Selznick to hire noted Scottish playwright James Bridie to write the complete screenplay. Disappointed with Bridie's work, Selznick took it upon himself to rewrite the entire screenplay, even while he was winding up post-production work on *Duel in the Sun*. He had scheduled *The Paradine Case* to begin shooting at the end of December 1946, and hoped to complete the screenplay in time.

Selznick intended to have a truly international cast. In the part of Mrs Paradine was Alida Valli from Italy; Selznick hoped to turn her into a new Ingrid Bergman. He signed her without having met her nor even seeing any screen performance, a move he undertook after advice from his executives. This indicates how deeply immersed he was in so many other areas simultaneously writing the screenplay, promoting *Duel in the Sun* and setting up production on *Portrait of Jennie* for Jennifer Jones.

Another new European star Selznick signed unseen to play Mrs Paradine's valet, was Louis Jourdan, then twenty-seven and highly popular in his native France. He told me, 'I met David in New York in 1946. Immediately, I could see that he liked me. He was happy that I had come. We got along beautifully, immediately. He was saying, "I did not make a mistake. That was the *right* decision." '

There was no doubt in Selznick's mind that Gregory Peck should star as the British lawyer who defends Mrs Paradine. But according to Jourdan, it became obvious over a dinner he had one night with Hitchcock and Anita Colby that Hitch hoped Peck would *not* do the film. 'He was talking about Emlyn Williams for the part. He wanted an English actor such as Laurence Olivier or Ronald Colman. And years later I discovered that Hitch hadn't wanted me at all but Robert Newton.' Selznick always got his way, and this was no exception.

Hitchcock set about trying to anglicize Peck's appearance by deciding he should have a moustache, until Ann Harris from

Selznick's London office reported that English barristers were always clean-shaven. So it was decided that greying Peck's dark hair a little would help to give his good looks a little English distinction.

From England came Ann Todd as the wife of the lawyer, and Charles Laughton as the chief prosecutor. With his fine cast but incomplete script, Hitchcock started filming on 19 December, 1946. He was used to starting work meticulously prepared, and was unhappy at being forced to work on a film with an unfinished screenplay. But he got on with what he had so far from Selznick, working on a budget of $3.2 million.

Charles Laughton was usually wary of he-man Hollywood types because of his secret homosexuality, which he feared would manifest itself on screen opposite more manly figures. But he had a considerable respect for Peck, telling him, 'You should be doing Shakespeare – you've got the voice, you've got the breath control and you've got the energy.' For the rest of the production, Peck and Laughton engaged in excited conversation about the prospect of doing Shakespeare together – an ambition never fulfilled.

Peck loved Laughton's outrageous style of acting. 'He was a ham – but a great one,' said Peck. 'I love actors like that. Too bad it's gone out of style. He was really a pussy cat – but he could be a threat. He was the kind of actor who always projected a sense of danger.'

After the first four days of shooting Selznick was dismayed to find Hitchcock was two days behind schedule already. At the end of the first week Selznick complained to his general manager, Daniel O'Shea, that Hitchcock was now three days behind schedule.

After three weeks Hitchcock had used up all the screenplay he'd been given, and from then on new pages arrived each day, which Hitchcock had to shoot without any kind of preparation. 'I'd never seen Hitch so unhappy,' said Peck. 'He decided to save time by setting up four cameras on the courtroom set to get as much coverage and cutaways as he could hope for in the shortest space of time. One camera was on the witness box, one on the prosecution, one on defence and one on the judge.

Each take, shot from four angles, took around ten minutes which should have resulted in faster filming. But somehow it didn't work in practice. Director and cinematographer, Lee Garmes, argued over the manner of filming because there was no way to light each shot individually, giving Garmes tremendous headaches over how to light the whole scene effectively for each of the four cameras.

While Hitch waited for new pages of script to arrive, he ordered work on the Old Bailey interior set to be modified, including the building of a ceiling, a move which horrified Selznick who complained that Hitchcock was holding up production. 'It wasn't a happy film from any standpoint,' said Peck. 'Selznick was a totally disorganized but essentially lovable man, while Hitchcock was not quite so lovable but totally organized. This created an unavoidable tension between them.'

Peck also noted, 'Hitch seemed really bored with the whole thing, and often we would look over to his chair after a take and he would be – or pretend to be – asleep.'

Peck found little time for any real relaxation during filming. He worked six days a week, and evenings were usually spent learning the new dialogue as it was being written. Greta had her own set of friends to keep her from living a virtually solitary life. He was free on Saturday nights, which developed into serious drinking sessions.

A regular guest at these Saturday sessions was Burl Ives, whose singing Peck recorded on wax discs. Ives tended to stay the whole weekend, sleeping through the whole of Sunday, waking for a further session of drinking and singing in the evening, then staying over and sleeping through Monday. Peck, by contrast, had to be at the studio at seven-thirty in the morning. Greg recalled how he would return at the end of Monday to find Ives curled up on the carpet 'like a beached whale'. Then there would be further carousing, which didn't particularly suit Peck, and only when he returned home at the end of Tuesday would he find Ives gone. But he loved the man.

Some Saturday evenings were spent at the home of Robert Mitchum and his wife at Mandeville Canyon. Other regulars included the Richard Widmarks, the Carusos and the Dean Jaggers; they were all known collectively as the Mandeville Canyon Gang. To these friends, Greg's marriage had all the outward appearance of a happy union. But, as the cracks widened, they saved their rowing for the privacy of their own home.

One day in February 1947, Peck was between takes on the courtroom set when he received a call from Darryl F. Zanuck who said he had just finished reading galleys of Laura Z. Hobson's latest novel, *Gentleman's Agreement*, about a journalist who pretends to be Jewish for an article he is writing about anti-Semitism in America. He wanted it to be Peck's second film for his studio, but he warned Peck it would be a controversial picture which would require all involved to show considerable courage. Peck couldn't resist it; he was hooked.

The other studios balked at the very idea of a film that would dare to suggest anti-Semitism existed in the United States, and a meeting was called at Warner Brothers in which all the major studio heads, many of them Jewish, tried to persuade Zanuck to drop the idea. 'Why make the picture?' they asked him. 'Why raise the subject at all?' They felt it was best to keep the whole subject hushed up so soon after the war and the revelations of the death camps.

Peck remembered, 'Zanuck politely told them to mind their own business.'

Further pressure came from the Catholic Church, which told Zanuck that the leading female character in the story, Kathy Lacey, was a divorced woman and so should not be presented as a heroine to the American public.

Peck himself felt the pressure. 'Some well-meaning friends fear that my screen popularity might be affected by such a role,' he said at the time, 'but I feel that an actor can't go wrong in a good picture, no matter how controversial the subject.' His agent was one of those who begged him not to do it, telling him it could wreck his career. Peck refused to listen; he was involved in a crusade that he could not resist.

Meanwhile, he still had *The Paradine Case* to wind up. Hitchcock found himself, by this time, unable to make the confused rewrites make any sense on the screen, and he later admitted that it was never clear exactly how Mrs Paradine had committed the self-confessed crime.

The budget ended up close to $4.3 million and the film had become a costly gamble for Selznick, especially considering that by the time it was finished, *Duel in the Sun* had not yet been released. Only time would tell if the Selznick Organization could survive.

Despite its problems it was quite a compelling courtroom drama. Howard Barnes of the *New York Herald Tribune* declared, 'Alfred Hitchcock has brought all his directorial cunning to a

71

screen tour de force.' Barnes's main criticism was that there was 'merely too much David O. Selznick' while for Hitchcock, he had only praise for his 'extraordinary imagination'. Peck, he said, 'is handsome and properly befuddled, adding still another striking portrayal to what is becoming an impressive list'.

Variety said that 'Hitchcock's penchant for suspense, unusual atmosphere and development get full play. Gregory Peck's stature as a performer of ability stands him in good stead among the extremely tough competition.'

Bosley Crowther of *The New York Times* thought different, noting that a courtroom mystery from Alfred Hitchcock should be 'a slick piece of static entertainment'. He added that in this case, 'it isn't,' and accused the film of being a 'too-well-written story – for the purposes of cinema, that is ... Peck is impressively impassioned as the famous young London barrister.'

Meanwhile at MGM, executives' hopes of Oscar nominations for *The Yearling* were realized when the list of hopefuls was published early in 1947. Peck had his second Best Actor nomination. Jane Wyman was nominated as Best Actress, as was Harold Kress for his editing, Cedric Gibbons and Paul Groesse for their colour art direction, and Charles Rosher, Leonard Smith and Arthur Arling for colour photography. In the event, *The Yearling*'s art directors and cinematographers won, and a special Oscar went to Claude Jarman Jr, as 'outstanding child actor of 1946'.

Peck lost out to Fredric March for *The Best Years of Our Lives*, but he did receive the Hollywood Foreign Press Association's Golden Globe as Best Actor. The film went on to gross more than $5.2 million in the domestic market, making it one of the studio's biggest successes of 1947.

The Macomber Affair opened at the Globe Theater in New York on 30 April 1947, shortly before the Oscars ceremony of that year. It might have done better but for the arrival of *Duel in the Sun*, which hit screens in May 1947. While many in Hollywood looked upon Selznick's epic lusty Western – which became known as *Lust in the Dust* – as an expensive gamble that could topple him, the undaunted producer set up his own distribution company, The Selznick Releasing Organization, because he was unwilling to trust any other distributor with the responsibility of making or breaking the picture. He spent almost $2 million alone on publicity.

Promotional material was dropped on to sporting events using thousands of war-surplus parachutes Selznick managed to acquire.

His publicity chief, Paul MacNamara, told Selznick that he thought the film was 'lousy' and that the best way to make a profit was to play the picture in as many situations as possible, to get it on and off before the inevitable disastrous reviews destroyed their chance of making back their money. Selznick reluctantly agreed. The traditional method of releasing a film was to show it first at a Manhattan theatre, and then move it to another borough. MacNamara booked the film into all five boroughs of New York. It was advertised as 'THE PICTURE OF A THOUSAND MEMORABLE MOMENTS'. The film was immediately denounced by the Roman Catholic Legion of decency for its immorality. They demanded several cuts to which Selznick reluctantly agreed, moaning, 'They can make me cut it, but they'll never make me like it.' The Legion rated the film 'B' which meant it was 'Morally Objectionable in Part for All.' The Legion's definition was, 'Films in this category are considered to contain elements dangerous to Christian morals or moral standards.' Other films which shared the distinction of being rated 'B' included Cecil B. De Mille's religious epic *The Sign of the Cross* and William Wyler's *The Best Years of Our Lives*.

Jennifer Jones came in for personal criticism from the Legion, which found her portrayal of the lusty Pearl Chavez an immoral contradiction of her portrayal of St Bernadette. Jones rightly responded, 'I was never Bernadette, nor was I Pearl Chavez. Each was simply a role I, as an actress, tried to interpret.'

The film was even condemned in the US House of Representatives in Washington. Nevertheless, MacNamara's ploy worked. In its first five days, the film took $750,000. It then opened in 300 theatres across the country and raked in a staggering $17 million. As late as 1970, the film appeared in the best twelve films of all time in a poll conducted by *Action*, the official magazine of the Director's Guild of America. But to Selznick's disappointment, *Duel in the Sun* failed to outdo *Gone with the Wind* in terms of popularity or critical appraisal.

Peck, whose popularity had never been in question, was now riding on a wave of public adulation that he was not completely comfortable with. Perhaps because of his sexual image in *Duel in the Sun*, his fan mail from women increased, many offering to pay for the chance to sleep with him. When his secretary asked him how to respond, he said, 'Tell them I'm all booked up.'

He spent hours personally signing requested photographs; many other stars had their autographs printed or simply signed by secretaries. But Peck never let the adulation go to his head, saying, 'I didn't feel like a tin god just because people wrote and asked for my autograph. It was just part of the job.'

It wasn't part of the job, though, to send money to the many who wrote asking for funds, and his secretary simply sent them polite letters rejecting their requests.

7

The 'Un-American' American

IN SPRING 1947 PECK began work on the film that many said might end his career – *Gentleman's Agreement.* It was his first opportunity to use his stardom to express some of his political views – and while it kicked up a lot of controversy, it was nothing compared to the brouhaha that his political views would stir up in the wake of anti-communism.

He had a first-class director, Elia Kazan, whom, Zanuck believed, could deliver a high-quality picture within schedule and within the set budget of $2 million, a considerable amount by 1947 standards, though modest compared to the amount Selznick had spent on *The Paradine Case.*

Peck played Phil Green, a widower who arrives in New York from California with his mother (played by character actress Anne Revere) and his young son (played by Dean Stockwell). Phil has a job with Smith's Weekly magazine and, at the suggestion of the publisher's niece, Kathy Lacey, writes a series of articles on anti-Semitism. Dorothy McGuire played Kathy, a divorcee of somewhat liberal but contradictory views who falls in love with Phil. Dorothy McGuire was delighted to discover that, having heard Peck suppos-edly had no sense of humour whatsoever, he was 'outrageously funny without ever trying'. They became lifelong friends.

As the fashion editor Anne Detrie, who carries a torch for Phil, Celeste Holm was exceptional and worthy of the Best Supporting Actress Oscar nomination she received. John Garfield too was outstanding as Dave, Phil's war veteran buddy. 'John was a sweet-heart,' Peck remembered. 'I got along great with him, and we tried to see if we could set up a repertory theatre in Los Angeles which we wanted to call The Actor's Company.' Shortly after finishing

Gentleman's Agreement, Garfield had a heart attack at the age of just thirty-eight. He refused to believe that at his age he really needed to take things easy and told Peck, 'Dammit, if I'm going to die, it'll be with my boots on. I'm not going to die an invalid.' He suffered one more, fatal, heart attack in 1952.

Scenes were shot on location in Darien, Connecticut, where 'gentlemen's agreements' between landowners excluded Jews from buying property. It was one town where Laura Z. Hobson's book had not been welcomed. But now the town welcomed the film stars, and the *Darien Review* reported,

> Hollywood came to Darien on Monday when the tall, handsome Gregory Peck and slender and pretty Dorothy McGuire enacted a scene at the Darien railroad station. Elia Kazan, who directed *Boomerang*, which was filmed in Stamford recently, was in charge of the proceedings. The scene is a minor one for the film *Gentleman's Agreement*, a story of real estate dealings.

The article prompted Bennett Cerf to comment wryly in the *Saturday Review*, 'The *Darien Review* finally has taken official note of Miss Hobson's best-selling blast against bigotry – particularly in Darien.'

The film never strayed into the realms of extreme bigotry but was all the more effective in exposing the more subtle forms of discrimination and intolerance practised by many in so-called polite company. In essence, the whole of American society came in for criticism, because those who were not overtly anti-Semitic kept silent and preferred, like many of the Hollywood studio moguls, to keep it under ground.

The film made its point in scenes such as the one where the neighbourhood children refuse to play with Phil's son and shout insults at him because they think he's Jewish. In his article, Phil describes one facet of anti-Semitism as 'an unending attack by adults on kids of seven and eight and ten and twelve'. When Phil and Kathy become engaged, she asks if she can tell her high-society friends that he isn't really Jewish. At many points in the story, those who claim to be non-discriminatory, even Kathy, are proved to be the opposite.

Screenwriter Moss Hart knew the film would not eradicate prejudice, and no one involved in the production had any such lofty hopes. But Hart did say that in making the film they were showing that 'the motion picture, if it gets courageous and grown-up, can be a wonderful medium'.

The whole cast believed they were involved in a politically important motion picture, and none of them was going to apologize for it. The film's director of photography, Arthur Miller, noted many years later, 'It was a way-out Left picture. Most of the cast were to the Left; Celeste Holm, Anne Revere, John Garfield, the whole damn lot. Jesus!' Many considered the film, and those involved, as un-American. But then, in post-war America, anything that in any way suggested any imperfection in American society was considered radical and unpatriotic. John Garfield, more than the others, was persecuted for his left-wing views, and was blacklisted in Hollywood by the House Un-American Activities Committee because he refused to name friends of his who were suspected of being Communists. Those close to him said that it was the blacklisting that killed him. Gregory Peck would also find himself accused of being un-American in due course.

The American film critics, however, were almost unanimous in their praise for it. 'A brilliant blow against racial and religious intolerance,' is how Howard Barnes described it in the *New York Herald Tribune*. 'Peck and the cast act as though they knew what they were up to and meant every minute of it.' 'An extraordinary achievement, a mature, honest and well-balanced drama,' thought *Cue* magazine.

'Every point about prejudice [in the book] has been made with superior illustration and more graphic demonstration in the film,' said Bosley Crowther in *The New York Times*, 'so that the sweep of Miss Hobson's moral indignation is not only widened but intensified.'

Crowther had one niggle; 'Although it is crisply and agreeably played by Gregory Peck, it is, in a careful analysis, an extraordinarily naive role. It is amazing that the writer should be so astonished to discover that anti-Semitism is cruel.' Peck defended the depiction, saying, 'Because the film needed to discover and experience the shock of anti-Semitism, it had to be done through Phil's eyes and experiences, so he was perhaps uncharacteristically naive.'

Elia Kazan said he wanted to make people think in relation to attitudes in films. 'Try to put yourself back in American films in 1946 when the word "Jew" was never mentioned. For the first time someone said that America is full of anti-Semitism'.

The *New Yorker* scoffed at the film, stating, 'the problem [of anti-Semitism] is quite a bit bigger than Mrs. Hobson and Mr. Hart make it out to be.'

Towards the end of filming on *Gentleman's Agreement*, Peck got The Actors' Company off the ground, with its base not in Los Angeles but at La Jolla. He persuaded Dorothy McGuire and Mel Ferrer to join him in founding the La Jolla Playhouse, through which they could indulge themselves in the pure pleasure of acting on a stage. Further interest in the project came from Joseph Cotten, Jack Benny, Rosalind Russell and Gene Kelly, and even David O. Selznick got involved by funding their theatre, which was the 500-seat auditorium of the La Jolla High School. Peck, McGuire and Ferrer figured the most they could expect to make on the box office was around $9,000 per play – $5,000 on a bad week. It would cost that and more just to produce each play. But the point of doing it at all was for the love of it. They also felt quite sure that ten plays a season featuring real movie stars would bring in plenty of business.

They planned to kick off the programme with *Rope*, starring Peck. Unfortunately, he ended up having to postpone it because he still had work to do on *Gentleman's Agreement*, and so the opening play became *Night Must Fall*, featuring the distinguished British character actress Dame May Whitty. Dorothy McGuire appeared in *Summer and Smoke*; Richard Baseheart, Ann Harding and Betsy Blaire starred in *The Glass Menagerie*; Jennifer Jones, Constance Collier and Louis Jourdan were in *Serena Blandish*; and Jose Ferrer appeared in *The Silver Whistle*. Peck closed the first season in *Gaslight*.

'A lot of actors come to us offering their services,' Peck told a reporter. 'They realize it's a good chance to be seen and to gain experience with experienced casts and capable directors.'

The La Jolla Playhouse kept Peck busy during the time he was not filming, and Greta got on with her life with her own friends.

Gentleman's Agreement was somewhat rushed through post-production and opened at the Mayfair Theater on Broadway on 11 November 1947. It stayed there for twenty-eight weeks, and by the time it had played throughout America it was Fox's top grossing film of 1947/48, making a net profit of $3.9 million. It was a landmark, proving that controversial films could be commercially viable at a time when the House Un-American Committee was conducting its Communist witch hunt in Hollywood. But in Spain the film was banned because, claimed the censor, anti-Semitism was not a problem in their country.

Honours and nominations were heaped upon the film. The New York Film Critic's Circle voted it Best Picture and named Elia Kazan Best Director. Kazan was awarded again by the National Board of Review, which named the film as one of the ten best of 1947. Golden Globes went to the picture, Kazan, Celeste Holm and Dean Stockwell as Best Juvenile Actor.

Oscars were handed out to the picture, Kazan and Celeste Holm. Peck received his third Best Actor nomination, while other nominees from the film were Dorothy McGuire (Best Actress) and Anne Revere (Best Supporting Actress). One of Peck's competitors for the Best Actor Oscar was Ronald Colman in *A Double Life*, and the manner in which the battle was fought out between studios was typical of the lobbying – some might even say rigging – that was prevalent in Hollywood. (Peck himself tried to stamp out such dubious practices when he served as President of the American Academy of Motion Picture Arts and Sciences from 1967 to 1970.) Universal took out space in magazines exclaiming surprise that so 'expert' an actor as Colman had not yet won an Oscar. Zanuck counteracted by organizing a rush of magazine stories on Peck. Colman personally arranged for his own supporters to speak up for him in paid advertisements. Colman won the Oscar.

The Paradine Case opened almost a year after its completion, on 31 December 1947. Despite an extensive advertising and publicity campaign, the public could not be persuaded to part with their money to see the film, which by June 1950 had earned little more than $2 million. *Portrait of Jennie* was an even bigger disaster and ended Selznick's independent reign in Hollywood. He did, however, co-produce a number of films in Europe with Alexander Korda, with whom he planned to remake *A Tale of Two Cities* (which Selznick had made for MGM in 1935), with Gregory Peck in the lead, but that was one that never got off the ground.

In spring 1948 Peck made his third film for Fox, *Yellow Sky*, directed by William A. Wellman and produced and written by Lamar Trotti. For this, his second western, remembering how he was almost killed by the show horse Selznick had found for him in *Duel in the Sun*, Peck decided to pick out his own mount. He went to a ranch in the San Fernando Valley and began trying out the available horses. The fourth horse seemed to be the best as Peck took it through various manoeuvres. He was turning it at a gallop when it suddenly slipped and went down on Peck's left leg. His ankle was broken. An ambulance was called and Peck was carted off to hospital.

The studio called the surgeons and asked if they could patch him up as quickly as possible, as they needed him to start work in four weeks; usually a broken ankle would take up to two months to heal properly. As he waited to be taken to surgery, he was given an injection of morphine by a nurse who was not particularly pretty or even young, but the effect of the morphine altered his perception and his behaviour. He reached up from the trolley he lay on, stroked her breasts and told her, 'you have the most beautiful breasts in the world. You are an angel. I love you.'

The nurse gently scolded him, 'Morphine addicts say that to all the girls.'

His ankle was reset, and four weeks later they released him after setting his ankle in a special cast that would allow him to walk, even though it was not fully repaired. Consequently, his ankle never did repair properly, and thereafter he had to resort to wearing a support to enable him to run – and he would only run if it was absolutely necessary. 'When I play tennis, I do some fast walking around the tennis courts,' he once said.

He went to work on *Yellow Sky* with the cast on his left leg, and for the first few weeks director Wellman shot him from the knees up or from his right side to keep the strapped foot out of shot.

The western was tough-looking and bleak, and the story an intriguing one, with Peck leading his gang of outlaws, including Richard Widmark, into a deserted ghost town where only an old man and his daughter, played by Anne Baxter, live. Patience between the outlaws becomes strained as they hole up there, while Peck and Baxter have the inevitable romance.

William Wellman was a tough director, who kept everyone working hard. According to Peck,

There was little time to sit in your canvas chair and relax between takes because he'd finish with a scene as quickly as he could by the expedient of keeping everything moving along at a gallop. And he never spoke – he shouted. And he swore profusely. But no one took exception to him because that was just his way of getting the best from everyone. He had a biting sarcasm that just made you enjoy the bumpy ride. And he was a master of the art of telling a story with pictures. Words are important but of secondary importance to these pioneer directors.

Yellow Sky is an excellent but largely forgotten film. Howard Barnes of the *New York Herald Tribune* called it 'an utterly implausible and vastly exciting horse opera. Peck is the bulwark of this Wild West epic who acts quietly. The dialogue is crisp and economical. The characters are always drawn in proper stature.'

'In this scorcher, the guns blaze, fists fly and passions tangle in the best realistic Western style,' wrote Bosley Crowther in *The New York Times*. 'Wellman has directed for steel-spring tension from beginning to end. It works out conventionally. But it's classy and exciting while it lasts.'

Peck made only one other film in 1948, *The Great Sinner*, a typically opulent production from Metro-Goldwyn-Mayer. The producer was Gottfried Reinhardt, son of Austrian stage impresario Max Reinhardt whom Peck had admired so much when he was directed by him on Broadway.

Set in nineteenth-century Russia, the film featured Peck as Fedja, a serious Russian writer who becomes a gambler. MGM writers Ladislas Fodor and Rene Fulop-Miller fashioned the story from segments of Dostoevsky's short novel *The Gambler*, but the author's name received no official screen billing whatsoever. The character was also partly based on Russian author Fyodor M. Dostoevsky, who wrote *Crime and Punishment* in 1866, and even elements from that book were incorporated without credit. The final screenplay was fashioned by Ladislas Fodor and Christopher Isherwood.

Peck found himself among some first-class actors, notably Walter Huston, Melvyn Douglas and Ethel Barrymore. Peck admired Walter Huston enormously and being young and looking to improve his craft, he asked Huston if he had any advice.

'Well, sonny,' Huston told him, 'give 'em a good show and always travel first class.'

Peck said, 'He'd never talk about ordinary stuff, acting. He didn't have much patience with it.' Peck soon learned, however, that Huston was an adept hand at upstaging his fellow actors. He recalled,

> When I'd do a two-shot with him – when two actors are seen in profile together – I'd find him taking hold of my arm and gently moving me until I'd have the back of my ear to the camera. I just thought it was his enthusiasm, but I came to realize he was just hogging the camera. But he looked at you with a twinkle in his eye, as if he were saying, "And just what are *you* going to do about it, young fellow?" Fortunately, I didn't have to do anything because I'd still have my close-ups shot, and in the end the editor has the final say. But he certainly liked to try it on before the camera.

Ava Gardner played Pauline Ostrovsky, a part again inspired by a real-life person, Polina Suslov, who was Dostoevsky's mistress. Ava was not only stunningly beautiful but a woman of great passion, who admitted to having flings with leading men such as Robert Taylor and Stewart Granger. She told me that such escapades between leading men and women were common, and when she made advances, few men could resist her. Peck, however did. Usually he refused to comment on his rumoured affairs with leading ladies, but in the case of Ava he was adamant that there was nothing between them. He said, 'The first thing you noticed about Ava was that exceptional beauty. As a young fellow, I was not as bowled over by that as the older fellows were. Our relationship was, and always has been, as pals. People say, "Oh, come on, this is one of the most desirable and beautiful women in the world, and you tell me you were just *pals*?" But that's the truth. It's quite possible for a young man and a young woman in their prime to be great friends.'

He admitted that he felt he had much in common with her 'because we were both products of middle-class, small America towns where everybody knew everybody. It was like we were young people from the same hometown, and it was on that basis we struck up an immediate friendship.'

Ava had come to the fore in movies because of her beauty – she knew that. Acting was something she did because it was a way of making profit from her looks. She was discouraged from trying to become a great actress by the studio which employed her. Some thought she was just lazy about acting, but the truth was that Metro-Goldwyn-Mayer, who had her under contract, never allowed her career to develop much beyond that of a pretty face. Peck said, 'Her development as an actress wasn't easy because everyone – directors, producers and even the critics and the audience – was perfectly happy just to look at her. It was OK if she just said her lines and walked through without being awkward or clumsy. She wasn't expected to try and get under the skin of a part, so she didn't attempt to.'

Peck was ambitious to develop as an actor, and he wanted to encourage her to do likewise. 'I worked more at the acting, did more homework, more preparation,' he said. 'I had a great respect for fine acting. Ava was more diffident about her talent, and I always had a tendency to encourage her and even, God help me, to coach her a little.'

The film's director, Robert Siodmak, made little impression on Peck, who usually relied heavily on guidance from his directors. Peck said of him:

He was an absolute nervous wreck. He was a hyperthyroid type, jittery and nervous. There was a nurse on the set who, a couple of times a day, would walk up to Siodmak when he was shouting and gesticulating at the actors or the cameraman, and she'd roll up his sleeve and jab a needle in his arm. I don't know if it was vitamins or a tranquillizer she was giving him to keep him from going through the roof. But he never paid any attention to it. So Ava and I had a mutually shared tendency to disregard him. He'd sit on the seat of the camera crane, and every now and then he'd mutter 'Up! Up! Up!' and off he'd go to hide eighteen feet above the rest of us while he collected his thoughts. And Ava and I would grin at each other and say, 'There he goes again!'

The Great Sinner was, as Howard Barnes called it in the *New York Herald Tribune*, 'a top heavy period piece ... pompous and dull entertainment. Peck has the arduous title role [and] plays with what might be termed a steady charm. He handles the romantic moments easily but he is far from persuasive when he calls upon religion for a preposterous regeneration. Ava Gardner is attractive and doleful but scarcely the type for the role.'

Peck was experiencing the first real slump in his career. The screenplay didn't give him much chance to do anything but play 'the fellow with sideburns and a Continental leer,' as the *New York Times*'s Bosley Crowther put it. 'Ava Gardner plays the lady with her emotions and her chest well exposed. The actors, entrapped by a weak script and fustian direction, are more sinned against than sinning, on the whole.'

Peck spent much of 1948 organizing the summer season at the La Jolla Playhouse with Dorothy McGuire and Mel Ferrer. As well as producing the plays, they did their best to try and persuade the biggest stars in Hollywood to appear in them. Peck asked Ava Gardner, suggesting it would do her good to 'work out, to learn'.

Gardner told him, 'OK, I'll do it if I can start with something small.'

Gardner recalled, 'Before I could commit, I had to ask Metro. They said, "Small part? Not the lead? Of course you can't do that. You either play the lead or nothing." I told them, "But I can't possibly play the lead." But little did they care. And that was the last time I allowed myself to even think about learning on the stage.'

The biggest stars were the most difficult to commit. When Peck asked Joan Crawford, she told him, 'You couldn't get me on that stage for a million dollars. It's one thing to act before a camera, but if I had to get up and act before all those people, I'd die of stage fright.' The truth was, many of Hollywood's biggest stars didn't have the courage to perform on a stage in front of a live audience. Yet even those who heartily joined in were not totally immune to a touch of stage fright. Dorothy McGuire admitted, 'We were all scared lots of times.' She recalled that there was little time to get the shows to performance level and they were often panic-stricken right up to opening night. 'And there were the dress rehearsals which were always before an audience, and that was really a full opening. You just took it for granted that you damned well got that show on and got it opened.'

During that second season, Peck appeared with Martha Scott in *The Male Animal,* James Thurber's comedy. Local critics described his performance as 'sensational', not realizing that comedy was a hidden forte of Peck's.

One of the plays he produced was *Born Yesterday*, which starred Robert Ryan. Peck and Ryan shared a liberal political philosophy.

They also both enjoyed drinking Scotch, and one night after a performance they sat and talked and drank until they were both 'completely pissed,' as Peck recalled it. In the early hours of the morning, having consumed copious amounts of whisky, they decided to clear their heads by stripping off and taking a swim in the sea. The next day, nursing a hangover, Peck realized that they were both lucky not to have drowned in their inebriated state.

Ryan still felt lousy by the time he had to go on for the next performance. Peck said that while watching the play, 'all I could think was that I was glad it wasn't *me* up there'.

His political interests sometimes led him to show support for various organizations whose views he shared. In China, revolution was a distinct possibility as Mao Tse-Tung prepared to overthrow General Chiang Kai-Shek, who was America's preferred choice of leader there. Peck approved of the activities of the China Conference Arrangements Committee, which opposed the current feudal system and pressed for true democracy.

He also supported the Committee for a Democratic Eastern Policy, which pushed for independence. He was certainly not alone in his involvement in the Committee for the First Amendment which was set up by many Hollywood personalities, including Humphrey Bogart, Lauren Bacall, William Wyler, Myrna Loy, Groucho Marx, Danny Kaye and Fredric March, to oppose the violation of civil rights that was beginning to harden as so-called un-American activities were investigated by Senator McCarthy. On the other side, aiding and abetting what had become a Communist witchhunt, were the likes of John Wayne, Robert Taylor, Ward Bond and John Ford.

Peck was also actively involved with the Hollywood Citizens' Committee of the Arts, Sciences and Professions, and the Progressive Citizens of America, but he resigned from both, explaining, 'I did feel that the stand these organizations were taking on several issues was too far to the left for my taste.'

The liberal views he and Ryan shared were not a great secret, but political poison was spreading throughout America in 1948, and Peck became a target. A book, *Treason in Hollywood*, was published in which author Myron C. Fagin named Gregory Peck, Fredric March, his wife Florence Eldridge, Eddie Cantor and Edward G. Robinson as Hollywood's communists and supporters. Peck, wrote Fagin, had been barred from making a personal appearance in Dublin because of 'his red activities'.

Peck refuted the claim, saying, 'There is more than one way to lose your liberty. It can be torn out of your hands by a tyrant – but it can also slip away day by day while you're too busy to notice and too confused or too scared.'

A huge can of worms opened up when the Joint Fact-Finding Committee to the California Legislature noted Peck's association with six organizations which they claimed were Communist fronts; they were the China Conference Arrangements Committee, the Committee for a Democratic Eastern Policy, the Committee for the First Amendment, the Hollywood Independent Citizens' Committee of the Arts Sciences and Professions, the Progressive Citizens of America, and The Actor's Laboratory.

In La Jolla, an alarmed Mrs C.P. Lineweaver, the chairwoman of the local chapter of the Pro-America organization, wrote to Peck expressing concern over his theatrical activities in her home town, saying that her members were 'anxious not to support any person or project through which encouragement and help might be given to radical groups who are seeking to undermine our Government'.

In response, Peck wrote a long, detailed letter in which he told Mrs Lineweaver that The Playhouse 'has absolutely no political motive,' and that he was a liberal Democrat to whom 'the domestic policies and the international views of President Roosevelt met, for the most part, with my humble approval'. He assured her that he would happily vote for a Republican president who offered 'the kind of leadership I, as an individual citizen, think is needed'. He stated that he held 'no brief for Communists or communistic doctrines' but he maintained anyone who did had a 'right to think and act independently within the law'.

Through his letter he challenged the Joint Fact-Finding Committee to 'instigate prosecution' against the six named organizations 'if laws are being violated'. He went on to explain that The Actor's Laboratory trained young actors and technicians who needed funds and he simply contributed $20 after seeing one of their plays. As for the other political organizations mentioned, he outlined their purposes and his reasons for supporting them, and ended by explaining why he had left two of them.

Shortly after, he was invited to meet with State Senator Hugh Burns, chairman of the Californian State Committee for Un-American Activities, who questioned him privately for forty-five minutes. Then he told Peck, 'I admire you for coming in and stating the truth. I believe you when you say that you were not a Communist and I'm going to report this to my committee.'

Consequently, Peck was not called to answer before Senator McCarthy in his hysterical investigation into Hollywood's Communists, and Mrs Lineweaver reasserted her support for the La Jolla Playhouse.

8

At War and Out West

PECK'S MARRIAGE WAS still rocky: he and Greta continued to share few interests apart from their sons, Jonathan and Stephen. Generally, he was dedicated to his work and she was fond of socializing. He knew from long experience that he couldn't tell her about his acting problems at the end of the day, and she knew he wasn't interested in the people she met and where she went during the day. But they did their best to make what passed for married life work, and late in 1948, Greta announced she was pregnant again.

Peck took on a new interest around this time. He became a rancher, although rather than buy his own homestead to grace the cattle he bought, he leased grazing land in Santa Barbara County, in Mercedo County, and also in Modesato. His financial advisors had told him that expenses for running ranch land were tax-deductible and the business itself would be a good investment, but in the end he did it simply for the love of it.

Yellow Sky opened with an all-star premiere on 1 February 1949 at New York's Roxy Theater. Danny Kaye was master of ceremonies, hosting the pre-screening show on stage, which featured Georgia Gibbs, Calvin Jackson and the Roxyettes. Curiously, the film never became a classic, considering the critical praise it received. There were no Oscars or Golden Globes for this picture, but Lamar Trotti and W.R. Burnett received awards for the 'Best-Written American Western' of 1949 by the Writers Guild of America.

MGM had great faith in Peck and cast him as young Roman general Marcus Vinicius in their lavish 1949 Roman epic *Quo Vadis*. John Huston was going to direct from his own magnificent screenplay that likened the Romans to the Nazis and Nero to Hitler. The persecution of the Christians was intended to remind the world of the attempt by the Nazis to exterminate the Jews. Gregory Peck saw tremendous integrity in Huston's vision. Elizabeth Taylor was to play Lygia the Christian girl he falls for, and Peter Ustinov would play Nero (who, it turns out, did not set Rome to the torch nor fiddle while it burned).

When Louis B. Mayer read Huston's script he complained that this was not the kind of film he had in mind. He wanted a big religious epic that would make grown men cry, and he proved it by weeping before Huston while singing 'Eli, Eli' on his knees. 'You see?' he asked Huston. 'That's what I want this picture to be.'

Huston left Mayer's office determined he would not make the film Mayer wanted, and got down to pre-production work. Then Peck caught an eye infection and filming had to be postponed. The film's producer, Arthur Hornblow, was criticized for the hold-ups as if he had personally been responsible for causing Peck's condition, and he resigned. So did Huston, who realized Mayer would not allow him artistic freedom. So did Peck. He was replaced by Robert Taylor, handsome and heroic but a lesser actor than Peck and far too old to play the young general. Elizabeth Taylor was by then unavailable, so Deborah Kerr played Lygia; Peter Ustinov hung on to his role and it made him a star. Mervyn LeRoy directed with a flair for spectacle but little drama.

The Great Sinner opened in June 1949; MGM was celebrating its twenty-fifth anniversary, so studio publicists came up with the idea of promoting some of its more lavish films as 'Silver Jubilee Productions'. This was one of them. But it was not one of the best as the critics were quick to point out. The public didn't go for it either, and it was an expensive flop.

A month before *The Great Sinner* opened, Peck was making *Twelve O'Clock High*. Darryl F. Zanuck had purchased the rights to Sy Bartlett's and Bernie Lay Jr's World War Two book. They had based their principal character, General Frank Savage, on a real officer, Major General Frank A. Armstrong, who had suffered a nervous breakdown while directing the first American daylight bombing air raids against German military installations from British airfields. Bartlett and Lay Jr had served under Armstrong after the general's recovery, and they made use of their own and his experience to write *Twelve O'Clock High*.

Zanuck wanted a film that, in contrast to the gung-ho heroics of current cinema, dealt with warfare realistically, with the emphasis on how the pilots fared under fire, using exciting aerial combat scenes purely as a background to the central drama. Zanuck told Peck he had been watching *Command Decision*, which told a similar story with a huge cast including Clark Gable, Walter Pidgeon and Van Johnson, over and over, and had realized the film was three quarters through before the audience could forget they were watching film stars and accept them as real characters. 'They were overwhelmed, overpowered by the stars,' said Zanuck. 'But that's not going to happen with *Twelve O'Clock High*. I want to make it with unknowns, except for you and Dean Jagger.'

Zanuck felt so strongly about the film that he decided to produce it himself. To direct the film to his specifications, he chose Henry King, whose considerable repertoire stretched back through the silent era and whose talkies included the classics *In Old Chicago*, *Alexander's Ragtime Band*, *Stanley and Livingstone* and *The Song of Bernadette*. Zanuck told King that he was his only choice as director, but King actually heard that the producer had first offered it to William Wyler, who had turned it down. Nevertheless, King liked Zanuck's vision, agreeing that the film should aim to show the emotional and physical effects on the commanding officers, whose job was to send young men into battle, and often to their deaths. 'It was a story exploring the responsibilities of officers to their men rather than merely a phase of aerial warfare,' King said.

Zanuck gave King the screenplay, which Sy Bartlett and Bernie Lay Jr had written from their own book, and told him to take Bartlett far away from the studio and work with him on polishing the script. The final version of the screenplay delighted Zanuck.

King was given every assistance by the American Air Force, which arranged for the film unit to use Algin Air Force base in Florida for shooting; the story may have been set in Britain but it was cheaper to shoot on home soil.

Zanuck wanted only Gregory Peck to play the war-weary General Savage. King said, 'Zanuck chose him for the part. He told me, "I think we can get Greg Peck for this. If we can, don't you think he'd be great for it?" I had seen him in one other picture and I said, "Yes, I do. I don't know of anyone who'd be better. It's either him or Burt Lancaster and I prefer Peck." Lancaster's a totally different kind of actor. A fine actor, but a different type.'

The union of Henry King and Gregory Peck would be something of a milestone in both their careers, and they went on to make six successful or critically acclaimed films together. Peck told me:

> I liked Henry King and he liked me. When we first met to discuss the part and the film, I told him that I'd had no military experience to help me prepare for the part. He told me, 'Well, you're going to live on a military base, and you're going to live military base life. I'll give you a man who'll instruct you in how to salute. He'll teach you everything you need to know. Just one more thing. Try to act like a general and not like a second lieutenant.'
>
> 'What's the difference?' I asked.
>
> He said, 'A second lieutenant is always trying to act like a general, like he thinks a general *should* be, and everything he does is very stiff. But a general is more relaxed.'
>
> I asked him about the symptoms of a man who is heading for a nervous breakdown, and King said he'd only ever observed one man who'd had such a breakdown, and leading up to it he used to sit and pull on his knees with his hands and rock back and forth, and he used to move his feet around a lot. So I remembered that bit of detail.

Peck's preparation for the role was thorough: he underwent special coaching from Elsa Schreiber, the Viennese actress who, at eighteen, had gained a huge reputation when she played Juliet for Max Reinhardt. She was often hired by film studios to coach stars like Tyrone Power and Rex Harrison, and she helped Peck to find the right approach to his role through disciplined sessions held in a small room. It was an experience Peck found so stimulating that he called on her for further coaching in future films.

He had by this time developed a technique of throwing himself so totally into a role that it tended to spill over into his private life; he often took his roles home with him. 'When you start rehearsing with Greg,' said Henry King, 'he's *in* the part there and then and stops being himself. He's the hardest worker I've ever seen.'

In the early summer of 1949 Gregory Peck and the rest of the cast and crew were loaded into a United Airlines DC-4 and flown to Florida; King flew himself in his own plane. 'Usually they put you on a train whenever you go off on location,' said Peck. 'When we shot *The Yearling* it took around ten days to get to Florida, but King had this big old DC-4 he'd chartered, and we did the trip in one go.'

Peck remembered what King had told him about the symptoms of a nervous breakdown, and he worked out how he was going to employ them in his performance. When they came to shoot a scene just prior to his breakdown, he sat at his desk and pulled on his knees.

'Peck, what in the world are you doing?' asked King.

'Well, you told me this is the symptom,' Peck replied.

King was genuinely impressed with the way Peck had worked out how he was going to play the scene. 'He is a very dedicated man,' said King. 'He's seeking information every minute. When he has a part to do, he is the part, even at home, he's so dedicated to do the best job with it.'

When asked if there was any one director who had helped him develop and hone his acting skills, Peck replied:

> I've worked with so many fine men – Kazan, Hitchcock, Zinnemann, Huston and the whole list of them – and I don't mean any disrespect or lack of regard for any of them when I say that the fellow who meant the most to me was Henry King. As a screen actor, I play to only one person – the director. He becomes a kind of confidante, a kind of brother, a father. He's your audience. With King I had like a kind of older-brother-younger-brother relationship. He didn't direct me all that much. He used to say something now and then but very often he wouldn't say anything at all. We didn't have to talk very much. He was just my kind of man and I wanted him to be pleased with my performance. He simply provided me with a one-man audience in whom I had complete trust. If I played to him and he liked it, then I was fairly confident that I was on the right track.

The American Air Force provided King with several B-17s for his combat scenes as well as actual aerial combat footage, which King and his editor Barbara McLean cut into the film. One shot King needed was a B-17 landing on its belly with its wheels up. No less than twenty actual pilots on the base volunteered to do the dangerous stunt, but their superiors forbade their involvement in anything so risky. So King called Hollywood's flying expert Paul Mantz, who was due to come down later to shoot aerial formation flying, and asked him to arrive sooner to do the belly-landing.

Mantz said he would do it but wanted a lot more money and quoted some astronomical fee that King knew was out of the question. So he immediately called the studio and told them he would do the stunt himself and instructed them to let Mantz know that. Mantz promptly halved the fee he had demanded and consequently did the stunt.

In one scene Peck had to take away the stripes of his clerk sergeant who had stowed himself on board a bomber when it took off for a raid. Peck went through his paces, displaying what seemed to be the requisite amount of anger. After Zanuck viewed the rushes in Hollywood, he called King and asked him to take another look at that scene, as he felt there was something wrong with it but couldn't put his finger on what it was.

Peck sat with King and watched the scene. Peck remarked, 'My heavens, that's an awful lot of acting.'

They decided to do the scene again, this time with Peck playing it totally differently, conveying not anger but pride in the clerk, while still having to maintain discipline. The change made all the difference.

While Peck was away in Florida filming, Greta gave birth to their third son, Carey Paul, on 17 June 1949, named after Peck's friend Harry Carey. When Greg returned to Hollywood, he moved his growing family into a bigger house. The arrival of a third child seemed to convey that all was well in the marriage. The fan magazines portrayed them as one of Hollywood's happiest couples. But Greg and Greta just seemed to make each other miserable. Having babies was not, they came to realize, the solution to their problems. But they doggedly stuck at it. Peck had known what it was for a child to suffer the trauma of a broken home, and he didn't want his children to go through it.

Post-production work on *Twelve O'Clock High* was completed in the fall and the finished picture opened in Los Angeles in December, before its formal New York premiere, to make it qualify for Oscar consideration. The actual premiere was on 26 January 1950, at New York's Roxy Theater, a date chosen because it celebrated the eighth anniversary of the formation of the 8th Army Air Force as well as the seventh anniversary of the first daylight precision bombing raid on Germany.

Time declared it to be 'the freshest and most convincing movie of the current cycle about World War II,' and praised Peck's 'strong, beautifully modulated performance that never lets the role down'. *Life* said, 'Gregory Peck gives a forthright performance at the head of a strong cast of male actors who recreate all the urgency and the strain of men face-to-face with the grim business of air warfare.' 'A topflight drama, polished and performed to the nth degree,' said *Variety*. 'Peck gives the character much credence as he suffers and sweats with his men. We can mark it down as just about his best work to date.' Bosley Crowther wrote in *The New York Times* that the general was 'beautifully played by Peck. He is magnificently, unselfishly heroic, even in his breakdown at the end.'

Peck received letters from William Wyler and Fred Zinnemann applauding his performance. Members of the American Academy saw fit to give him his fourth Oscar nomination. Also nominated were Dean Jagger in a supporting performance, Thomas T. Moulton for sound, and the picture itself. Curiously, Henry King received no nomination. As it happened, it was the year *All the King's Men* won most of the substantial awards, and Peck lost out to Broderick Crawford. He did, however, get the thumbs up from the New York Film Critics Circle with their Best Actor award.

The American Air Force was so impressed with the picture that they used it for many years as a training film about the stress men suffer under combat conditions.

Despite his political differences with John Ford, Peck readily agreed to take a supporting role in the World War One play, *What Price Glory*, which Ford directed on stage at Grauman's Chinese Theater in aid of the Purple Heart recreation centre for war veterans in the San Fernando Valley. Leading characters were played by Ward Bond and Pat O'Brien, while John Wayne, in the rarest of stage appearances, performed a supporting role.

Before the premiere of *Twelve O'Clock High*, Peck had started work on his next film for Fox, a western called *The Gunfighter*. He played Johnny Ringo, an ageing gunfighter trying to live down his reputation as the fastest gun in the west. He is anxious to try for a reunion with his wife (played by Helen Westcott) and the young son who's never known him. But his past catches up with him and he is killed in a gunfight with the three brothers of one of the many young gunmen who has tried to outdraw him. With his dying breath, he tells the one who finally got him, 'In every town you go, there will be someone itching to kill the man who got Johnny Ringo.'

Zanuck had sent the script to Peck who recalled, 'I remember reading the script and feeling certain right away that this was going to work into a fine picture. Johnny Ringo had an innate intelligence, and could, in other circumstances, have gone on to become a senator.'

Zanuck went off to Europe, leaving Nunnally Johnson to produce the film. Peck, now with considerable star power to his acting elbow, had made it clear he wanted Henry King to direct it. Johnson had already spoken to King about the project, but suggested Peck also approach him. When Peck went to meet him, King hadn't read the script.

'Please read it,' Peck told him, 'because if you do it, I'll do it too.'

King read it, and liked it. He told Peck he should grow an authentic-looking moustache. 'In those days,' said the director, 'every man had to have a moustache or he wasn't a man at all.'

Peck not only grew the moustache but had himself given a basin haircut. When King saw him, he said, 'That's it. Perfect. Don't grow the moustache any more.'

When the first rushes were viewed by Nunnally Johnson, he immediately called King and told him he didn't think much of Peck's moustache and was sure Zanuck would object too.

'Do you want me to take him out of uniform and turn him from gunman to general?' asked King. 'He has to have the right look, the right clothes.'

'Well, I don't like the clothes either,' said Johnson who was sure that Peck's overall appearance would disappoint his female fans and have an adverse effect on the box office.

King refused to make any changes to Peck's appearance, and when Spyros Skouras, president of Twentieth Century-Fox, watched the rushes, he began shouting, 'Take off that ... that ...' but was too distraught at the sight of Peck's moustache to complete the sentence.

King and Peck went to see the production manager and asked how much it would cost to reshoot all they'd filmed over the past two weeks in order to remove the offending moustache. It worked out at $150,000.

As a boy Eldred Gregory Peck dreamed of being a sailor, but after his first boat
sank, he decided to become a doctor – an ambition which also sank

With his first wife, Greta, in happy times during their early days in Hollywood. Greta loved the Hollywood life while Greg preferred a quieter existence. Their opposing lifestyles eventually led to divorce

In his second film, *The Keys of the Kingdom* (1944), there was no place for romance. He played a priest who sacrifices all for missionary work in China and his leading lady, Rose Stradner (*right*), was the Mother Superior. The female population of America fell in love with the new star and he received his first Oscar nomination

Ingrid Bergman attempts to cure amnesiac Peck whose lost memory may hold the key to a murder in Alfred Hitchcock's *Spellbound* (1945). Bergman said, 'Greg was a very handsome man – very sexy. It was difficult not to be attracted to him'

Sizzling screen sex 1946-style as outlaw Peck and outcast Jennifer Jones
set the screen alight in David O. Selznick's grandiose western *Duel in the Sun*. It
looks tame today yet had the defenders of American morals objecting strenuously
– but the public loved what became known as *Lust in the Dust*

There was a second Best Actor nomination for Peck in *Twelve O'Clock High* (1949) in which he played the commander of a US bomber unit who comes increasingly under stress despite support from his superior officer played by Millard Mitchell (*right*)

Sporting a handlebar moustache and unflattering costume, Peck played Ringo, an ageing gunman, in *The Gunfighter* (1950), who, though desperate to hang up his guns, is forced by circumstances to keep them trained on the likes of Anthony Ross (*left*)

Peck as David, the biblical shepherd king, who got into divine trouble over a woman in the guise of Susan Hayward. *David and Bathsheba* (1951) was the first in a spate of money-spinning biblical epics produced by Twentieth-Century Fox during the fifties, but it was Peck's only foray into that genre

Ava Gardner provided Peck with his love interest during the long flashback sequences in *The Snows of Kilimanjaro* (1952). Close friends off-screen – but never lovers, insisted Ava – he encouraged her to develop her acting ability which her studio invariably suppressed

Gregory Peck in typical serious, handsome, reliable, authoritative pose in *The Snows of Kilimanjaro*

Gregory Peck with second wife, Veronique, a French journalist he met while making *Roman Holiday* and went on to romance after he and Greta split

Peck told the production manager, 'Tell Mr Skouras it's going to cost $300,000.'

'I can't do that. My job depends on my being absolutely accurate.' But Peck and King persuaded him to send a memo to Skouras to the effect that it would cost $300,000 to re-shoot. Skouras was furious, knowing he couldn't order retakes at that cost, and he told Zanuck that he'd contribute $25,000 himself to the budget just to get rid of the moustache if someone else would pay the rest. There were no offers. The moustache stayed.

Skouras was proven correct; the female fans did stay away, and the picture flopped, despite being a critical success. 'There's never a sag or off moment in the footage,' said *Variety*. 'Gregory Peck perfectly portrays the title role, a man doomed to live out his span killing to keep from being killed. He gives it great sympathy and a type of rugged individualism that makes it real.'

Despite its commercial failure, the film has continued to gain respect and admiration. Film director Lindsay Anderson declared that it 'preserves throughout a respectable level of intelligence and invention'.

Peck was back in the saddle for his next picture, a cavalry western, *Only the Valiant*, and was distinctly unhappy. The failure of *The Paradine Case* had been a severe blow to Selznick, who suffered another flop with his expensive *Portrait of Jennie*. He had to recoup some money by loaning his stars out, and he took advantage of just such a contract he had signed with Peck. When Warner Brothers wanted Peck for *Only the Valiant*, Selznick struck a deal that earned him $150,000. Peck got just $65,000.

Peck didn't know anything about the deal until he received a call telling him to report to Warner Brothers for wardrobe fittings. When he read the script, he was dismayed to say the least. It was the most inferior screenplay he'd yet been given – just a routine, predictable adventure yarn. He was to play a US Cavalry captain, whose small detachment has to make a stand in a desert fort to hold off an Indian attack until reinforcements have time to arrive.

'I raised holy hell about it,' said Peck, who demanded that a better screen vehicle be found for him under the Selznick contract. A Selznick executive told him, 'David needs the money. He won't discuss it.'

Peck accepted the fact that he was in a no-win situation, but he consoled himself with the thought that by doing the film it would be one more commitment to Selznick out of the way.

Among the supporting cast were Ward Bond as an alcoholic corporal, Lon Chaney Jr, as an Arab whose presence in the US cavalry is never fully explained, and Gig Young as a lieutenant whom Peck sends on a deadly mission. Playing Young's sweetheart was blonde starlet Barbara Payton, who spends most of the film hating Peck but in the end falls in love with him. The relief column arrives with a Gatling gun, by which time there are just three survivors.

For its type of picture, it was actually quite good, and when it opened in April 1951 more than one critic credited Peck with making the film more watchable than it might otherwise have been. 'Thanks to Gregory Peck's physical authority and his ability as an actor to imbue a synthetic character with a degree of conviction that would be lost to a lesser performer, the spectator is not, at least, overwhelmed by the banality of the plot,' thought Thomas M. Petcher in *The New York Times*.

'Peck gives a strong performance,' said Otis L. Guernsey in the *New York Herald Tribune*, who thought the picture 'a good cavalry-and-Indians melodrama which might be much better if the first thirty minutes were cut down to five'.

Because he wanted to make a concerted effort not to become associated with westerns, he turned down a role that Carl Foreman offered him, that of Marshall Caine in *High Noon*. Gary Cooper was therefore cast, and the role won him a Best Actor Oscar. Peck considered his rejection of the film 'the greatest mistake I ever made'. He admitted that when he saw Cooper collect his Oscar, it occurred to him that it could have been him up there instead. 'But he was perfect in it,' said Peck. 'I'm not a plaster saint, without envy.'

He was still named 'Cowboy Star of the Year' by American exhibitors.

9

Black Clouds and High Seas

DURING THE SUMMER OF 1950, Peck spent much of his time at La Jolla working on a season of plays. His father and his wife, Harriet, came to visit to be with Greg and the boys. Greta was conspicuously absent from the family get-together. Life for her and Greg had by now become miserable for both of them, and Greg had actually packed his bags and moved out a couple of times, but always returned for the sake of his boys.

There was a black cloud hovering above him as he began to realize that his personal life was a shambles and he seemed powerless to do anything about it. He eased the emotional trauma with a daily dose of Scotch, which he complemented with tranquillizers. He was on a downward spiral that he felt helpless to stop.

Darryl F. Zanuck had a new script for Peck in 1950, *David and Bathsheba*. It was to be a $3 million biblical epic to ride on the bandwagon set in motion by Cecil B. De Mille's *Samson and Delilah* the year before.

Peck wasn't convinced he was right for the role and expressed his doubts to Zanuck in his large studio office. Zanuck showed him a book which itemized the costs and the profits of all the films Peck had made for Fox, revealing that he had made the studio in the region of $100 million.

'I think you *are* right for this picture,' Zanuck told him. 'But it wouldn't matter what I thought if your pictures didn't do well at the box office. You shouldn't forget that. We're not sentimental in this business. I don't give you good roles because I like you – although I do – but because you're box office.'

Peck told me, 'That's when I learned that while it's pleasing to get good reviews and be well liked by directors what really counts is that your pictures make money. It's a *business.*'

Early one morning in October, Peck was undergoing make-up tests for the part of David at the Fox studio. He suddenly felt his left arm go numb and an agonizing constriction in his chest. He broke into a sweat and told the make-up man, 'I think I'm having a heart attack.'

He was rushed straight to hospital. He recalled that although he was convinced he was about to die, he felt strangely calm and realized that it was the stress in his life that had finally brought him to this point. An electrocardiogram revealed that he hadn't suffered a full-blown heart attack, but it was an early warning. He was sent home, whereupon he managed to get into a blazing row with Greta. He hurriedly packed a suitcase and drove off to an isolated resort at Apple Valley in the Upper Mojave Desert where he rented a bungalow at an exclusive resort.

There he stayed for a month, reading classic books and eating good food brought to his bungalow by the woman who ran the resort. Recognized that he had developed something of a drinking habit, he abstained from alcohol. He began to feel physically better, and hired a horse to go riding over the desert and even took to walking in the wilderness. It was a time of enforced relaxation and self-analysis; it was also the longest time he had ever spent in virtual isolation. He came to the conclusion that his marriage had failed, but that he should try to make the best of it for his children's sake.

He returned home to maintain the outward appearance of a happily married man, and when the press asked him how he managed to stay well adjusted with all the fame and money his success had brought him, he told them, 'I'm lucky. I've a very tolerant wife.'

Henry King spent more than a year working on *David and Bathsheba*. Peck's stint was limited to a few months, but he found, somewhat to his surprise, that he enjoyed it. King had a method of pacing up and down before shooting a scene, going through the motions of the characters and trying to decide how best to film it all. He didn't like to be watched, and when he once noticed Peck observing him, he said, 'Greg, please, don't you do the scene the way I'm doing it. I'm just trying to design the scene.'

'Well,' replied Peck, 'it doesn't look too bad to me.'

His leading lady was Susan Hayward, and for some reason they failed to hit it off socially. They didn't argue or backbite about each other, but they just never took the time to get to know each other personally and seemed not to want to. Or perhaps Peck simply felt that he'd prefer not to get too friendly with any woman at this time, while he was trying to save his marriage.

Zanuck announced that, in making *David and Bathsheba*, 'Twentieth Century-Fox would be known as a filmer of great dramas instead of a maker of mere spectacle.' This decision was probably due more to cost than artistic integrity. De Mille's film and MGM's *Quo Vadis* were huge successes because they looked historically accurate, but also had tremendous spectacle created at enormous cost. Fox wanted to keep costs down, although Henry King insisted, 'We never went out for spectacle, never had it in mind. That picture was done purely. Everything was from the Bible.' Which is pretty much what De Mille said about *Samson and Delilah*.

The film's publicity highlighted the appointment of Dr Chester C. McCown, a renowned authority on Bible archaeology and history, as technical advisor, claiming Zanuck wanted his film to be the most authentic biblical film to date. That didn't stop the screenwriter Philip Dunne rewriting the Bible to give the film an uplifting ending; in the original, King David is actually damned for his sins. Most critics weren't fooled. The *Saturday Review* thought it was 'a misguided effort to beat Cecil B. De Mille at his own game. Gregory Peck lends dignity and his virile good looks to the role of David.'

'The producers have obviously intended to follow in the footsteps of Cecil B. De Mille,' said the *New York Herald Tribune*, 'but they have failed to come up with eye-filling mass movements of men and material which such an extravaganza requires. Peck is properly dignified, though there is less fire in his acting than is indicated in the heroic legends.'

Look felt that it didn't have 'the blustering showmanship of *Samson and Delilah*, but it is certainly a more creditable attempt to bring biblical history to the screen in a reverent, poetic and tasteful manner'. Abe Weiler of *The New York Times* called it 'a reverential and sometimes majestic treatment. In Gregory Peck's delineation the producers have an authoritative performance.'

Variety called it 'a big picture in every respect. It has scope, pageantry, sex, cast names, colour – everything. Peck is a commanding personality. He shades his character expertly. His emotional reflexes are not as static as the sultry Miss Hayward's.'

Peck was still locked into history for his next picture, *Captain Horatio Hornblower*, based on C.S. Forester's book about Nelson's adventurous but fictional contemporary. In fact, Forester had a hand in writing the script, a script that also passed through the typewriters of Ivan Goff and Ben Roberts before Raoul Walsh was satisfied. Walsh was producing and directing for Warner Brothers. The company had some money frozen in England that couldn't be transferred to the United States, so they decided to shoot at Denham Studios in London. The sea sequences were to be shot just off Villefranche in the south of France.

When Peck heard that Jack Warner wanted Virginia Mayo to play the part of Lady Barbara, Hornblower's love interest, he told Raoul Walsh that he thought English actress Margaret Leighton would be a much better choice.

'Don't know the broad,' said Walsh. 'Is she any good?'

Peck explained that he had seen her on the New York stage with Laurence Olivier and that she was perfect for the part.

'Okay,' said Walsh, 'I'll tell Jack and see what he says.'

A few days later Walsh told Peck, 'It's Virginia Mayo.'

'But what's the matter with Margaret Leighton?' asked Peck.

'Simple. No tits.'

To prepare for the part, Peck had some coaching sessions with Elsa Schreiber and read all of the Hornblower books, imagining himself in the part in each story. Of the role, he said:

> I thought Captain Hornblower was an interesting character. I never believe in heroes who are unmitigated and unadulterated heroes who never know the meaning of fear. I just don't believe that. I think it's inhuman. I like a hero, particularly a seagoing hero, who gets seasick, who gets nervous before every battle, because I think people are like that and I don't really subscribe to the hard-nosed guy who's afraid of nothing. That's a cinematic cliché. I'd rather play someone who's like the rest of us.

Greta and the children went with Greg to London, and lived in a house in Gloucester Square which came complete with three Irish girls to wait upon them. Peck told a friend, 'It's all very fine –

except the cooking. But the girls are such nice rosy girls that I don't have the heart to release them.'

Walsh had a casual way of directing, giving his actors little in the way of instruction, except to say, 'Speed it up. Keep it moving.' He was something of a high-liver, and he liked to dress meticulously. One day he told Peck, 'You're a lousy dresser, you know that?'

'I've always let the studio worry about how I dressed,' Peck replied.

'You come with me,' said Walsh, who took him to Huntsman & Co. in Savile Row, where the director proceeded to pick out Peck's new wardrobe. Thereafter Peck ordered virtually all his suits from there.

During filming at Denham Studios, Princess Margaret, in a well-stage-managed piece of PR, came to watch Peck at work. She said, 'I think it's fine to see such an exceptionally good-looking man who is also such a fine actor. I think he is wonderful.'

When the studio work was complete, the unit moved to the south of France and were ensconced at La Réserve Hotel in Beaulieu. There were no Sundays off, but one Saturday night Walsh led his principal actors and technicians to the Château Madrid on the Haute Corniche where a quartet of musicians were playing chamber music. They all got so loaded, said Peck, that 'none of us could feel any pain'.

The drunken assistant director told the band to play, 'Yes Sir, that's My Baby' and Peck insisted they play 'Home on the Range'. He even sang it for them while the assistant director and members of the crew demonstrated American football to the dozen diners who only wanted to eat their meals in peace.

The film party finally left at four in the morning, and were on set at eight, looking the worse for wear. Walsh suffered no ill-effects whatsoever, and told them, 'If you want to stay up all night, fine, but you'll still have to work all day.'

Walsh produced a fine, unpretentious film. As Bosley Crowther of *The New York Times* pointed out, 'This bright-colored sea-adventure picture ... should please those mateys who like the boom of cannon and the swish of swords. The conduct of those who made it will be brought to the attention of the Admiralty. A portion of rum all round!'

Arthur Knight of the *Saturday Review* prescribed it as 'just the thing for those hot nights. All the gusto, sweep and color that endeared the Hornblower series to millions of readers has been preserved in Walsh's rapid and muscular direction.'

Otis L. Guernsey of the *New York Herald Tribune* thought, 'Peck cuts a fine figure as the capable, laconic and embarrassed captain. Walsh has put on a good visual show. It is a good job, fun to watch for the most part, respectful of its source and presenting a colorful sequence of romantic sea events.'

Peck loved London, and not long after *Hornblower* was completed returned there with Greta and the children to attend the Royal Command Performance. There they put on a performance of their own for the newspaper photographers – that of a happily married couple. But behind closed doors there was further rowing. Greta was concerned that so much travelling was unsettling for their sons, while Greg thought that it did them good. He also thought it important that they were together when he had to travel, although while he was working they saw little of each other, home or abroad. Greg still spent much of his time at the La Jolla Playhouse, as well as enjoying his life as a would-be rancher. But desperate not to become a failed father, he ensured that he took time out to take them on picnics, and horseback riding in the mountains.

In January 1951, Peck received the Henrietta, an award from the Foreign Press Association, proclaiming him as the World Film Favourite, based on a worldwide poll that garnered more than a million votes.

With that honour, Peck went to work again for Zanuck, who personally produced *The Snows of Kilimanjaro* in 1951. Henry King was to direct from a screenplay by Casey Robinson, based on a short story by Ernest Hemingway about a writer (played in the film by Peck) who lies dangerously ill at the base of Mount Kilimanjaro in Tanzania, reliving his misspent life. Robinson's job was to expand the story to include memories of the Spanish Civil War, during which he loved and lost the beautiful Cynthia, played by Ava Gardner. Susan Hayward assumed the less colourful role of his wife.

King thought Robinson's adaptation was first-class, saying, 'On his writing on this you couldn't tell where Hemingway's writing quit and Robinson's began. He developed a Hemingway style and drew a little bit on everything Hemingway had written.'

Robinson wrote the role of Cynthia especially for Ava Gardner, basing the character, which was only suggested in Hemingway's story, on Lady Brett Ashley in Hemingway's *The Sun Also Rises*. Curiously, Gardner would play that role in the movie version King directed a few years later.

Ava loved the role, saying, 'I really felt comfortable in that part. I could understand the girl I played so well. She was a good average girl with normal impulses. I didn't have to pretend.'

Peck said he recognized that 'this was certainly a wholehearted attempt, a serious effort to make a fine Hemingway picture. We had, of course, a very good director in Henry King. I loved him and respected him, and I think Ava did too. I believe her work was much more subtle, and that she acquired much more confidence under his direction. She did things in that picture which she could not have done three years earlier in *The Great Sinner*. Henry was an old-time director who understood his trade and he understood actors, and Ava felt good with him.'

Peck felt that under King's direction, Gardner was allowed to follow her own emotions. 'She began to get a sense of what acting is really like, how to allow her emotion to dictate what she was saying and doing externally,' said Peck. 'In some of her scenes, she was very moving and touching, and very, very sympathetic.'

Much of the film was shot on Stage 8 at the Fox studio, which was turned into an African hunting camp with a 350-feet-long cyclorama with Mount Kilimanjaro painted on it. Apparently, some of the props, like the elephant foot stool, came direct from Zanuck's office. For the scene in which Peck shot a charging hippo, he simply had to be photographed against back projection, waiting for a tiny light to flash that signalled the exact moment he needed to fire the rifle.

Exteriors were shot on the Fox back lot. During the Spanish Civil War flashback scene in which Peck carries wounded Ava Gardner out of a shell hole, he pulled a ligament in his left knee and had to spend the next two weeks in a plaster cast. He continued to work but Henry King had to postpone all action sequences and was careful to keep Peck's bad leg out of shot.

Ava had not long been married to Frank Sinatra, who was suffering from a decline in his career, and she wanted to be with him in New York as soon as possible. Sinatra had agreed that she could spend only ten days on the film. When King came to shoot one of

the Spanish Civil War scenes involving thousands of extras, it took
a day longer than had been planned, and so Ava did her work
under considerable pressure, knowing that her husband would
blow his top because she was a day overdue. Despite that, Peck
said, 'I don't know of anyone who could match her performance
in *The Snows of Kilimanjaro*.'

King said, 'It's the best picture I have ever made. Hemingway's
story is vital and the performances are magnificent. Greg plays an
age span from 17 to 40, and you'll believe the 17.'

Otis L. Guernsey of the *New York Herald Tribune*, agreed about
Peck, though not the film:

> It is a lumpy grab bag of adventurous thrills and soul-searching
> loosely tied together by the wisps of Hemingway's original tale.
> Peck's performance is a good one; he gives off a lot of the interior
> doubts and exterior hardness of a Hemingway hero and manages to
> hold himself together even while hanging intoxicated over a bar.
> His vision of a frustrated man is presented in a well-controlled style
> – there is not a sign of the breast-beating type of acting in it – and
> his moments of excitement are all the more effective in contrast to
> the calmness with which he plays through most of the scenes.

Bosley Crowther of *The New York Times* thought it 'a handsome
and generally absorbing film. A vivid performance by Gregory
Peck who by the very force and vigour of his physical attitudes,
suggests a man of burning temper and melancholy moods.'

Newsweek complained, 'The succinct and vivid qualities associated with Hemingway are rarely evoked, and what has been substi-
tuted is for the most part meandering, pretentious and more or
less maudlin romance.'

Exhibitors were alarmed by the title. Robert A. Wile, executive
secretary of the Independent Theater Owners of Ohio, wrote to Al
Litchman, chief of Fox's distribution, stating, 'Several exhibitors
on this state have asked me to convey to you their apprehension
over the box-office possibilities of *Snow* because of the picture's
title. It is felt that people will not go to see a picture whose name
they cannot pronounce. They hope that you will see fit to change
this title before the picture is released.'

W.C. Gering, a Fox sales assistant, responded by admitting that
it was indeed 'an odd title, but it is a very famous one'. He assured

Mr Wile that all the Fox executives, including Mr Skouras, 'are sure that the title is just right, the picture is great and will be a huge box-office success.'

Before that could be proved, *David and Bathsheba* opened on 14 August 1951, at the Rivoli Theater in New York. Despite its critical drubbing, it was named 'the outstanding film of 1951' by The Protestant Motion Picture Council. Philip Dunne's script and Leon Shamroy's colour photography were Oscar-nominated, and the domestic box office was $7 million, making it Fox's biggest money maker of 1951.

Captain Horatio Hornblower opened at Radio City Music Hall on 13 September, and returned $3 million domestic, pushing it into the top twenty films of 1951. It remained a personal favourite of Peck's. He was disappointed, though, to have to give up the La Jolla Playhouse. He had to give something up in his hectic schedule, and his treasured Playhouse programme was it.

10

Holiday in Rome, Honeymoon in Paris

PECK HAD BEEN GENTLY complaining that he was not being offered any good comedy roles and that he was keen to show he could perform *à la* Cary Grant. It so happened that Cary Grant had been offered a good script, *Roman Holiday*, by Ian McLellan Hunter and John Dighton.

Frank Capra wanted to make the film under the banner of Liberty Films, which was formed after the war by Capra, William Wyler and George Stevens. These three directors were to make nine pictures between them for RKO, including *Roman Holiday* with Cary Grant as an American newspaperman and Elizabeth Taylor as the princess he meets in Rome. But Capra's first Liberty film, *State of the Union*, in 1948 was such a commercial failure that the partners decided to sell all their properties to Paramount. That studio had a cost-control programme which allowed no single budget to go over $1.5 million, and Capra felt he couldn't make *Roman Holiday* for so little and abandoned the project.

Paramount offered it to Wyler, who accepted it on condition that he could shoot the film on location in Rome. The studio said it could be shot on their back lot. Wyler argued, 'You can't build me the Colosseum or the Spanish Steps. I'll shoot the whole picture in Rome or else I won't make it.'

Paramount gave in. Wyler had one other condition. He wanted to find an unknown actress to play the princess. Paramount still wanted Elizabeth Taylor.

'I don't need a leading lady,' Wyler insisted. 'I want a girl without an American accent to play the princess, someone you can *believe* has been brought up as a princess.'

The studio pointed out that Taylor wasn't American; she was

British.

'Yeah, but she sounds so goddam American that nobody would believe she wasn't,' said Wyler.

Paramount then announced they were going to cast Jean Simmons, who had no American accent, thus defeating Wyler in his argument. But Simmons proved to be unavailable. Finally Paramount decided that their major male star could basically sell the picture, so they would allow Wyler to cast an unknown actress.

Wyler decided he didn't want Cary Grant to play the reporter; Grant was, he knew, perfect for the part and would be cast to type. Grant's name also had the requisite marquee value Paramount demanded. But Wyler wanted to be just a little dangerous and cast an actor who would be working somewhat against the grain. So during the summer of 1951 he sent the script to Gregory Peck.

Peck turned it down. The actor generally renowned for his lack of ego discovered he had one after all, when he realized his role would be secondary to the princess's.

Wyler told Peck, 'You surprise me. If you didn't like the story, OK, I could understand that. But because somebody else's part is a little better than yours – *that's* no reason to turn down a film. I didn't think you were the kind of actor who measures the size of the roles.'

Wyler's words had a way of bringing Peck down to earth. He reconsidered and accepted the part for a fee of $120,000 plus a percentage of the profits. If studio estimates of the potential box office were to prove true, this arrangement would give Peck an additional $350,000.

Wyler began searching for his Ruritanian princess, watching scores of films featuring young British actresses. Among them was a rough-cut of *The Secret People* in which 22-year-old Audrey Hepburn had her first major part after appearing in supporting roles in a handful of British films. He decided to audition her in London along with several other actresses. Then he went to Paris and Rome to see some European actresses, during which time Paramount became enthusiastic about Hepburn and arranged for her to have a screen test at Pinewood Studios in England. She played two scenes from the *Roman Holiday* script. The results were seen by Gregory Peck at the Paramount studios, and he agreed with Wyler, who said, 'You could believe her as a princess. If you hadn't known otherwise, you'd have assumed she was one.' There was one snag: she was due to star on Broadway in *Gigi* and would not be available for a year.

Wyler decided she was so perfect for the part that they would delay production until she was available. Meanwhile, Peck started work for Raoul Walsh in *The World In His Arms* in autumn 1951 on the Universal lot. Peck played a seal-poaching sea captain who meets a Russian countess (Ann Blyth) in old San Francisco. Playing his rival for the affections of the countess and the seals was the fiery Mexican-Irish actor Anthony Quinn who could, if let loose, chew up the scenery with his broad style of acting.

Walsh, as usual, didn't waste words on instructing his actors. Anthony Quinn recalled that the usual command he heard was, 'Tony, too much garlic!' Or 'Do it again with more garlic!' Which meant that he was indeed chewing up the scenery, while Peck was advancing his usual, more subtle approach. The two actors liked each other and were friendly enough, but in front of the camera a touch of rivalry was evident. 'He does everything he can think of to attract attention to himself,' said Peck. 'I don't mind that. He's a good, salty actor, one of the best. There's always room for the two of us on the screen. Our relationship is friendly rivalry.' Ann Blyth supplied the romantic interest.

Each lunch Walsh took Peck to a particular restaurant, where they ordered the biggest steaks available, washed down with Jack Daniels. They may have been enjoying a special camaraderie, but it was not the best way for Peck to kick off the afternoon's work, as he tended to get a bit sleepy. He didn't actually nod off on the set but he did slow right down on occasions, and then Walsh would yell at him, 'Wake up, Greg! Give it all your energy.'

To wake himself, Peck would grab one of the chamois leathers that were stocked in an ice box to help cool down the actors in the intense heat of the studio arc lights, and thoroughly wash his face. 'Keep going, Greg,' Walsh would shout. 'Run till you drop, like a thoroughbred.'

Peck later reflected that he should never have had those lunches with the tough old director. But the film did what it set out to do, as Bosley Crowther confirmed in *The New York Times*: 'The screen never stops quivering and the watcher never has time to spot the story's seams. Peck is only a shade more restrained than Anthony Quinn who plays a Portuguese captain as though he were animated by hot-feet and rum. It is really that race between the schooners that you'll go to this picture to see.'

Otis L. Guernsey of the *New York Herald Tribune*, found it to be 'a brawling, colorful tale of adventure and romance. The whole thing is as stereotyped as the sea language of command, but it is delivered with a flair and a laugh that makes it irresistible.'

In September 1952, *The Snows of Kilimanjaro* opened at the Rivoli Theater, and although the critics were not wholeheartedly enthusiastic, the public turned it into a big hit. Then *The World in His Arms* opened on 9 October 1952 at the Mayfair Theater in New York and took $3 million. Of all his recent films, only *The Gunfighter*, in which he had disguised his considerable good looks for the sake of authenticity, had been an outright flop. He was in the almost unique position of being one of Hollywood's very few top stars under the age of forty.

Just before *Roman Holiday* began filming in June 1952, Paramount threw a pre-production party where Peck met Audrey Hepburn for the first time. She told me, 'The first time I met him, I was like a young fan because he was such an idol.' He thought she was 'enchanting'.

Audrey Hepburn arrived fresh from her success in *Gigi* on Broadway, where she had established herself as a star. Suddenly the previously unknown Audrey Hepburn was not quite so unknown. But she was still largely untried on the world's cinema screen. And she was not yet used to the trappings of the movie star's life. When she found herself booked into one of Rome's best hotels, she told the press that the hotel was 'way over my head. I could never afford them before.'

Peck, Greta and the children – Jonathan, eight; Stephen, six; and Carey, three – rented a palatial villa with views of vineyards at Alabano, fifteen miles from Rome. It came complete with exotic gardens and a marble swimming pool filled with water that poured from the gaping mouth of a nude Roman statue.

'On our first day on the set,' recalled Peck, 'Wyler called his cast together and said, "Now, boys and girls, there's just one prima donna on this picture and I'm that one. And I want that understood from the beginning!" '

The first several days of filming concentrated on scenes revolving exclusively around the princess, so right from the start Audrey Hepburn was taking the heat. And heat is exactly what she experienced; it was 95 degrees in the summer sun outside, but inside the

Palazzo Brancaccio, where Wyler filmed the princess in her royal boudoir, the temperature was 104. 'Now I know what it's like to be a star,' Audrey told a reporter. 'It's warmer, more uncomfortable, and the hours are longer.' Each day started at six-thirty in the morning and usually ended around eight-thirty in the evening.

Peck was eager to get to work on the picture, and especially anxious to know how well Audrey Hepburn would do in her first major motion picture. Within a few days he had made up his mind that a major new star had been discovered. He called his agent, George Chasin, in Hollywood, and asked, 'What's my billing?'

'You've got top of the bill as usual,' Chasin answered, surprised that Peck should seem concerned. 'Greg, nobody can be billed above you and nobody can be billed with you.'

'But the real star of this picture is Audrey Hepburn,' Peck told him. 'It would be pretentious of me to take the billing alone. Go to the studio and tell them I want Audrey Hepburn to be billed on the same line.'

So Chasin sent a cable to Paramount: 'Suggest Audrey Hepburn is given co-star billing in *Roman Holiday*.'

Production chief Frank Freeman called Chasin and told him, 'Absolutely not. This is an unknown girl. Our job is to sell Gregory Peck.'

'Mr Freeman, you're going to have a very unhappy actor,' Chasin warned.

Freeman paused, and then said, 'Leave it to me. I'll get back.' A meeting at the studio was held with the publicity department, and afterwards Freeman called Chasin and told him, 'We've decided to go along with the idea of projecting a new star. Audrey Hepburn gets co-star billing.'

Early in production, Peck was interviewed by an attractive teenage Parisian journalist, Véronique Passani, for *France Soir*. It was, by all accounts, just a typical interview: Peck talked about the film, about working with Wyler, about Audrey Hepburn. But something more was going on; Greg was very attracted to his interviewer. He was thirty-six; she was almost twenty years younger. A few weeks later he received a copy of the article she had written. The content of the article would not remain as indelible in his memory as the woman who wrote it.

On the set there was a great deal of laughter going on between Peck and Hepburn in between takes. 'I'm enchanted with Greg,' she told reporters, 'because he's so marvellously normal, so genuine, so downright *real!* There's nothing of the "making-like-a-star" routine, no phoniness in him.'

Peck told newspapers, 'Audrey is not the type who, bit by bit, turns to granite until they are a walking career.' She was, he said, 'as lovable as an over-strung tennis racquet.'

The joy Peck experienced with Audrey on the set contrasted starkly to the misery that was setting in back at his villa in Alabano. His working hours were long and sometimes they filmed through the night. When they filmed at the Colosseum, he worked for twenty-two hours straight, but nevertheless found the experience exhilarating. It didn't help his domestic life that he was, as usual, quite consumed by his part. The script called for him to be enchanted by the princess, and rumours abounded that Peck was having an affair with Audrey. Peck maintained silence over the tittle-tattle, refusing to confirm or deny them.

He and Audrey certainly had a great rapport on the set, discovering they shared an instinctive feel for what would and wouldn't work; they knew they were a good team. Whether or not they were lovers, they were certainly great friends.

'Rumours were flying about Greg and I for a year,' Audrey Hepburn told me.

> If there was anything going on, it didn't last long because most of our time was taken up with work. It's true that I had an enormous crush on him. But I was engaged at the time [to Jimmy Hanson, son of a wealthy Huddersfield businessman] and I even had my wedding gown hanging in the wardrobe of my Roman hotel suite. And Greg was married to Greta. I knew that he wasn't happy, that his marriage was not good even though they had three lovely children. Maybe he did feel something for me, maybe there was a little chemistry between us that made our scenes work. I was in Rome, being treated like a princess, and it was not difficult for me to believe I was the princess in the film, and it was not difficult for me to believe that I was in love with Gregory Peck.

Suddenly, Greta packed her bags and took the children off to Finland. The truth was, *Roman Holiday* spelled the end of the marriage. A new honeymoon would soon begin in Paris, but not with Greta. Peck insisted that there was no marital rift, saying, 'All

I want to say is that my wife is homesick. I have to stay on here to work. That's all.' He was much happier to talk about working with William Wyler:

> Wyler is a known taskmaster. He's terribly difficult to satisfy and he'll have you play a scene maybe forty or even fifty times. He doesn't usually tell you what he wants – he could not always explain it the way he wanted it. But when you did it right, he knew it. He took that many takes because he had a purpose, but he had to see it happen before he knew if it was right. This makes some actors upset because you can be up to take 41 and he still can't tell you what you want. This can make you feel pretty lousy, but I always had confidence because I knew that he simply wanted everybody to be at their best, and that gave me confidence knowing that and that would give you a good performance. Wyler gave you the chance to give it your best, and I loved working with him for that reason. What went on the screen was your best, when you had reached your peak. I realize this has baffled some actors who don't understand his way of working. But in the end your best was what the public saw.

Wyler had a reputation for tearing a strip off his actors on occasions, and Peck was shocked when Wyler turned his guns on Audrey when they were filming in the Roman Forum. Audrey had to shed tears. Peck recalled:

> Audrey was a very good comedienne, and a really fine actress, but she didn't know how to shed tears. The make-up man blew menthol in her eyes to get some tears, and then we began shooting – take after take. After about thirty takes Willy just wasn't satisfied because she had not found it in her to summon up the right kind of emotion. Willy just suddenly shouted, 'Goddammit Audrey, it's lousy! I don't believe a goddamned word of it! Now get into it and give me something!'
>
> She was so frightened and embarrassed by this sudden outburst of anger against her that she did it perfectly on the very next take. It wasn't the emotion of the scene that made her do it, it was because Willy had just scared the living daylights out of her. But it worked.

Making the film was hard work but a joy; all involved in it felt confident they had a marvellous film on their hands. Critics generally felt the same. Otis L. Guernsey of the *New York Herald Tribune* wrote, 'Hepburn makes the sad skylarking of a princess lovely, and carries off the finale with a nicety that leaves one a little haunted. Gregory Peck portrays the reporter with alternate abandon and thoughtfulness.'

A.H. Weiler of *The New York Times* called the film 'a royal lark in the modern idiom, a bittersweet legend with laughs that leaves the spirits soaring. Audrey Hepburn is a slender, elfin and wistful beauty, alternately regal and childlike. Gregory Peck makes a stalwart and manly escort and lover, whose eyes belie his restrained exterior.'

'What Wyler has done is to fashion one of the gayest, most original and endearing comedies to be credited to Hollywood in recent years,' reported *Newsweek.*

One day on the set Wyler told Peck, 'It's a hell of a thrill to make a movie. We start with just an idea, get it on paper, put it before a camera and then people pay money to look at a blank wall to see what we've put up there.' From that moment Peck began to seriously consider the prospect of producing films of his own.

Towards the end of filming, Greta returned to Rome with the children. As Peck was due to stay on in Europe to film *Night People* at the beginning of 1953, they decided to rent a house in France. They found a place just west of Paris, at Les Temps La Ville. Early winter was setting in. And the final curtain was slowly coming down on their marriage. The change of scenery did not keep them from rowing, and they soon realized that this was having a detrimental effect on the boys. They agreed on one thing – that it would be better for the boys if Greta took them back to California while Greg remained in France. He even suggested she ought to begin divorce proceedings.

They vacated the house and he made arrangements to stay in a hotel in Paris. Then he drove his family to the quayside to see them on to the *Ile de France* that would take them on the cruise home. It was no pleasant leave-taking. The boys were in tears, as were Greg and Greta. Then he hit the road to Paris in his Jaguar, feeling thoroughly wretched. He later recalled that his feeling that day had been 'very Dostoevskian, practically suicidal'. He stopped at a café *en route* and knocked back two double cognacs.

When he finally arrived at the hotel, he locked himself in his room and stayed there for virtually two weeks. This second bout of solitary confinement was worse this time than his stint in the Arizona desert. Then he had abstained from alcohol and had eaten well. This time he drank heavily and ate little. He emerged from his room only to walk the streets on his own, sometimes for hours. He would stop at a bistro for a brandy and maybe a coffee. Then he'd return to the hotel.

Towards the end of the bleakest fortnight of his life thus far, he began considering how best to pick up the pieces of his fractured life. He began thinking of Véronique Passani. He decided to ring the offices of *France Soir*. He learned that she had left to work at *Paris Presse*. He dialled again, and asked to speak to Véronique Passani. When he was asked for his name, he gave it.

He could hear Véronique being paged, and when he heard his name mentioned, the sound of typewriters in the background suddenly stopped. When she came on the phone she seemed distinctly unimpressed. He said, 'Hello, I'm Gregory Peck. Do you remember me?'

'Yes, of course,' she replied coolly.

He asked her to come with him to the race track at Auteuil, and when she did not answer immediately, he inquired, 'Are you still there?'

'Yes,' she said. She didn't explain that she couldn't just take the afternoon off as she had an interview with Albert Schweitzer.

'Well? Last chance,' he said.

She quickly calculated that she could do the interview and make the races, and so finally she said, 'Yes, I will come with you.'

As it turned out, Dr Schweitzer didn't show up at the apartment of his cousin, Jean-Paul Sartre, where the interview was to take place. Finally, at around three in the afternoon, she left the apartment and went to the races with Gregory Peck. Then he took her to dinner. Afterwards, she took him back to meet her mother and grandmother.

Greg and Véronique saw each other regularly, then he had to leave to go to Berlin to begin filming *Night People*. The romance had begun in Paris, and continued in Berlin; she went with him.

Nunnally Johnson wrote the screenplay of the cold war spy thriller *Night People* for Twentieth Century-Fox, and was also directing it. When he first asked Zanuck if he could direct, Zanuck said that it depended on Peck's approval. Peck knew that Johnson had the vision of a director, and agreed.

The film was shot entirely in Berlin and Munich. Even in Germany, Peck could not escape the Hollywood gossip. Back in America Audrey Hepburn was fighting off the rumours of their alleged affair. She told *Photoplay*, 'I know all about those stories. Who starts them? And how could they be true, especially when I'm so fond of Greta? I saw her coming out of Romanoff's the other day, and she asked me to spend next Sunday swimming in the pool of her home. Does *that* sound like I'm a home-breaker?'

Peck refused to rise to any bait the press dangled in front of him. He said, 'I believe in the old maxim, "Never complain or explain."'

What he was not making public was the fact that he and Véronique were now a definite item. It is possible that Greta didn't even know at that time, and when she was pressed by reporters to explain why she was in America while her husband was in Europe, she explained, 'I do my best to make our home worth coming back to. Warm, friendly and interesting. It was impractical to remain together and have the children travelling all over Europe.'

Because it was impractical for Zanuck to be away from Hollywood, he could not personally produce *Night People*, so he assigned his former German ski instructor, Otto Lang, to stand in for him. Production manager Gerd Oswald, also a German, had special instructions from Zanuck to act as an unofficial co-producer.

Peck had to go to London for costume fittings and there met Otto Lang for the first time. When Peck was put into army uniform that had huge shoulders stuffed with cotton wool, he told Lang, 'This is so out of date I look like an usher at Radio City Music Hall.'

'What do you mean?' replied Lang. 'You look like a powerful man, tough, with big shoulders.'

'But you don't have to prove I'm tough by padding my shoulders with cotton wool.' Peck refused to wear it and after a row with Lang, he stormed out, got in a taxi and went to Huntsman in Savile Row and was measured for an authentic uniform.

He caught the plane to Germany, expecting the usual VIP treatment, which was normally just a PR exercise; American star flies in, is met by producer and waves to gathered photographers. But Otto Lang was not there, nor was the production manager. Only a publicity man was sent there to welcome him. Peck was getting angry about the whole thing.

He checked into his hotel and had hardly unpacked when he received a call from George Chasin in the States, asking 'What the hell are you doing?'

'What do you mean?' asked Peck.

'It says on the front page of today's *Hollywood Reporter* that you're holding up production and being difficult.'

'I'm not doing any such thing. I'm ready to start. I've still got to meet with Nunnally. What's it all about?'

Chasin read the article over the phone; Otto Lang had accused Peck of being difficult over his wardrobe and delaying filming. Now Greg was really furious. He got in touch with Nunnally Johnson and demanded a meeting. His anger was boiling over as Johnson tried to calm him down, assuring him he had made the right decision about the uniform.

The next day, when they began filming, Peck was still simmering as he went through a scene with Broderick Crawford, watched by the producer and production manager. The script called for him to erupt in anger at Crawford, so he simply channelled all his real anger against the producer and production manager towards Crawford. The scene, scheduled to take two days, was wrapped in two hours. Nunnally Johnson was delighted and told the producer and production manager he needed the next set ready. They informed him that they hadn't expected it to be needed so soon, so it wasn't ready. Johnson was furious with them, but Peck left the studio that afternoon feeling a lot better.

The film was shot in CinemaScope, Peck's first widescreen experience. The night people of the title were the Russians, who as the *New Yorker* pointed out, 'do all their dirty work after dark, which, of course, makes things difficult for the Americans, sun-lovers to a man. As the colonel, Gregory Peck is every inch a heroic defender of democracy.'

Otis L. Guernsey of the *New York Herald Tribune* thought that 'Johnson's script is slashingly written and action is paced like a rapier duel. Peck issues his commands and crushes interference in the very personification of authority. He is hard-boiled and sarcastic, yet sympathetic with the underdog.'

Bosley Crowther in *The New York Times* called the film 'a first-rate commercial melodrama – big, noisy, colorful and good. It may be the sheerest piece of fiction, and a reckless piece at that, but it is fun.'

Roman Holiday opened on 27 August 1953 at Radio City Music Hall. Oscars were awarded to Audrey Hepburn as Best Actress, Ian McLellan Hunter for his original screen story, and to Edith Head for her costumes. Nominations were for Best Picture, Best Supporting Actor (Eddie Albert), Best Screenplay, and Black and White Photography.

There were further awards, one from the New York Film Critics Circle for Audrey Hepburn, one from the Writers Guild of America, which named it Best Written American Comedy, and one for Wyler from the Directors Guild for 'Outstanding Directorial Achievement'.

The film was a hit, although *Variety* reported that business was 40 per cent below expectation, so Peck did not earn as much as had been originally estimated. Nevertheless, the world fell in love with Audrey Hepburn. And the press fell in love with the idea that Audrey had to be in love with Gregory Peck. While she went back to playing *Gigi* on a tour of America, he returned to Paris to promote *Roman Holiday*. Even while he was undergoing a gruelling schedule of non-stop interviews, he found time to mix business with pleasure, since Véronique was with him. One evening she was included in a dinner he had with some of the Paramount publicity people accompanying him.

In her notebook, she wrote, 'Dined with G. tonight. He likes me. We eat by candlelight and he takes my hand in his. The hairs prickle on the back of his hand. He has sex, this one. I laugh because they all talk about Audrey Hepburn. Studio talk. He says so. Why else would he be with me? I think I am beginning to fall in love …'

11

Whale of a Time

DURING THE SUMMER OF 1953 Peck made the first of two films in Britain, *The Million Pound Note*, based on Mark Twain's 1893 short story. Peck was paid $350,000 for the two – the other being *The Purple Plain*. In *The Million Pound Note* he played a penniless American in Edwardian England who is given a million pounds by Wilfred Hyde White and Ronald Squire, who bet how long Peck could last without ever spending a penny of the money. The note establishes him as a millionaire and makes him welcome everywhere and living in luxury without ever having to break into the million pound note.

One of Peck's great pleasures while making the film was working with A.E. Matthews, who was then in his eighties and had to be fed his lines on the set for each take. But what impressed Peck was the perfect timing and delivery with which he spoke them. Matthews complained that he was being sent to famed London costumier Monty Berman to be fitted with a riding outfit *circa* 1900. 'Great bore, fittings are,' Matthews complained. When Peck heard about this, he turned up with a riding outfit of his own, which, with its tweed jacket and bowler, were perfect for Matthews to wear in the film.

The film, called *Man in a Million* in America, was regarded as something of a disappointment, yet it nevertheless makes for a pleasing 92 minutes of screen entertainment, and Peck is engaging in it. Bosley Crowther of *The New York Times* noted, 'The lack of cleverness, we fear, is the film's one weakness. Peck is skilful and handsome. The rest of the cast is refined. The production in colour is delicious, the direction smooth. The picture doesn't sparkle with humor, doesn't flash the satire on money-madness that is lodged in the yarn.'

Otis L. Guernsey of the *New York Herald Tribune* thought it 'a production shimmering with the Technicolor elegance of the horse-and-carriage era. After the first few surprises, though, its humor becomes laborious. Gregory Peck looks like a man of promise even in rags. His touch with comedy is light but guarded, almost suspicious.'

Saturday Review liked it: 'That rare and remarkable quality of complete accord, of deft interplay not merely between the actors but between the entire production team on a film, is again visible in a delicious comedy. Peck reveals unsuspected comic gifts.'

It was just a short air flight for Véronique, who came to stay with him at the Grosvenor Square apartment he rented, complete with a wonderful Hungarian cook. A constant stream of visitors from the British film industry passed through, including Ronald Neame, the Leo Genns and many others he had befriended on the set of *Captain Horatio Hornblower*. Véronique became a permanent fixture, in London and in his life.

When he heard that Audrey Hepburn was at last returning home after her exhausting tour of *Gigi* (which ended triumphantly in Los Angeles), he decided to throw a party for her. He invited his friend Mel Ferrer, who was in England filming *Knights of the Round Table*. Audrey had, by this time, broken off her engagement to Jimmy Hanson, and she and Ferrer, who was estranged from his wife Frances hit it off immediately. 'We began talking about the theatre,' recalled Ferrer. 'She knew all about the La Jolla Playhouse Summer Theater where Greg and I had been co-producing plays for years. She also said she'd seen me three times in the movie *Lili*. Finally, she said she'd like to do a play with me, and she asked me to send her a likely script if I found one.'

Their interest in each other went beyond wanting to do plays, and in due course they fell in love and married; Peck hoped once and for all that the rumours about him and Audrey would end. But he was wrong. When Greta Peck threw her own party for Audrey in Hollywood, someone remarked, 'I wonder if Greta knows about all those dinners Audrey and Greg had together in London?'

By this time Greta couldn't have cared; she liked Audrey, and she accepted her marriage to Greg was over – they had been separated now for eight months. Peck had kept quiet up till now, partly because he didn't want the world to know about Véronique yet. In a desperate effort to quash the rumours once and for all, he told the press that it was 'ridiculous' to connect him romantically with Audrey Hepburn, and it was 'unfair' to link her with 'a married man'. But he didn't admit he wouldn't be married for much longer, nor that he and Greta were officially separated.

For her part, Greta was still fending off suggestions that there was a rift in the marriage, and when asked by a reporter if rumours of an impending divorce were true, she replied, 'I've taken no steps along those lines.' But the truth was that Greg had decided that as soon as he could get back to America, he would instigate divorce proceedings.

When *Night People* opened on 12 March 1954 at the Roxy Theater in New York, the ads proclaimed: 'YOU HAVE NEVER REALLY SEEN GREGORY PECK UNTIL YOU SEE HIM IN CINEMASCOPE.' Apart from the slight distortion that early CinemaScope produced with close-ups, this was not, strictly speaking, true.

In June 1954, *Man With a Million* opened at New York's Sutton Theater. It was popular in England, less so in America.

That year Greta began divorce proceedings. It was a most amicable affair. When she was asked to explain her statement that 'Gregory Peck has pursued a course of conduct towards his wife of such character as to constitute in law extreme cruelty,' she replied, 'He is cruel because he stayed away from home nights.'

Peck, meanwhile, flew to Sri Lanka – then still called Ceylon – to begin his second British film, *The Purple Plain*. It was written by Eric Ambler, based on H.E. Bates's story of a Canadian squadron leader who suffers from shattered nerves during the Burma campaign in World War Two, but regains his composure during an arduous trek to escape from the jungle.

The Sri Lankan heat and humidity was unyielding. Peck and his director, Robert Parrish, shared a sense of mischief that helped make conditions bearable. It turned out that the half-Burmese, half-German leading lady, Win Min Than, had a fiancé, a tough-looking tycoon from Rangoon who was suspected of being a Japanese collaborator during the war. He was so jealous about Win Min that he refused to leave the set. Peck and Parrish concocted a plan to teach him a lesson. They told Win Min that a new scene had been added, which required Peck to make love to her. She was horrified at the thought of what such a scene would do to her fiancé.

The next day she arrived on the set wreaking of garlic and displaying unsightly bright red gums. Her fiancé had insisted she eat cloves, garlic and betel nuts to turn her gums blood red and make it virtually impossible for anyone to make love to her. Parrish and Peck caught sight of him lurking in the bushes. The whole cast and crew had been primed and behaved as though they didn't notice the smell. Win Min couldn't understand why no one noticed her garlic breath, so she covered her hair in coconut oil which turned rancid in the heat. 'She smelled like a badger,' recalled Peck, 'but she looked perfect for the camera.'

The time came for the love scene. Peck had to endure the terrible stench but was motivated by the sight of the alarmed fiancé dashing from palm tree to palm tree. Parish called for 'Action!' and Peck slipped an arm around her waist. She was trembling as he gently eased her head against his shoulder. The fiancé was seen raging with fury. Then without so much as a kiss happening between Peck and Win Min, Parrish called, 'Cut! Print. Next scene.'

Parrish and Peck had agreed that the scene would simply end with a romantic fade-out. The tycoon from Rangoon was so overcome with joy that his fiancé had not been made love to by Gregory Peck that he began a dance of joy among the palm trees. Parrish, Peck and everyone else were in hysterics.

When the location wrapped, the unit returned to England and interiors were shot at Pinewood Studios in England. The results on screen were good.

The film reached the screens in April 1955. William Zinnser in the *New York Herald Tribune* said, 'Ambler's sardonic script makes the characters real. Peck is his old competent self. Win Min Than would beguile any man away from his troubles.' Bosley Crowther wrote in *The New York Times*, 'Gregory Peck shows the stuff of which heroes are made. He plays his role with stolid drive. The extent of his agony is impressively transmitted to the audience in vivid and unrelenting scenes. One suffers with him as he doggedly sweats and strains to save himself and his ineffectual companions.'

Peck had become an actor others less successful looked up to and emulated, either out of pure respect or just green envy. One such actor was Gary Merrill, who was then Bette Davis's fourth husband and had worked with Peck in *Twelve O'Clock High*. During one of their typically stormy marital evenings, Merrill told her, 'I wish I were Gregory Peck, so I'd only have to do one good movie a year and make some decent money.'

Bette Davis's response was not only cutting towards her husband and a prelude to one of their famous rows, but was also indicative of her own sour opinion of Peck; she said, 'If you're going to pick an actor to be, at least pick a good one.'

During the summer of 1955 Audrey Hepburn signed with Italy's movie moguls Carlo Ponti and Dino de Laurentiis. They had got together to produce a massive film version of *War and Peace*. Audrey, who was to play Natasha, made it clear that she hoped they would cast Mel Ferrer as Prince Andrei, which they did, even though director King Vidor opposed it. For the principal role of Pierre, Vidor wanted Gregory Peck or Marlon Brando.

Brando didn't want to do it, and Ferrer, friend to Peck though he was, was not totally convinced that Audrey was completely over her 'crush' with Greg. As his wife's manager and general decision-maker, he persuaded her and the producers that Henry Fonda would be better suited to play Pierre.

Peck was not disappointed; he got to play the most challenging role of his career to date in John Huston's version of Herman Melville's *Moby Dick*. Huston had long planned to make the film, with his father, Walter, as Captain Ahab. But Walter died in 1950 before son John could get the film launched. He tried to cast Orson Welles, but Welles was then considered to be box-office poison. Knowing that Gregory Peck was one of the most bankable stars, he approached him and at first Peck misunderstood, thinking Huston wanted him to play Starbuck.

'No, no,' said Huston. 'I want you to play Ahab.'

For Peck, that was a challenge he could not turn down.

A special wooden leg was constructed and sent to Peck's London house so he could practise with it. He wanted to ensure that when he came to start filming, he would be able to walk about with his real leg strapped tightly behind him, using the false leg as though he'd had it for years. 'Huston was a fiend for realism,' Peck recalled. 'We were all set on an old seafaring leg called a "Chelsea peg". But that didn't satisfy John. He pointed out that Ahab had lost his leg in the South Pacific and that Melville described the peg as being carved out of whalebone by the ship's carpenter, so he wanted the one I wore to look as if it had been made at sea under rough conditions. He even showed me how to walk with it.'

Huston sent a second unit to the Azores to film actual whaling, while he took the first unit to Youghal, on the Irish Channel coast north of Cork, which resembled the New Bedford setting. Scenes were also shot across the Irish Sea, just off the coast of Wales.

The giant whale of the title was built on the hull of an ancient derelict Irish potato schooner with an engine built into it to spout water and make the tail wag. Huston told me:

I needed Peck to ride the whale himself because I needed close-ups of him – a stunt man could not fill in. There was a hole in the body for Greg to put his leg in and he had to be securely fastened to it because it was going to revolve and he would go round with it. We attached the whale to the end of a long pier and we had wind machines roaring and torrents of water whipped up over Greg as he was submerged time and again with the harpoon lines wrapping around his body. It suddenly occurred to me, *what would happen if the damned whale got stuck while Greg was under water?* I held my breath and I am sure he did every time he went under, but it all worked perfectly on the first take.

But Greg said, 'Let's do it again, John.' I told him we had the shot but he insisted. He said, 'We can't come back and do it again if the film gets ruined so let's do it again.' So we did.

Of that experience, Peck said, 'I think for the first time in my life, I experienced real physical fear.' His own recollection of filming that scene did not paint himself in quite so brave a light.

By then I had a severe head cold. The wind machines were roaring away and I was half drowned by torrents of water. Huston told me, 'I want you with your eyes staring open as you slowly come out of the sea on that whale's back with your dead hand beckoning the men to their doom.' What I didn't know was that the winch they were using to rotate the section I was tied to was hand-operated. Later I learned that when they'd first tried it out, the damn thing jammed. I could have *really* come up dead, which I think would have secretly pleased John – providing the last touch of realism he was after.

126

Peck began the film expecting to work for twelve weeks, but as problems plagued the production the schedule was extended to twenty-seven weeks. Many of the cast sustained injuries: Richard Basehart broke three bones in his foot jumping into a whaleboat; Leo Genn slipped a disc and caught pneumonia; and Peck hurt his kneecap. At least twelve of the film crew were injured at sea. 'It could have been worse,' mused Huston.

'There was always something to worry us,' Peck recalled. 'When John told us he was going to shoot the typhoon scenes right on the ship during an actual storm at sea we all tried to tell him that such a thing had never been done and it was impossible. But it's a mistake to tell John that something can't be done. That guarantees he'll go ahead and do it. We began thinking of John as a real-life Ahab.'

Sure enough, Huston took the ship out into a storm and filmed from cameras which were hung on elasticized ropes so they swung in the wind as the ship battled mountainous waves. 'Three times we were sure we'd lost the ship and three times she lost her mast,' said Peck. 'It's a miracle we survived.'

'Greg brought a superb dignity to the role,' Huston told me.

He revealed Ahab's obsession through softly spoken words but with a controlled intensity in thought and action. I can't imagine any actor giving the speech "It's a mild, mild day ..." any better than Greg did it. He had never tackled anything like Ahab. Melville's character is a complex man at war with God. He sees the mask of the whale as the mask which deity wears and so he sees deity as a malignant beast out to torment men and all other creatures.

The film confounded the critics and Peck's performance was hammered. 'Peck's make-up for his role is expert,' wrote Hollis Alpert in the *Saturday Review*, 'but the force needed for conviction is seldom present.' *Variety* thought the film 'is interesting more often than exciting. Peck actually does quite well with the stylized speech but often seems understated and much too gentlemanly for a man supposedly consumed by insane fury.'

The film didn't do well commercially, but there were some compensations for Huston who was awarded the 'year's best direction' from the Motion Picture National Board of Review, and was named Best Director by the New York Film Critics.

Huston always felt that his film was one which would come into its own in the future. 'I think the next generation will appreciate it more than the last,' he said in 1980, 'and Greg Peck is getting the applause he always deserved.'

The problem, however, is that the scenes of whales being killed tend to jar in an age of conservation awareness and to a filmgoing generation who have learned to love the whale. Great white sharks, meanwhile, have taken over as the horrors of the deep. Huston's *Moby Dick* is, in the final analysis, a rather magnificent misfit.

Despite Huston's admiration for Peck, and Peck's admiration for Huston's work, what had quickly developed into a great friendship suddenly ended. Said Huston:

Greg is one of the straightest, nicest guys I've ever known and I had a great affection for him during the making of *Moby Dick*. After that I wanted to do *Typee* with him which the Mirisch Brothers had purchased but it proved too expensive to mount. Then Greg and I talked about doing *The Bridge in the Jungle* which would actually have given him only a comparatively small role, but he said he would do it for me and then I would make a picture for him with us both working for the same fee so money would never be an obstacle in our future work. But that film didn't come off either.

After that whenever I was in California I'd call him up and we'd get together and talk art or horses. I simply enjoyed being with him. I went to see him while he was making a film and Véronique was with him in his dressing room. Something inexplicable happened. I went to kiss her on the cheek, as I always did, and she backed away and threw a look at Greg, like she was appealing to him for something. I thought that maybe he'd simply turned jealous and didn't want anyone kissing his wife. But that was not in Greg's character. But from that moment on he began to avoid me.

I'd call and leave messages at his house, at his office, but he never called back. I valued my friendship with him too much to just say 'To hell with him,' and I tried to recall what I must have done to offend him. I called my business manager because Greg and I had been partners in a racehorse, and asked him to find out. But Greg refused to talk to him about it.

Then one day I came face to face with Greg at Universal where he had an office. He walked in, acknowledged me with a nod, turned around and walked out. I tried to phone his office but his secretary told me he wasn't in. I called half an hour later and was told the same. I never heard back from him.

Years later I met Greg and he seemed genuinely pleased to see me and seemed to want to talk. But I felt it was too late. This time *I* turned around and walked out.

Huston never found out what had upset Peck, and Peck, typically, never explained.

Peck was relieved to leave the high seas behind for the business and financial world of contemporary New York in *The Man in the Gray Flannel Suit*. He played Tom Rath, an American suburbanite who has a chance at being a big businessman in the city. In time he comes to realize that his preference is for a nice nine-to-five job and a family life. When he tells his wife, Betsy, that he had had an affair in Rome during the war that produced a child, his marriage falls apart.

Peck hoped the picture would be in the order of *The Best Years of Our Lives* ten years on when Zanuck suggested the idea to him. The film was actually Zanuck's last as production chief at Fox, and the fifth and last film of Peck's which he would personally produce. Nunnally Johnson directed from his own screenplay, based on the book by Sloan Wilson. Peck loved the idea of working with Johnson again, as well as the chance to make another picture with Jennifer Jones, whom Zanuck was trying to cast as his wife. By now David O. Selznick was in the business of hiring out his contract stars and Jones was his biggest commodity. He would never loan her out without getting the best price possible, so he and Zanuck got engaged in some furious haggling.

Peck prepared himself for the role by going on a visit to New York two weeks before filming began, in October 1955. He went down Madison Avenue to observe its inhabitants, visited the offices of numerous advertising agencies, explored the executive offices of the NBC television and radio network in Rockefeller Center, where he'd once been a tour guide, and caught an afternoon commuter train to Larchmont. He began adopting an air of an executive to the extent that during these prearranged and secretive visits, few recognized him as Gregory Peck, the movie actor.

When they started filming, Zanuck had still not struck a final deal with Selznick for Jennifer Jones, so when the first scenes were shot at the Westport, Connecticut, station of the New Haven Railroad, a female extra in the film was chosen to stand in for the wife. She had to wear a headscarf to hide her hair, and Johnson had to film her at a distance. He would cut in close-ups of the actual leading lady at a later time.

Peck was asked by a local reporter if he was disturbed by the crowd of onlookers who came down to watch the filming at Westport. 'Not at all,' said Peck. 'In Rome, where we were making *Roman Holiday,* we had everywhere from five to fifteen thousand people watching while we were shooting.'

When the unit returned to Hollywood for the studio-bound scenes, Zanuck finally agreed a deal with Selznick, and Jones arrived for work on her second film with Peck. He was delighted to be working with her again, but Nunnally Johnson, while happy with her performance, came under increasing pressure from Selznick, who bombarded him with memoranda telling him how Jones should be photographed, and how she should be treated generally. Johnson would write back with the same response each time: 'Thank you very much, David. I passed your notes on to Mr. Zanuck.' Zanuck ignored Selznick's memoranda, and Johnson shot Jones as he pleased, although he did send one note to Selznick which read, 'In case your wife is too modest to tell you, I want you to know that she did a scene today that was absolutely marvellous. P.S. Don't answer this.'

Peck found the film rather tame after the rigours of *Moby Dick.*

> The film was peppered with some very fine scenes, but the Madison Avenue part was not very interesting; it just became a sort of soap opera. My favourite sequences which I felt were among the most successfully realized scenes in the film were the flashbacks to the war and the romance with Maria [played by Marisa Pavan] in Italy. I think, too, the film had some very good performances, but in all it didn't quite live up to what I'd hoped it would be.

Not all the critics agreed with him. *Cue* said, 'Nunnally Johnson and a fine cast combine their distinguished talents to help make this an eminently satisfying, full-bodied, honest and mature drama of real people and real situations.' Kate Cameron of the *New York Daily News* called it 'a work well done, a deeply moving domestic drama. The various roles are so realistically acted that the audience becomes absorbed in the action. Peck gives a full-bodied, well-rounded characterization.'

Bosley Crowther of *The New York Times* found it 'a mature, fascinating and often quite tender and touching film. Mr. Peck is a human, troubled Tom Rath. Mr. Zanuck's expensive production gives proper setting to this intelligent film.'

Time didn't like it: 'The movie relentlessly envelops every idea, obscures every issue in a smug smog of suburbaninity. It is a vice of the picture that it can't tell a human being from an overage Boy Scout. Peck is presented as a red-white-and-blue wonder boy just because he tells the boss man a smart truth rather than a dumb lie.'

12

Big Trouble in Big Country

PECK'S DIVORCE WAS MADE FINAL on 30 December 1955. The Los Angeles judge ordered Greg to pay Greta more than $100,000 a year, plus $700 a month for the boys.

The day after the divorce, New Year's Eve, Greg married Véronique at the Santa Barbara ranch of friend Channing Peak. His father and Harriet attended, as did his mother and Joseph. The celebrations went on for the first few days of 1956, then the couple went on a honeymoon through the United States, including Texas, where Véronique became an honorary citizen, Chicago and New York. It was Véronique's first time in America, but she easily slipped into Peck's lifestyle and enjoyed watching the Yankees play baseball. 'It is not exaggerating to say that we were wildly happy,' said Peck.

They invited Véronique's divorced father, an architect, over to Los Angeles, and took him to Manhattan to see the famous skyscrapers for himself. Greg also arranged for Véronique's brother, Cornelius, to come to America and attend Harvard University and UCLA Medical School.

Then Greg suffered a severe financial blow. He didn't object to the alimony he had to pay Greta, but he objected strongly when a new tax law came in which demanded that 80 per cent of his income from his European films had to be taxed. It cost him $900,000.

For the first and only time in his career Gregory Peck was fired from a movie. He had accepted a guest appearance in Michael Todd's epic extravaganza *Around the World in Eighty Days*, but, according to Todd's son, he had to be replaced for 'not taking his role as a cavalry major seriously enough'.

133

On 12 April 1956, there was a benefit premiere of *The Man in the Gray Flannel Suit* for the March of Dimes charity at New York's Roxy Theater. In May, Greg and Véronique went to the London premiere of *The Man in the Gray Flannel Suit*. The couple were now recognized as such, and *Look* magazine featured them on the cover, quoting Greg as saying, 'Véronique is very special.' She was also very pregnant. In October, Véronique gave birth to a son, Anthony. 'This is the greatest thing that could happen to us,' Peck announced.

Moby Dick was released in the summer of 1956. After the critical pounding he received, he said, 'I'm not sure it can be done at all. I was relieved when I saw both the previous versions that they were terrible too.'

Designing Woman was a chance in 1956 to have another stab at comedy, at the same time as fulfilling his commitment to MGM. He played a sports reporter who marries a dress designer and finds that their common interests are few. It was a fairly sophisticated comedy directed by Vincente Minnelli.

The studio wanted Grace Kelly to play the dress designer, but as Lauren Bacall recalled, 'She was in Europe preparing to become Princess Grace of Monaco. So I called Dore Schary at Metro and told him I could play it, I wanted to, and when I cut my salary in half, he finally said yes. It was a lovely, funny script, a terrific part.'

Until then her career had been on hold while she nursed husband Humphrey Bogart. That March, he had undergone an operation for cancer in which the whole of his oesophagus had been removed, along with two lymph nodes and part of his stomach. It was a miracle that he survived at all. Bacall said, 'I was happy about working. I wasn't sure about leaving Bogie to work, but he wanted me to.'

Through working with Bacall, Peck got to know Bogart well. Although weak and obviously dying, Bogart came to watch the first day's filming, which took place at the pool of the Beverly Hills Hotel. When Peck and Bacall had to spend some days filming on a sailboat, Bogart came by in his yacht, the *Santana*, to provide his wife and new friend with lunch.

'That movie was one of my happiest film experiences,' said Bacall. 'It had one of my all-time favourite lines: "Open your eyes, Maxie, and go to sleep." '

Making the film also gave her emotions, which were kept in

check at home, a way to manifest themselves. She said, 'I seemed to be constantly running toward Greg or away from him, so I had emotional and physical release to compensate for keeping everything inside at home.'

Even after *Designing Woman* was over, Peck maintained his friendship with the Bogarts, visiting the ailing film icon at every opportunity. He watched him wasting away. But Bogie never lost his sharp wit. When he discovered that Peck was a Catholic, Bogie pointed a finger at him and said, 'What is this Immaculate Conception thing? Explain that, will you?'

When they last met, Bogie weighed just 85 pounds. Peck tried to cheer him with a joke. It turned out to be a rather long joke, and though he tried to cut it short, Bogie finally exclaimed, 'Greg, if you don't get to the end of this soon, I won't be around for the punchline.'

Three days later, on 14 January 1957, Bogart died. Greg and Véronique attended the funeral, where the eulogy was read by John Huston. Almost the whole of Hollywood turned out to fill the church. Lauren Bacall insisted that no flowers should be sent; instead contributions should be made to the American Cancer Society. It was Bacall who first got Peck interested in doing some kind of work on behalf of the society.

Designing Woman opened later that year and was modestly successful. One day Peck happened to bump into George Burns, who told him, 'I saw *Designing Woman*. That was so funny.' Peck later reflected, 'That was worth more than an Oscar, to be told I could make George Burns laugh.'

That summer Peck went with Henry King to Mexico to film *The Bravados* at Morelia, San Jose and Guadalajara; Greg said he loved the country and the people.

He played an embittered stranger on the trail of the four outlaws be believes raped and murdered his wife. He kills them one by one until, finally, he discovers they were not responsible after all. The outlaw leader was played by Stephen Boyd, who became seriously ill with a raging temperature during production. His band of outlaws included Lee Van Cleef, who told me, 'I've been shot in westerns by Clint Eastwood, John Wayne and a lot of other big stars, but the sweetest man who ever shot me was Gregory Peck.'

Providing the love interest (completely irrelevant to the main story but necessary for box-office appeal) was 25-year-old Joan Collins. She recalled, 'My memory of making *The Bravados* was nursing Stephen Boyd when he got sick, and being made to ride a horse by Gregory Peck, who basically pushed me into the saddle while the head wrangler held on to the reins.'

Peck recalled, 'Joan Collins was a sensational young girl, kind of a knockout'.

Henry King later related the story of a young and inexperienced actor (not named) who after finishing a scene was asked by King to do it again. 'Why?' asked the actor. 'I know the scene perfectly.'

'It isn't just knowing your lines,' King told him. 'I didn't believe a damned word you said.' Then he pointed to Peck, who was a long way up the street set, just walking back and forth. 'See Gregory Peck?' King asked the young actor.

'What's he doing?'

'He's preparing himself physically and mentally for his next scene.' King suggested the young actor try emulating a star who knew his craft thoroughly.

Although he didn't want to be associated too much with westerns, Peck had become something of a real cowboy with his own cattle spread over 150 square miles of California. He dreamed of having a homestead of his own one day but knew that ranching was a full-time occupation, and he had no thoughts of retiring yet. He had to settle for being a partner with other ranchers and being boss over other men, who took care of his small herds on rented grazing land.

He also fantasized about entering a horse in the Grand National. He felt that no other steeplechase in the world could compare with the British Grand National. He bought a horse in England called Tetread from the Anglo-Irish Blood Stock Agency, and brought it over to California where he had it trained in the hope of its becoming a winner. Unfortunately, it never did.

Peck's next film was intended to be *Thieves' Market*. William Wyler was to direct as well as co-produce. Peck and Wyler were so eager to work together again and to become producing partners that they turned down other more lucrative offers to make *Thieves' Market*. But they couldn't get a satisfactory script and decided they ought to drop the whole project and try for something else. George Chasin suggested *The Big Country*. He had a treatment, based on a story, later novelized, by Donald Hamilton in the *Saturday Evening Post*, which was intended for Marlon Brando and which United Artists was keen to make.

'United Artists want to get this one tied up very quickly,' said Chasin.

'I've made westerns in six days,' replied Wyler.

Wyler and Peck decided to make the film together, and contracts were drawn up. They agreed that Wyler would be the boss on the set and would be responsible for editing. Peck would hire the horses and cattle and authentic western props. The responsibility for casting would be shared. Then they agreed with United Artists that they would each take 25 per cent of the profits. They both stood to make millions from the film. Star and director agreed that what they wanted to do was make 'a good commercial movie'. The budget was set at $1,100,000.

Jessamyn West, who'd scripted *Friendly Persuasion* for Wyler, was assigned to write the screenplay. Dissatisfied with it, Wyler and Peck brought on Leon Uris to improve it. Uris told the producers that the original script by West was 'bullshit, all cliché, totally unplayable'. By now the budget had risen to $1,500,000. After spending three weeks on it, Uris met with Wyler and Peck, and writer and director got into a furious row, after which it was left to Peck to work with Uris. Then Wyler had his brother, Robert, take over from Uris, and then another writer, Robert Wilder, was added. Even Donald Hamilton had a go. James R. Webb and Sy Bartlett fashioned the final draft, which retained some of Uris's work; it ran to 170 pages.

The story centred on the arrival of sailor James McKay, played by Peck, at the Terrill Ranch to wed Patricia (Carroll Baker), daughter of tough former major Terrill (Charles Bickford). He soon finds himself caught up in a violent feud between the Terrills and the trashy Hannasseys over water. McKay is a fish out of water who refuses to do what a man's gotta do out west, much to the shame of Patricia.

Various subplots focused on tangled relationships, as big, oafish Chuck Connors tried to woo schoolteacher Jean Simmons and Charlton Heston tried to steal Carroll Baker from Greg Peck. '*The Big Country* is a sort of *Grand Hotel* western with a whole gallery of characters,' said Peck. 'They all have big scenes and fit into the main theme.'

Wyler cast most of the actors, including Charles Bickford, who, it turned out, could no longer mount a horse in as sprightly a fashion as he had done in the old days. He had to be doubled in many shots. Wyler also convinced Charlton Heston, then established as a strong leading man, to take a supporting role as Terrill's foreman. But it was Peck's idea to cast burly singer Burl Ives as old man Hannassey, convincing Wyler that Ives had the bulk to be threatening and the voice to suggest a man of reason behind the menace.

Filming began on 1 August 1957, by which time the budget had risen to $3 million. Wyler chose to film in Technirama, the new widescreen process that Technicolor had developed. Its considerable advantage was that it eliminated the distortions that bedevilled CinemaScope. Wyler had a fine time working with cinematographer Franz Planer composing shots to emphasize the vast landscapes, against which were played the lives of the small-minded characters. And he didn't rush to get the shots he needed.

Heston recalled that twelve days into the shoot, Wyler 'pottered around endlessly, kicking little clods of dirt into the stream and chewing on a stick, then gave Franz a set-up that would show as much as you could hope to see of a stampede'.

Peck discovered many truths about producing with which he had not had to concern himself before. 'The main thing I discovered,' he said, 'is that a producer is always aware of money going down the drain.' The budget was revised to $3.5 million.

Despite the escalating costs, Peck arranged for 4,000 head of cattle, at $10 each, to be used for the shot in which he comes out of the house on his first morning at the Terrill Ranch and surveys the vast landscape covered in cattle. It took Peck the producer several days to arrange for the vast herd to be gathered from various ranches for the single day, and he considered the cost worthwhile for the effect. But he arrived on the set to find only 400 cattle; Wyler had cut the numbers to save money.

Peck stormed over to Wyler, demanding, 'What's happened? Where's our panoramic shot? Where's the vast herd?'

'It'll be enough,' Wyler assured him.

'But this was *my* decision,' roared Peck.

'Goddammit,' yelled Wyler, $40,000 for just one shot!'

It is actually one of the most disappointing shots in the film, and a rare mistake for a director who had the reputation of going to great pains and expense to get what he wanted. Peck found himself worrying more and more about escalating costs and tried to put pressure on Wyler to speed up filming.

One of the film's highlights was a simple fist fight between Peck and Heston which Wyler shot largely in extreme long shot, in keeping with the film's visual style. Said Heston, 'That was a day I damn well earned my pay. Greg and I wore our asses off on that fight till nearly six.'

The two actors, who did all the shots themselves without doubles, grew tired and careless. Heston recalled, 'I missed a mark and got thrown on my back on a rock.' But Wyler did get the scene in one day.

While Wyler spent endless time setting up shots and doing dozens of retakes, Peck grew ever more tense – not an ideal situation for the leading actor to find himself in. Lest it spoil the performance he was giving, he tried hard to keep his worries as producer separate from his worries as an actor. Ironically, it was the very nature of Wyler's method, to do up to thirty or forty takes, that ensured that Peck's best came out on screen.

But Peck lost faith in Wyler's assessment, and objected to a close-up of himself and Carroll Baker on a buckboard. 'We must do that again,' he insisted. 'I was like an amateur in it.'

Wyler had already decided not to reshoot it, but rather than risk another row, he simply said, 'We'll see.' Several times Peck pressed Wyler to retake the close-up until the exasperated director eventually told him, 'We're not going to do it. I can cut around it. I'm sick and tired of hearing about it.'

Peck stormed back to his trailer, then made up his mind to go back to Los Angeles. His working relationship with Wyler as a co-producer was well and truly shattered. 'I can't understand how it all happened,' reflected Peck. 'Especially since Wyler is one of the directors I love and respect the most. Somehow, though, you lose touch with reality and little matters become magnified out of all proportion.'

Wyler decided that he could finish the film at the studio where all the interiors were to be shot, but Peck, unusually petulant, refused to return for the final week of filming. George Chasin and Véronique finally persuaded him to change his mind. Wyler insisted Peck made a public apology for his tantrum, but Peck refused, and Wyler had to drop his demands or risk not getting the film finished. Peck reported for work at the studio and for the final week the atmosphere could have been cut with a knife.

Carroll Baker recalled, 'It was difficult for all of us but especially for them. We all loved them both and there was no taking sides.' Heston remembered, 'Whatever their differences, by and large they kept them to themselves without involving anybody else. Whatever Greg had to say about Willy, he said it to his face, not behind his back.'

When the film was completed in November 1957 Wyler told a New York reporter, 'I'll never make another picture with Greg Peck. And you can quote me.'

The feud wasn't over. Wyler supervised the editing and delivered a film to United Artists that ran four hours. Peck complained, 'He's overshot by an hour's length, which had to be cut. We went way over our budget and in the end spent $4.1 million.'

Wyler tried to stop Peck's name going on as co-producer and lawyers were called in to fight it out. Véronique and Wyler's wife, Talli, tried to get them to sort out their problems amicably, but both men stubbornly stood their ground.

After the troubles of the film, Greg took a long break from filming to recover, and as time went by, he began to regret his fall-out with Wyler. Peck missed his chance to mend fences before *The Big Country* could hit the screens, because Wyler went off to Rome to shoot *Ben Hur* early in 1958. By then Peck had family matters on his mind; his first and only daughter, Cecilia, was born in May.

The Big Country had its Gala Premiere on 1 October 1958, at New York's Astor Theater, in aid of the National Jewish Hospital at Denver, a non-sectarian treatment centre for tuberculosis and respiratory diseases. The next day the newspapers published their reviews.

Paul V. Beckley of the *New York Herald Tribune* called it 'king-size and astutely and enthusiastically made. Wyler, in giving full attention to the themes and incidents of his story, has shown such relish in the telling, such a richness, that the workmanship becomes economical, always to the point, never diffuse. The acting is good throughout. This is pre-eminently a director's picture and among Westerns a real beauty.'

Bosley Crowther wrote in *The New York Times* that Wyler and Peck

> have attempted to make the most bellicose hymn to peace ever seen. Those verbal encounters and violent battles are like something on the windy plains of Troy. This quality is best represented by Mr. Bickford and Mr. Ives who glare and roar at each other like a couple of fur-bearing gladiators. [Peck and Heston] stoke up the spirit of contention to a lesser degree. For all this film's mighty pretensions, it does not get far beneath the skin of its conventional Western situation and its stock Western characters.

Time called it 'a starkly beautiful, carefully written, classic Western. Wyler's drama hinges not on a fateful clash but on a succession of real choices to be made by each of the characters, each choice affecting the lives of all the others, and creating in turn a new set of choices. The story is acted out against a landscape in which the splash of blood provides the only bright colour.'

The buckboard shot which Peck had thought would be so awful and embarrassing was virtually eliminated, and what there was of it was cut into the scene so deftly that nobody but he would even have been aware of it.

13

Subversive Fall-out

AFTER THE BREAKDOWN of Peck's partnership with William Wyler, he formed a new co-producing partnership with Sy Bartlett to form Melville. James R. Webb brought to Peck's attention a book by US Army Brigadier General S.L.A. Marshall, who was regarded as one of the world's foremost military historians. It was an account of the battle for Pork Chop Hill in the Korean War. *Pork Chop Hill* became Melville's first venture in 1958.

James R. Webb wrote the screenplay and Peck and Bartlett asked Lewis Milestone to direct. Milestone accepted, partly because the film would complete what was for him a trilogy that covered the three major wars fought by America in his lifetime. His classic war films were *All Quiet on the Western Front*, set in World War One, and *A Walk in the Sun*, set in World War Two.

A cast of generally unknown actors was introduced to the public, including George Peppard, Harry Guardino, Robert Blake and Martin Landau. Peck said, 'It's one of the outstanding war dramas, with a cast of men who really seem to belong. They are not "names" but each boy contributes a great performance. What more can one ask?'

Time argued that 'the fighting scenes are almost too spectacularly realistic, and too often they transpire in the middle distance, surrounding the spectator but somehow never quite touching him. The moviegoer never really gets to know the fighting men, but then, on the other hand, the film does not sentimentalize or patronize its heroes.'

Bosley Crowther wrote in *The New York Times*, 'Milestone knows how to stage these things and he has here the further advantage of a highly responsive cast. Gregory Peck is convincingly stalwart. A good dozen other fellows – notably Woody Strode – are moving and amusing in G.I. roles. And the audacity of Sy Bartlett in producing such a grim and rugged film, which tacitly points out the obsoleteness of ground warfare, merits applause.'

Variety said, 'Peck's performance is completely believable. He comes through as a born leader, and yet has his moments of doubt and uncertainty. This is no customary Hollywood hero and the picture gains immeasurably from the human factor with which Peck imbues the role.'

When the film opened in May 1959, it was a big hit. However, Milestone is reported as saying that the film suffered because much of the footage that did not feature Peck was cut out, allegedly at the suggestion of Mrs. Peck.

For the first time in ages, Greg's personal life was settled. He told reporters, 'Véronique is the woman of my life and I couldn't ask for more. I'm the luckiest man in the world.'

Greta had custody of the children, but when Jonathan asked if he could live with his father, it was arranged without argument. The other boys were also allowed to stay with their father whenever they wanted and his hectic schedule allowed. Greta and Greg didn't agree, however, about the children's schooling. Greg wanted them away from Hollywood, which he felt was never a healthy environment for children to be raised in, but Greta, understandably, wanted them at home. She sent Jonathan to Harvard School, California, where he proved to be an exceptional athlete. Of all his brothers, he looked most like his father, a fact which really got to him during his college years when his peers teased him about it. Greg and Véronique always went to watch Jonathan run in competition when they were not globe-trotting. Carey soon followed Jonathan to Harvard School, then Jonathan moved on to Occidental, a liberal arts college in Los Angeles that boasted outstanding track teams.

Reporters tried hard to get Peck to open up and talk about his life away from the film set, but he told one persistent newspaperman, 'It's all rather second-rate to expose one's insides to the public view. I'm not interested by the vogue for actors to tell all. I think it's in poor taste. My performances are the only forms of self-revelation that I go in for.'

Peck became excited about the prospect of co-starring with Clark Gable in a film called *Toward the Unknown*. When George Chasin, who represented both stars, brought up the tricky subject of who would take top billing, Peck told him, 'Me take first billing over Clark Gable? Out of the question.' Unfortunately, the two actors could not fit the film into their individual schedules, and it was eventually made with William Holden and Lloyd Nolan.

Instead, Peck made *On the Beach* for Stanley Kramer, leaving to film in Australia towards the end of 1958, and taking Véronique, Anthony and Cecilia with him.

The film, based on Nevil Shute's bestseller, was a bleak drama about the end of the world after a nuclear war has wiped out most of civilization. Peck played the commander of an American submarine which happened to be submerged just off Australia at the time. Australia is untouched by the war but radiation fall-out is heading its way. Ava Gardner starred as the last woman Peck makes love to.

Kramer said, 'I wanted *On the Beach* to transcend politics and nationalist ideologies. I wanted to make a film that reflected the primary hopes and fears on the minds of everyone at that time.'

Peck said 'Stanley Kramer wanted to say something about crucial matters of world importance. He said, "I'm going to make a picture and perhaps I can have some effect on people's attitude, perhaps I can change their minds about the dangers of nuclear build-up." I think we all became somewhat imbued with Stanley's mission; we all wanted to help him do it, including Ava. I believe that she felt good about being in that picture.'

She did feel good. She said, 'Stanley's script made me weep. It was compelling, tragic, moving, chilling.' She said that everyone involved in the film knew that it was a scenario that could happen. 'That added a dimension of reality to the unreal world of filmmaking that none of us had experienced before.'

Peck modelled his character of US Navy Captain Dwight Lionel Towers after US Navy Commander W.R. Anderson of the first American nuclear submarine, *Nautilus*. But he objected to the part of the script that called for him to take Ava to bed on the grounds that she was almost the last woman on earth he could now have a relationship with. 'It was a violation of the novel and out of character,' he argued. He felt the captain should have remained hopeful that his wife might still be alive. 'My character goes out the window when I do the expected thing and go to bed with Ava. The character, the peculiar twist that makes him interesting and differ-

145

ent, goes down the drain.' Nevil Shute objected to virtually everything Kramer had done to his novel and characters, and he boycotted the film entirely.

For Fred Astaire the film offered his first real straight dramatic role as a nuclear scientist, even though it was his thirty-first film since making his screen debut with *Dancing Lady* in 1933. He and Peck hadn't really had the chance to meet and get to know each other before, but they became firm friends from the time they began working on this picture to Astaire's death in 1987.

Australia was not exactly geared up to accommodate the filming of a major Hollywood picture in 1958, and Kramer had to have most of the equipment, including two mobile generators and dressing-room trailers, shipped over from the United States. The populace of Melbourne, where much of the film was shot, were so excited about the prospect of having a Hollywood movie shot on their doorstep that they gathered everywhere the unit set up its lights and cameras. Great crowds became a constant audience for the actors, blocking streets and bringing complaints from the city's leaders. When a city block was cordoned off one Sunday morning, preventing worshippers from getting to their church, one of Australia's leading churchmen denounced Stanley Kramer for interfering with 'one of the fundamental freedoms – freedom of worship'.

The Australian Navy were more accommodating, lending Kramer an aircraft carrier, while the Royal Navy provided a submarine, HMS *Andrew*. Studio space was at a premium, so Kramer acquired the Royal Showgrounds. The wardrobe department took up residence in a warehouse that stored farm tools, and a car showroom became the production office.

Peck rented a big Victorian house where Gardner, Astaire, Anthony Perkins and Stanley Kramer spent most evenings. Australian laws closed bars and pubs at 6 p.m. and wine could only be served in restaurants up to 9 p.m., but at Peck's house alcohol was available at any hour.

Anthony Perkins was then only twenty-six but had already made nine films and been nominated for an Oscar (for *Friendly Persuasion*). He played an Australian naval officer. Gary Cooper, who had worked with him in *Friendly Persuasion*, had told Greg, 'He needs to spend a summer on a ranch.' Peck now agreed, saying, 'He's a very good young performer but perhaps not too unlike the neurotic characters he tended to play.'

Much of the principal photography was done by Giuseppe Rotunno, who had to invent new techniques to satisfy Kramer's visual flair. When Peck kissed Ava Gardner in front of a campfire, Kramer wanted the camera to do a 360-degree turn. Some of the technicians said it was impossible, but it worked because, said Gardner, 'of the genius of Pepe Rotunno. By the time the cameras finished circling, it must have qualified for the longest screen kiss in screen history. Hanging in there for almost two minutes was very exhausting.'

Ava Gardner said that one shot, towards the end of the film, remained etched in her memory. She had to kiss Peck goodbye before he returns to America, where his men chose to be when the end came. 'You can just see our two profiles come together as the sun sets between our lips,' she said. 'Pepe was shooting straight into the sun, but he made it work, and I personally think it's one of the greatest shots in cinema history.'

Peck recalled the love scenes in the film as being extremely uncomfortable.

> It was terribly hot, sometimes over a hundred degrees. Ava and I were trying to play a light-hearted romantic scene on a beach where the air was thick with flies which almost blackened the skies. There would be thousands of flies crawling on Ava's forehead and in her hair, and the effects men would rush in with a smoke gun to blow smoke in our faces. That would get rid of the flies for a minute or two and allow us to say a few lines before they came back again.
>
> Ava took it like a trouper. I have worked with a few actresses who will remain nameless who would never work under those conditions. But Ava never complained. We just kept plugging away at it despite everything until we had the scene.

Peck felt that Ava was by then a much better actress. He also recognized that she suffered as an actress because of her exceptional beauty: 'I always felt that she was underrated because people were deceived by her beauty and did not expect more from her. By the time we did *On the Beach*, Ava had a wonderful style, and there were certain things she did that I think no one could equal. To my mind she developed into a fine actress. I've been telling her that for years, and she always waves it off.'

During production Peck came across a horse he thought had promise, and when filming in Australia wrapped, he shipped the horse back to the States, hoping it would finally fulfil his hopes of winning the Grand National.

Kramer spent months working meticulously on post-production back in Hollywood. Meanwhile, Peck had to star in only one more film to fulfil his contract with Fox, so when he was offered *Beloved Infidel*, based on a book by Hollywood columnist Sheilah Graham about her relationship with F. Scott Fitzgerald, he thought it over carefully. There were two schools of thought at Fox about the project – whether to make a film about F. Scott Fitzgerald with Sheilah Graham as an incidental character, or make a film about Graham in which Fitzgerald is just an incidental character. The end result was a film according equal weight to both.

Peck was reluctant to do the film at all, knowing that past attempts at Hollywood biopics had been ripped apart because fictitious elements were included in deference to commercial interests. It was only because his friend Henry King was going to direct that brought him round to the idea.

Producer Jerry Wald took the screenplay by Al Hayes to Sheilah Graham for her approval. She hated it.

'Which part?' asked Wald.

'All of it!'

Peck didn't like the Hayes script either. He found Fitzgerald, as written in the screenplay, thoroughly unattractive and declared, 'I just could not see what charm she could have found in such a person.'

Robert Alan Arthur did a rewrite, but his work also failed to please Peck, who felt that the production should now be put on ice. Unfortunately, Deborah Kerr, who was playing Sheilah Graham, was committed later on, so work had to begin on schedule. Peck suggested they start filming using portions of the script that were acceptable – very few – while Sy Bartlett did the rewrites.

Deborah Kerr had mixed feelings about the changes Peck was insisting on. She told me,

> I was most upset that the film was not what it set out to be, although I understood Greg's point of view and I wanted to work with him. It became something that fell between Sheilah Graham's original

book, the first script and Gregory Peck's rewrite. Half of Sheilah's personality was cut out and I was just unable to characterize her. It was just impossible to pick up the threads of her life half way. I couldn't show where she came from, which I thought was important to do, and why she became the way she was.

The role of Fitzgerald was certainly a change of pace for Peck, who had to play the alcoholic writer in all his drunken glory without becoming repugnant. 'I'm no night-club imitator,' he said. 'I can only do what I can do to capture the essence of the man and hope that his friends will feel that I haven't done him violence.'

The script called for him to call Graham a 'silly bitch', and when the Production Code's representative Geoffrey M. Shurlock found out he told Peck and King that the word 'bitch' was forbidden. Star and director argued that the word was important and justifiable. They lost the argument, so a decision was taken to defy the code and keep it in.

Peck saw it as 'a story of a man who is trying to recapture his talent and a rather silly girl he happened to meet and fall in love [with]. Somehow they bring out the best in each other.' But he knew that what the film lacked was a sense of what really made Fitzgerald an interesting character. The film failed to explain what made him into the person and the artist he was. 'Somewhere between its conception and its release,' said Peck, 'Fitzgerald got lost. The picture turned out to be a soap opera about a Cinderella from London who came to Hollywood and took care of a noisy drunk.'

Paul V. Beckley of the *New York Herald Tribune* managed to find some of its virtues: 'It is an intensely told love story with some tender moments and some fairly desperate ones. Peck, although his manner and mannerisms won't persuade most writers that he is one of them, nevertheless manages to turn in one of his most pungent performances.'

Bosley Crowther of *The New York Times* complained that Jerry Wald and Henry King 'went on the evident assumption that the simple dropping of names, the unrestrained calling of "Scott" and the mention of the novels of Mr. Fitzgerald would be sufficient to impress an audience. There is no more reality in these names than there is in the postured performance of Gregory Peck.'

Peck's most bitter critic was Sheilah Graham herself, who found his portrait of Fitzgerald so unbelievable that, she said, 'even Bing Crosby' would have been better in the part. As for the film, she said it was 'dreadful!'

'It is impossible to put one's finger on what went wrong with *Beloved Infidel*,' said Henry King. 'It was a passable movie. Not every work can be a masterpiece of movie-making.'

In 1959 Peck agreed to star opposite the most exciting female star of the time, Marilyn Monroe, in *The Billionaire*, to be produced by Jerry Wald. Norman Krasna had written the original screenplay. Peck liked the part, which was a Howard Hughes-type character, and he thought that to star with Monroe would be a good move because she was simply the biggest female star in the world.

Before Monroe discovered that Peck was to be her co-star, the question came up at the studio of who of the two leads would get first billing, always a difficult problem to solve among star egos. George Chasin, who also represented Monroe, was called in to meet her and Lew Schrieber, an executive at Twentieth Century-Fox, and was asked to explain his way out of the dilemma. Chasin pointed out that Marilyn's contract said that she had first billing – unless she was co-starring with a male star who was more important in the industry than she was. Then he told her that Gregory Peck had shown interest, to which she responded with, 'Then there's absolutely no problem. Of course he should be billed first.' And that was that.

Peck had to sing and dance in the film, which was another challenge or two he could not resist. Tap-dancing lessons ensued and he learned, as he put it, to 'croak' three songs. Fox was talking about casting Bing Crosby as the singing coach in the film, with Milton Berle and Lee J. Cobb taking major roles; Peck approved their names. Monroe had director approval, and she opted for George Cukor, a director Peck admired and looked forward to working with.

Monroe arrived at the studio with writer-husband Arthur Miller, and her drama coach Paula Strasberg in tow. Peck met with Cukor, who mentioned that some rewriting on the script was being done. Peck got a bad feeling and asked what the rewrites were for; he said he thought the script was fine as it stood. Cukor, who had a reputation for favouring his female stars above the males, explained that Arthur Miller was going to 'sharpen it up, put more into it.'

Jerry Wald, who was producing, confirmed that changes were being made. 'We are deepening the character a little for Marilyn and writing in some special parts for her,' he said.

'God Almighty!' exclaimed Peck. 'The whole thing's going up the spout.'

Peck read the new version virtually as the pages scrolled off the typewriter, and he began to see how his role was being diminished while Monroe's got bigger. Cukor urged him to wait until he saw the new script in its entirety, so he agreed to be a little more patient.

On 17 November 1959, *Beloved Infidel* was premiered at the Paramount Theater in aid of the Damon Runyon Fund, and went on to become the first commercial Hollywood production to be entered in the San Francisco Film festival, then in its third year. The day after the premiere it was publicly announced that Peck would not be co-starring with Marilyn Monroe in *The Billionaire* after all. He had seen the final script and realized it was now no longer about the billionaire but about Marilyn Monroe. He met with George Cukor and told him that what had started out as a funny story was no longer making him laugh. Cukor was dismayed, and kept repeating, 'What shall we do? What shall we do?'

Peck diplomatically offered to bow out of the project, telling the studio he wouldn't hold them to a contract and he wouldn't take any money. Fox agreed to release Peck from his obligations to the film, which allowed him to meet the starting date of his next picture, *The Guns of Navarone*, which was to begin filming in the Greek islands in the spring of 1960.

The Billionaire was eventually made as *Let's Make Love*, and Peck's replacement was French star Yves Montand, who had a passionate affair with Marilyn.

Before *On the Beach*, Peck attended a press conference, where he responded to the suggestion that the film's theme was too controversial with: 'It is a subject which needs airing, which needs dramatizing.'

Some suggested his career might be harmed by the film's controversial nature, to which he replied that some well-meaning friends had warned him his career would be jeopardized by making *Gentleman's Agreement*, and yet the role had helped rather than hindered his standing in the industry.

Kramer wanted to premiere *On the Beach* simultaneously in twenty-five cities around the world on 17 December 1959, including Moscow, making it the first American feature film to have a premiere in the Soviet Union. Kramer personally worked with United Artists in handling the Moscow premiere, and Greg and Véronique arrived the night before as guests of the Soviet government, which bent over backwards to accommodate their sightseeing. Peck said, 'We were only in town for two days and we wanted to see everything.'

Peck had been concerned that the Russians might take offence at the picture, but, he said, 'No one I talked to, including many high in the Soviet cultural programme, found the film controversial. They called it "a dramatic warning".'

The day after the premiere the Russian newspapers gave the film unanimously good reviews. When Peck returned to the United States, he said at a press conference, 'There were no political slants or angles in the reviews. They took it as a good theme, didn't see anything political in it at all.'

The New York premiere took place on the same date at the Astor Theater, with a benefit celebrating the seventy-fifth anniversary of the American Academy of Dramatic Arts. The next day the film's reviews reflected the film's controversial nature. *Esquire's* Dwight MacDonald described it as 'slick, vulgar, sentimental, phoney, equipped with a plot of special banality.' John McCarten wrote in the *New Yorker* that the principal character's personal dramas seemed 'pretty irrelevant if we remember that we are supposed to be looking at the way the world might die.'

Arthur Knight of the *Saturday Review* liked it, but with reservations. 'The earlier, landlocked passages are heavy with the sense of actors acting. But once the *Sawfish* casts anchor, the screen begins to tingle with excitement. The film aims at something big and emerges as something tremendous.'

Bosley Crowther of *The New York Times* thought the film was 'splendidly done – crisply written, with intelligence and economy, wisely directed by Kramer in a clear terse style, and played by a cast that is uniformly fine in every role.'

John Beaufort praised the film in the *Christian Science Monitor*, saying it 'matches the somber warning of its theme with the jolting impact of its dramatic force.'

The more politically conservative *New York Daily News* launched its own attack on the film: 'This is a would-be shocker which plays right up the alley of (a) the Kremlin and (b) the Western defeatists of the H-bomb. See this picture if you must (it seems bound to be much talked about), but keep in mind that the thinking points the way toward eventual Communist enslavement of the entire human race.'

The film became front-page news, and the New York-based *Journal-American* ran the headline, 'ON THE BEACH HITS LIKE AN ATOM BOMB'. After a special screening for Washington officials, Senator Wallace F. Bennett of Utah decried the film, calling it 'an imaginative piece of science fiction, a fantasy, and not a dramatization of what would probably happen in the event of a nuclear war'.

The New York Times, however, devoted an entire 'Topics of the Times' page to the film, saying 'Its message is so vigorous and meaningful for all of us [that] seldom has a filmed message been conceived on so grand a scale.'

New York governor Nelson Rockefeller thought the film was subversive, saying, 'A basic objective of any military operation is to break the people's will to resist. I don't know how many of you have seen the movie *On the Beach*. I know some of my kids saw it, and I want to tell you that it is a great way to destroy people's will to resist, because they come out of that movie saying, "There is nothing we can do".'

Bosley Crowther responded to the political attacks on the film by writing a further piece in *The New York Times*, saying, 'The acerbity with which some authorities have lashed out at the film is indeed uncommonly surprising and hard to understand. It is as if they have peevishly resented its awesome warning about nuclear war and have missed the obvious point that its drama is purposefully based on an extreme hypothesis.' He went on, 'It appears that the impact of this picture is profound. People leave it in sober, contemplative and evidently resolute moods.'

Ava Gardner said she didn't care what anybody else thought of the film. 'I was proud of being part of this film, proud of what it said.' She was, however, amused with one personal notice she got from *Newsweek*, which said, 'Miss Gardner has never looked worse or been more effective.'

14

How the War and the West were Won

IN MAY 1960, PECK ATTENDED the Oscars ceremony, and was waiting in the wings to go on stage when William Wyler walked by clutching the Oscar he had just won as Best Director for *Ben Hur*. Peck immediately held out his hand and said, 'Congratulations, Willy, you really deserve it.'

Wyler smiled, shook his hand and said, 'Thanks. But I still won't retake that buckboard scene!' The three-year-long feud was over, and they remained friends until Wyler died in 1981.

Peck took Véronique, Anthony, and Stephen on holiday in France before heading for the island of Rhodes to make *The Guns of Navarone* in 1960. Alistair Maclean's World War Two book – about six commandos who scale impossible cliff-faces on an Aegean island, blow up the biggest guns in the world and so free 2,000 trapped British soldiers – was published in 1957 and became an immediate bestseller. Writer-producer Carl Foreman bought the screen rights and planned to cast it with Hugh O'Brien, Trevor Howard, Alec Guinness, Marlon Brando and Cary Grant. Then the names of Kenneth More, William Holden, Jack Hawkins and Gary Cooper were added to or replaced the original cast, but in the event the team heading for Navarone was Gregory Peck, Anthony Quinn, David Niven, James Darren, Anthony Quayle and Stanley Baker.

Peck admired Carl Foreman for the way he had worked virtually single-handed for more than a year to get the film made. He also admired him for the way he had re-established himself in Britain after being blacklisted by anti-communist witch hunters. Peck studiously went through Foreman's script and sent Foreman memos, suggesting changes that Foreman implemented.

Foreman originally chose Alexander Mackendrick to direct, but a week before filming he fell out with Mackendrick and fired him. Foreman, in Athens, cabled Peck, then in Paris, saying he'd like to offer J. Lee Thompson the directing job. 'He was always my first choice but not available originally,' said Foreman. 'He is the hottest director in England at this time.'

Peck flew to Athens to sit with Foreman in the private cinema of the King George Hotel and watched Thompson's films for three days, finally agreeing that Thompson seemed the best bet. Three days later filming began on the island of Rhodes, where Peck was accompanied by Véronique. The star cast met on the set. J. Lee Thompson told me:

> There was a certain amount of rivalry on the set between Gregory Peck, David Niven and Anthony Quinn – friendly rivalry. The first night we all met on the location in Athens David Niven was very cheery but he felt anxious that he was just going to be left standing around a lot with nothing to do while all the other stars got on with the action. It was true that his character was not as well developed as some of the others and he felt, rightly, that all the characters had been written as supermen without much depth to them. He thought he would be forgotten among all those stars like Peck and Quinn. But he had only just won an Oscar [for *Separate Tables*] and was insecure that Gregory Peck and Anthony Quinn would get all the best acting moments. And there was Peck convinced Tony Quinn would try to out-act him, and Quinn was aware that Niven had won an Oscar, and so they were all eyeing each other warily. Nothing unpleasant, but I felt the tension. Then Tony Quinn brought out little portable chess sets and they all got hooked on playing chess and took out all the rivalry on the chess board instead of before the cameras.

About those chess sets, Anthony Quinn told me:

> I thought that playing chess would reveal everyone's character. There was David Niven, the Errol Flynn of the chessboard, charging around with his queen, crying, 'Idiotic move, what, eh? Well never mind, on we go. Charge!' Then there was Peck – calm – like Lincoln – contemplating every move – deep in thought – you couldn't rush him. Stanley Baker was a competitive spirit who displayed terrible fury when defeated but great joy when victorious. Tony Quayle

156

moved his pieces like a general, planning his strategy, studying the board and knowing what his moves would be way ahead. Carl Foreman played too. When he lost you could see centuries of persecution in his face. And there was me. When I lost I just threw the board at them!

According to Anthony Quayle, 'Tony Quinn was not always easy to get on with. Because Gregory Peck was a big Hollywood star you felt he was in charge and you could trust him. But for me the delight of the film was working with David Niven, who never failed to say, "Hello, old bean, how are you?"' Peck also recalled Niven with exceptional affection. 'He was always so incredibly cheerful that when you asked why he was, he'd just say, "Well, old bean, life is really so bloody awful that I feel it's my absolute duty to be chirpy and try and make everybody else happy too."'

Peck and the rest of the cast knew the film's plot should not be taken too seriously. He said:

> Those five or six commandos were miracle workers, overcoming a whole German regiment by getting right in the middle of them, stealing their uniforms and pretending to be Nazis. Those Germans had 500 opportunities to kill us before we even got onto that island. They were like the Keystone Cops. But to bring that sort of yarn off you have to do it with complete conviction. We knew it could so easily have slipped over into parody.
>
> Early in production I told Carl Foreman, 'Here's the real plot of the picture. It's really a love story. David Niven really loves Tony Quayle and Gregory Peck loves Anthony Quinn. Tony Quayle breaks a leg and is sent off to hospital. Tony Quinn falls in love with Irene Papas and David Niven and Peck catch each other on the rebound and live happily ever after.'
>
> Carl said, 'You clever rascal, you've caught me out.'

When the location wrapped, the unit returned to England to shoot interiors at Shepperton Studios. Peck hoped to see the Grand National, but filming prevented him from doing so; he hoped one day to enter one of his own horses into the great race and win it. At least he and his family were living in a house in Ascot, so Greg and Véronique were able to see some horse racing with the Nivens on rare days off.

Peck was provided with a chauffeur, Mike, who drove him to and from the studio by day, and to the theatre in London by night. Mike was a genial chap who liked to bet on the greyhounds and gave Peck tips on a few winners. Most days, after Mike dropped Greg off at the studio, he'd take Anthony to the playground.

While the Pecks were at the theatre one night, their house was burgled; Véronique lost two fur coats and some jewellery. Fortunately, the children were unharmed, asleep in their beds, and the staff had noticed nothing untoward while watching television. The police discovered that the burglars had climbed up a ladder placed against the wall of the house and crept in through an open window on the second floor. They never caught the burglars nor retrieved the stolen goods.

Much of the filming at Shepperton was done in the studio tank where scenes of the shipwreck were filmed. The actors almost froze in the water and were warmed up with copious amounts of brandy. David Niven recalled that often they would all be quite drunk, except for Peck. 'He could match us drink for drink, yet he never so much as staggered or slurred his words. It was really quite disgusting to see a man able to handle his liquor like that.'

The scenes were dangerous to shoot. Peck received a head injury and Niven cut his lip, which turned septic and landed him in hospital. While the doctors struggled to contain the infection, production shut down for two weeks. All that remained was the scene where Peck and Niven rig the guns. Columbia executives flew in from the States to meet with Foreman and Thompson to discuss what they would do if Niven died. When news of this reached Niven he discharged himself against doctors' advice and went back to work. The rigging scenes were completed in three days, then Niven had a relapse and spent seven weeks convalescing. He recalled: 'The studio brass didn't so much as send me a grape.'

All the trials and tribulations were worth it though. Archer Winstein of the *New York Post* wrote: 'What makes the suspense all the more impressive is the caliber of the men, those sterling actors, who know how to toss a quip or a grenade with equal sangfroid. Coolest, of course, is Gregory Peck, but Anthony Quinn, David Niven and Stanley Baker are hardly less so. The picture grips you with an astounding power.'

Cue called it 'a rip-roaring spectacular movie entertainment ...

pure movie adventure, filled with clichés but presented so skilfully and so jam-packed with action that you haven't time to sneer before you start to cheer. The cast could hardly have been bettered.'

Time found it 'the most enjoyable consignment of baloney in months.' The *New Yorker*'s critic said it was 'one of those great big bow-wow, or maybe I should say bang-bang, movies that are no less thrilling because they are so preposterous. I was held more or less spellbound all the way through this many-colored rubbish.'

Bosley Crowther of *The New York Times* thought it was 'one of those muscle-loaded pictures which moves swiftly and gets where it is going. J. Lee Thompson has directed with pace and seen to it that the actors give the impression of being stout and bold.'

Paul V. Beckley, in the *New York Herald Tribune*, called it 'a good, bone-hard, manly military adventure. Peck may seem at times a trifle wooden, but his not too introspective, somewhat baffled manner is manly and fitted to the role he plays.'

At the end of filming, Peck gave inscribed Cartier gold watches to his stand-in, his make-up man, his wardrobe assistant and Mike, the chauffeur. Then he flew his family to California. A few weeks later an assistant at Cartier's of Bond Street phoned Peck and said that a dozen watches had been ordered on his account by the chauffeur, who claimed he was acting on Peck's instructions. Peck cancelled the order. Then he received a statement from the Connaught Hotel in London where Mike had booked a suite in Peck's name and ordered copious amounts of champagne for himself and a ladyfriend. Peck did some delving and discovered Mike had a prison record. Putting two and two together Peck realized that Mike had been the one who tipped off the burglars about the furs and jewels to be had at his Ascot house and had hidden the ladder for them to find. But he couldn't prove it. Nevertheless, he had Mike charged with fraud and put back behind bars.

Peck returned to England for post-synching while Véronique took the children to their new villa at Cap Ferrat on the French Riviera; her father had helped design and build it to their specifications. Then Greg flew out to join them for a long holiday, during which he and Véronique made a decision to have their marriage blessed.

On their return to Los Angeles, Greg asked Greta to give the necessary written approval required by the Catholic Church that their marriage was officially over. At the Catholic church in Santa Barbara, Jesuit Father Jim Deasy, a friend of the Pecks, blessed their marriage in front of a single witness, Channing Peak.

In May 1961, Peck did a guest spot in the Western epic *How the West Was Won.* MGM and Cinerama had entered into a deal that would give some of its profits to St John's Hospital at Santa Monica. Veteran actress Irene Dunne, as St John's representative, was unofficial casting director for the film, persuading some of Hollywood's biggest stars to appear for a set fee of $5,000 a week, including John Wayne, Henry Fonda, James Stewart, Carroll Baker, Richard Widmark, Debbie Reynolds and Karl Malden.

I made the mistake, when meeting Peck for the first time, of telling him how much I enjoyed the film and his performance. He said, 'I wish I hadn't done it. I was charmingly seduced into it by Irene Dunne. I wasn't happy with the role but it was the best they could find for me. Irene had appealed to me as a Catholic, and I agreed – against my better judgement. I should have just given Irene a big donation instead.'

Originally, Peck was to work only one week but ended up doing three, adding to his bad mood throughout production. None of this ill-temper seeps through on screen. He comes across as an amiable con-man out to woo frontierswoman Debbie Reynolds because he thinks she is rich. 'I thought the picture was predictable and corny,' said Peck. 'I didn't like working in Cinerama and artistically I think it fell short, even though it was a box-office success. If it comes on TV, I run to the set to turn it off.'

He thought his own performance was lousy, but *Variety* disagreed, saying, 'Peck gives a suave and polished gloss to his role of the gambler, and though it's an undemanding part he gives it notable distinction.'

Peck hated working in the clumsy Cinerama process, which was achieved by using a camera that was actually three cameras in one, with three separate films running through three lens gates. It was projected on to a giant curved screen through three projectors to create one big picture but with the joins between the films clearly visible. Nevertheless, it was an extraordinary effect which, since 1952, had been used successfully for feature-length Cinerama travelogues. But because the three camera lenses crossed each other's field of vision, the three individual images were filmed at different angles. Peck said, 'I couldn't look directly at Debbie Reynolds when I spoke to her because it would look like I was talking to the nearest tree. So I had to look past her, and as every actor knows, so much of acting is in eye contact. With Cinerama, there was little eye contact. You were looking round the corner instead.'

Co-director Henry Hathaway complained, 'That goddamned Cinerama. Do you know, a waist shot is as close as you could get with that thing?'

Not all the cast were unhappy. In fact Carroll Baker, James Stewart and George Peppard told me they enjoyed making the film. Of the three co-directors, Henry Hathaway, George Marshall and John Ford, the former was Peck's director, and it marked the first time they worked together. Hathaway had a habit of shouting at every one, so Debbie Reynolds pretended to faint every time he raised his voice at her until, finally, he promised to stop yelling at her.

Peck has since refused to do cameos in big-star productions. Once when he was asked to do a big cast film in aid of retarded children, he simply wrote out a cheque as a donation rather than do the film.

Bosley Crowther of *The New York Times* agreed with Peck's appraisal of the film, writing, 'With little or no imagination and, indeed, with no pictorial style, the three directors have fashioned a lot of random episodes, horribly written by James Webb, into a mat of outdoor adventure vignettes that tell you nothing of history.'

Kate Cameron of the *Daily News* gave it a four-star rating, stating, 'Here is as thrilling a picture as we have ever seen. It is the Western to end all Westerns.'

'Cinerama has always been big,' wrote Paul V. Beckley in the *New York Herald Tribune*, 'but now it is bigger. The movie has given it dramatic dimensions that it never had. There may be a tendency to corn, but corn here is growing the way it ought to. It's not only a tribute to the American past, but to American movie-making.'

Whether the public would watch a three-hour dramatic movie in Cinerama remained to be seen, but its outcome meant little to Peck. More important to him was *The Guns of Navarone*, which opened in June 1961, at the Criterion and Murray Hill Theatres in New York. Readers of the *Film Daily* voted it the best picture of 1961, and it received an Oscar for its special effects; it was also nominated for Best Picture, Direction and Screenplay. The Hollywood Foreign Press Association named it Best Picture and awarded Dimitri Tiomkin's music Best Score. The film cost $6 million and took $13 million in the domestic market, a figure that was more than doubled by the worldwide box office takings.

15

Killing Down South

PECK AGAIN CO-PRODUCED with Sy Bartlett on his next film, *Cape Fear*, based on John D. MacDonald's 1958 novel *The Executioner*. J. Lee Thompson directed what was Peck's first attempt at a shocker: the grisly story of a sadistic ex-convict who gets his revenge on a small-town lawyer and his wife and daughter, culminating in a terrifying climax in the swamps of Georgia.

Peck could easily have given himself the meaty role of the sex criminal, but he decided to cast Robert Mitchum, whom he felt could do the better job. Instead he cast himself in the less exacting role of the lawyer. It turned out that Rod Steiger had wanted to play the ex-con, and his agent kept calling Peck to complain, 'What's the matter, don't you want a good actor in the part?' Peck politely informed him that he had one in Mitchum.

Filming began in Savannah, Georgia. Mitchum arrived on the first day, singing, 'How dear to my heart are the scenes of my childhood; when fond recollection presents them to view.' This puzzled J. Lee Thompson, until Mitchum told him, 'These are the scenes of my childhood, man, and they are very dear, very dear indeed to my heart.' Mitchum had returned to the location of his misspent youth.

Throughout filming Peck raised his eyes to the heavens every time Mitchum opened his mouth to reporters. 'I show up at nine and punch out at six – that's all I do,' he told them. 'The picture belongs to other guys and I don't care too much.' Nevertheless, Mitchum proved very supportive of his co-stars – particularly the women. Barrie Chase, a dancer, was making her acting debut and was convinced she was doing a terrible job; Mitchum talked her out of quitting. Thompson said that Mitchum gave her the encouragement that allowed her to produce 'an extraordinary performance'.

But after the filming was over, Mitchum failed to endear himself to Peck when he claimed he had acted Peck off the screen. 'I had given him the role and had paid him a terrific amount of money,' said Peck. 'It was obvious he had the better role. I thought he would understand that, but he apparently thought he acted me off the screen. I didn't think highly of him for that.' Nevertheless, Peck told a reporter, 'It's Bob's picture. Best performance he ever gave.'

When the film opened in April 1962, the reviews were generally favourable. *Saturday Review*'s Arthur Knight thought it 'has no purpose beyond scaring the daylights out of you. Mitchum proves again to be a resourceful and expressive performer. Gregory Peck is equally commendable in a role that is, I suspect, far more difficult – that of the man who is acted upon.'

'A cold-blooded, calculated build-up of sadistic menace and shivering dread is accomplished with frightening adroitness,' wrote Bosley Crowther in *The New York Times*. Paul V. Beckley of the *New York Herald Tribune* called it 'a *tour de force* study in terror that verges on the horror genre'.

For some the film proved to be too strong. Thompson recalled, 'We ran into trouble with the British censor who demanded 161 cuts. Lord Morrison of the British Board of Film Censors decided that it was a – quote – "nasty film" – unquote. I just thought that many cuts would mutilate and emasculate the film. So I talked to Gregory Peck and Sy Bartlett and said we should withhold the film from release in Britain rather than give in to the censor. In the end the film was shown with about six minutes cut from it.'

After *Cape Fear*, Peck went to his office at Universal Studios, and wondered what picture he could next produce. Then he heard that Rock Hudson was trying to persuade Universal to buy the rights to *To Kill a Mockingbird*, based on Harper Lee's wonderful reminiscences of childhood in Alabama during the Great Depression years when her father was a lawyer. Universal, however, didn't rise to the bait.

Producer Alan J. Pakula and director Robert Mulligan had worked together on *Fear Strikes Out* with Karl Malden and Anthony Perkins, and were looking for a second picture together. They decided to try to turn Harper Lee's book into a movie, and when they approached Lee's agent, they discovered that studios were vying for the screen rights. They persuaded Miss Lee to withhold sale until they could make their own bid. They immediately sent a copy to Gregory Peck, hoping he would agree to play Atticus Finch, the wise, gentle but formidable lawyer who defends a black man falsely accused of rape. Miss Lee based Atticus on her own father.

'Gregory Peck was the only actor we ever had in mind,' said Pakula. 'He was our first and only choice for the role of Atticus Finch.' Apparently, he was the actor Miss Lee had in mind, too.

They knew that if they could get his name tied to the project, they'd have more chance of getting a studio to finance the film. Peck recalled:

> I hadn't known these two young fellows, but I had seen a picture about a baseball player called Jim Piersall they had made which I thought was well done and sensitively directed. That's all I knew about them. When they sent me the book and asked me to read it, I sat up all night and read it straight through. At about eight the next morning I called them and said, 'If you want me to play Atticus, when do you want me to start? I'd love to play it.' I thought the novel was a really fine piece of writing – I was right about that because it won the Pulitzer Prize and is still being read in high-school literature classes. But beyond that, I felt it was something I could identify with quite easily because I felt I knew those two children. My own childhood was very much like that. It was not in the true South, of course, it was in Southern California. But it was a small town and I did the same things the two children in the book did. So I fell into that very readily, both as the father and with an understanding of the children. I felt I could climb into Atticus's shoes and *be* him.

George Chasin tried to talk Peck out of doing it, because films with a racial theme often proved too controversial, failing at the box office and damaging the careers of those involved. He told Peck, 'You will lose the entire South.' That was not a good argument to convince Peck, who decided that the racial theme was a very good reason to do it.

With Peck's name to help sell the film, Pakula and Mulligan

went to Universal, which this time agreed to put up the money to purchase the screen rights. By this time the book had been on the bestseller list for six weeks; it went on to sell six million copies.

Pakula and Mulligan were determined to keep the film faithful to the book, and asked Miss Lee to write the screenplay. She was unable to accept the assignment as she was working on a new book in Monroeville, Alabama, where she lived with her father, Amasa Lee. Moreover, she was most reluctant to leave her home town to come to Hollywood. So Pakula and Mulligan assigned Horton Foote, who was himself a Southerner, a detail which greatly pleased Miss Lee.

The film makers conducted an intensive search to cast the three principal child roles. Nine-year-old Mary Badham, the daughter of a retired Army general, had never acted before, but was chosen to play Scout. Thirteen-year-old Phillip Alford, who'd only ever acted in the school pageants in his home town of Birmingham, was picked to play Jem. Only nine-year-old John Megna, who was cast as Dil, had real acting experience, having appeared on Broadway in *All the Way Home.*

Pakula and Mulligan felt that the film could only be shot in the South, and at first they considered shooting it in Monroeville, which had been Miss Lee's original model for the fictional town of Maycomb, but it had changed too much in the past thirty years. Finally, it was decided to film it entirely on the back lot of Universal, where art director Alexander Golitzen and Henry Bumpstead constructed Maycomb over fifteen acres.

Peck met with Amasa Lee, who was crippled with arthritis but full of pride for his daughter's success as a Southern writer. Peck learned that Lee had actually raised his children on his own and had also defended innocent black men in court. That meeting was invaluable preparation for Peck's work. When Miss Lee told Peck that her father had a habit of toying with a pocket watch in court, he decided to do the same, so she showed him exactly how Amasa used to do it.

Filming began in February 1962, and when Harper Lee visited the set and saw Peck for the first time in a three-piece suit and Panama hat, she burst into tears. 'My God!' she cried, 'he's got a little pot belly just like Daddy.'

'That's no pot belly, dear,' replied Peck. 'That's great acting.'

Making the film was one of the most satisfying experiences of
Peck's career.

> Working with the children was absolutely marvellous. Robert
> Mulligan wanted natural performances from them, and because two
> of them were not professional actors at all, and because of the sensi-
> tive and delicate way in which Mulligan worked with them, they
> were hugely successful with what they had to do. With the children
> around there was, for me, a feeling of family on the set the whole
> time, which I think helped the children give such marvellous and
> natural performances.

During filming, Peck was asked by a reporter if he felt such a
picture might have some sort of power to soften hard hearts in the
cause of justice and so create a kind of empathy. To this Peck
replied:

> You can never be sure what effect a picture of this kind that does
> deal with a social issue will have. I never overrate the importance of
> a social philosophy or message, if you like, in a film. But I think one
> does perhaps get the idea that people will not only be moved and
> held and entertained but perhaps they'll carry a thought away with
> them. Perhaps they'll carry it with them for a while, perhaps they'll
> discuss it with their friends and it may have some effect eventually
> in a change of social attitude one way or another. I think that's as
> much as we can be sure of, but that sort of thing does happen.

His own daughter, Cecilia, was on the set with him on the final
day of shooting to join in the closing party. Peck scooped her up in
his arms and waltzed her around. Before leaving the set for the last
time, Harper Lee approached him with her father's pocket watch.
Amasa had recently died, so Harper gave his watch to Peck. Since
that time he has rarely been without it on his person.

Peck took his family on another holiday in France, while Robert
Mulligan supervised the post-production. Universal, feeling they
had a film worthy of Oscars, opened the movie in Los Angeles in
December 1962, to qualify it for the Academy Awards the following
year. Its formal premiere was on 14 February 1963, at New York's
Radio City Music Hall.

Said *Time*, 'Harper Lee made a tomboy poem as full of hick fun as Huck Finn, a sensitive feminine testament to the Great American Childhood. Robert Mulligan and Horton Foote have translated both testament and melodrama into one of the year's most fetching and effecting pictures. Gregory Peck, though he is generally excellent, lays it on a bit thick at times.'

Bosley Crowther called it 'a fine film' in *The New York Times*. 'There is so much feeling for children, so much delightful observation of their spirit, energy and charm that it comes as a bit of a letdown at the end to realize that it doesn't tell us very much of how they feel as their father, superbly played by Gregory Peck, goes through a lengthy melodrama of defending a Negro, [but it is] a bewitching indication of the excitement and thrill of being a child.'

Judith Crist, writing for the *New York Herald Tribune*, said, 'Gregory Peck is indeed impressive as the father with loving wisdom, the lawyer dedicated to striving to give his motherless children a sense of decency amid the indecencies of bigotry in a small Southern town. But the scene stealers in this excellent film are Mary Badham, Phillip Alford and John Megna.'

'The children in particular are strikingly good,' wrote Richard Mallet in *Punch*, 'good enough to distract from the excellence of Mr. Peck's performance. Here is a stolid, kindly, dignified, conscientious citizen; never before has he shown so much authority.'

Harper Lee said, 'I can only say that I am a happy author. They have made my story into a beautiful and moving motion picture. I am very proud and very grateful.'

The month after its premiere it was announced that the film had been awarded Oscar nominations for Best Picture, Direction, Supporting Actress (Mary Badham), Screenplay Based on Material from Another Medium, Black-and-White Cinematography, Art Direction and a fifth Best Actor nomination for Gregory Peck. He was among stiff competition; the other nominated Best Actors were Burt Lancaster for *The Birdman of Alcatraz*, Jack Lemmon for *Days of Wine and Roses*, Marcello Mastroianni for *Divorce – Italian Style* and Peter O'Toole for *Lawrence of Arabia*.

The week before the Oscar show was a frantically busy one for Peck. He was well into filming *Captain Newman M.D.* Professional reader Syl Lamont, a long time friend of Peck's, had decided that the book of the same name by Leo Rosten would make a good film, and persuaded Peck to read it. Set in an army hospital during World War Two, it concentrates on three cases treated by Captain Newman M.D.: those of a decorated corporal who believes he's a coward, a crazy colonel plagued with guilt about sending men to their death, and an escapee from Nazi-occupied territory who feels shame for having hid in a cellar for more than a year. The story swung from high drama to heart-warming comedy.

Peck said, 'Syl shoved me into a corner, pushed me into a chair and handed me the book. I could see that it would make a picture even though I knew it had been kicking around Hollywood with no takers since its publication.'

He liked it enough to take it to Universal, and with Peck's own recommendation the studio decided to produce it, paying out $250,000 to Leo Rosten for the screen rights. The studio assigned their own producer, Robert Arthur, to oversee it, and Richard L. Breen wrote the first draft of the screenplay. David Miller was assigned as director, but he felt more work was needed on the screenplay, so he passed it to husband and wife team Henry and Phoebe Ephron, who'd written *There's No Business Like Show Business* and *Take Her She's Mine.*

To prepare him for the role of Captain Newman, Peck read scores of articles and journals about mental health, and spent hours with several Beverly Hills psychiatrists, watching them at work and talking to them. He also spent several more days visiting a mental hospital to observe the staff and patients. Filming began on location at Fort Huachuca, a former US Cavalry outpost in the Arizona desert, east of Nogales. Then the cast and crew returned to Hollywood to complete interiors at Universal Studios.

Peck played Captain Newman, giving a performance that was, according to *Variety*, 'characteristically restrained and intelligent'. The secondary role of an orderly, a resourceful operator from New Jersey, went to Tony Curtis. *Variety* thought, 'Curtis has some good moments, but essentially he is the pivotal figure in the film's secondary comic shenanigans.' Peck enjoyed working with Tony Curtis and was captivated by Curtis's skill at conjuring, which he'd learned when making *Houdini.*

Judith Crist of the *New York Herald Tribune* called it, 'that rare Hollywood film about mental illness that does not reduce it to the level of low comedy and/or Grand Guignol. This, with the more positive virtues of good humour and some excellent characterizations, is almost enough to make us overlook the fact that the film is, au fond, a sort of *Ben Casey* cum *Dr Kildare* in Khaki, with comparatively judicious admixture of schmaltz and corn. On the plus side, we have Gregory Peck's stability to lend authority to Newman.'

Midway through production, Peck arranged time off to race his new horse, Owen's Sedge, in the Grand National, just two days before Oscars night. As much as winning the Oscar, he wanted to win the steeplechase.

He and Véronique flew to Heathrow, and were driven to Aintree, near Liverpool, where they got straight into evening dress and joined the owners' party. They finally fell into bed for just two hours' sleep, then dressed and drove off in the rain to the racecourse. His horse didn't win but stayed the course, finishing seventh. Then he and Véronique were driven back to Heathrow to catch the plane to Los Angeles. They arrived for the Oscars ceremony looking fresh but feeling exhausted.

That night Horton Foote received the award for his screenplay of *To Kill a Mockingbird*, and the film's art directors were also honoured. Mary Badham lost out to Patty Duke for her performance in *The Miracle Worker*, while most of the year's other major Oscars went to *Lawrence of Arabia*.

Peck toyed with Amasa Lee's pocket watch throughout the proceedings, and when the nominations for Best Actor were read out, he gripped the watch tightly. Then the envelope was opened and his name was read out. He rose, passed Jack Lemmon, whom he thought would have been a deserving winner that year, and patted his shoulder. On winning at last, Peck said:

> It was wonderful being given the Oscar, but I feel deep down I've done better acting in more unsuccessful pictures that didn't come off as a whole. I cannot say that playing Atticus Finch was the most difficult thing I've had to do. On the contrary, it was one of the easiest. The part fitted me so well it was like climbing into a favorite suit of clothes. I knew all about that man, those children and that small-town background because of my own early life. Still, *To Kill a Mockingbird* is my favourite film, without any question. And without being falsely modest, I think I was good in the picture.

The pocket watch became a talisman to Peck, like the crucifix he still carried from St John's Military Academy. Peck, the watch and the movie went that year to the Cannes Film Festival of 1963, causing some controversy when its screening was met with bursts of applause from some and catcalls from others as Atticus put up the defence of his black client. Afterwards, at a press conference, Peck met the European critics, who were clearly split in their appraisal of the film, and he faced a barrage of questions about American race relations from both friendly and hostile reporters.

Curiously, considering he was now at the peak of his career, he began telling friends and family that he thought he probably only had another five good years as an actor and would then retire.

How the West Was Won finally hit the giant Cinerama screen on 27 March 1963, at Loew's Cinerama Theater. Peck probably couldn't care less that the public response was tremendous. The film won a handful of Oscars for its screenplay, sound and editing. There were also nominations for Best Picture and for its photography. Even its success was Cinerama-sized, earning more than $50 million, no mean feat in 1963.

In 1963 Doc Peck died. Greg had always been close to his father, despite his frequent enforced separations in early years. Over the years Greg and his stepmother, Harriet, had grown closer, and would grow closer still following the Doc's death.

That same year Peck made a film for which he had high hopes. Few of these were fulfilled, despite the fact that it was directed by one of the most respected and careful directors, Fred Zinnemann. *Behold a Pale Horse* was based on Emeric Pressburger's novel *Killing a Mouse on Sunday*, the story of a Spanish guerrilla who goes into exile at the end of the Spanish Civil War and twenty years later is persuaded to return to kill a brutal police chief.

Peck was co-producer with Zinnemann and Alexander Rauner, and together they agreed on the film's title, suggested by Revelations 6:8, 'And I looked and beheld a pale horse, and his name that sat on him was death. And Hell followed with him.'

With backing from Columbia Pictures, Peck and Zinnemann hoped to film in Spain, but as Peck remembers,

When the Spanish censor read the script he found a single line which he found objectionable and insisted we cut it out. Well, Fred Zinnemann insisted that not one line of dialogue would be cut, and that stirred up something much bigger. We were forbidden to shoot in Spain so we moved across the border into France and shot in the Basque country, which looks just like the terrain on the other side of the Pyrenees. Then the Spanish authorities withdrew all of Columbia Pictures' films from distribution and froze all the revenue that the country owed to Columbia for some time.

Filming in the province of Béarn took place during the summer of 1963. As the production progressed, Peck found himself doubting the film's commercial viability. Zinnemann merely posed many questions and supplied few answers, taking no moral stand in his telling of the story. Zinnemann also had nagging doubts about the film's commercial prospects. 'Zinnemann and I did realize that the background and the Spanish character would be a bit obscure for Americans,' said Peck. 'And since the film is so understated, I was always a little doubtful about how it would go over in America.'

He was concerned that modern American audiences, who had had no previous emotional experience of the Spanish Civil War, might remain unmoved by the film. Peck, analysing the movie some years later, came to the conclusion that it failed to convey the many ramifications with any conviction and thereby rise to a suitably noble and tragic climax, which, he felt, the material demanded. 'It is still a film with many lovely things in it,' he said, 'and much of Zinnemann's work is beautiful and meticulously done. But our biggest problem was in refusing to take a point of view of the war, and not to take sides. You can't not take sides about the Spanish Civil War.'

On 28 August 1963, Peck joined the Arts Group, which included Marlon Brando, Sidney Poitier, Burt Lancaster, Charlton Heston, Paul Newman, Harry Belafonte and many more of Hollywood's cream, as well as musicians and other creative artists, for the Civil Rights march on Washington to hear Dr Martin Luther King. The formation of the Arts Group was a measure of the disgust felt among many in Hollywood at racial bigotry, a subject that had always had a place in Peck's heart, as attested by his work in *Gentleman's Agreement* and *To Kill a Mockingbird*.

On 22 November 1963, President Kennedy was assassinated. The next day Peck received by mail an invitation, postmarked 21 November, for himself and Véronique to attend a White House luncheon. The president was hoping to show his appreciation to

Peck for his work on behalf of the president's 'New Frontier' program.

Later, the United States Information Agency asked Peck to narrate the official filmed tribute to the president, *John F. Kennedy: Years of Lightning, Day of Drums*; curiously, it took two years before the film was passed by Congress for showing in America. Then, in 1964, President Lyndon B. Johnson appointed Peck to membership of the newly formed National Council on the Arts for a two-year term. Peck travelled around America to promote regional theatre.

Captain Newman M.D. made its appearance in February 1964 at the Radio City Music Hall in New York. Around that time, actors William Lundigan and William Gargam, who had both suffered from cancer, came to Peck to try and persuade him to accept the role of California Chairman for the American Cancer Society. Unsure of what kind of a meaningful contribution he could make, Peck was reluctant to accept, but he did. He was genuinely surprised when his presence attracted great crowds to fund-raising rallies. When other volunteers told him how much he was an inspiration to them, he made up his mind to devote as much of his free time to the charity as he could.

Sparing the time to be an actor again, he went to Switzerland to make a World War One drama, *The Bells of Hell Go Ting-a-Ling-a-Ling*. Cast and crew stood by for six weeks as terrible weather made filming impossible. Finally, the picture was abandoned.

That year, Peck was back at Aintree to re-enter Owen's Sedge in the Grand National. Greg loved that horse but didn't get to see much of him, because he was being trained in Ireland. In preparation for the National, Peck entered him in a race at Kempton Park. Owen's Sedge fell after taking a fence, landing spread-eagled and breaking his pelvis. He somehow managed to get up and stagger on several yards, but dropped down dead.

Perhaps the death of Owen's Sedge was an omen for *Behold a Pale Horse*, which premiered on 13 August 1964, at the Victoria and Sutton Theaters in New York. Peck attended the gala premiere at the Victoria, where the audience's reception was conspicuously low-key. Peck recalled, 'There seemed to be problems with the sound and acoustics, and I sweated through every frame.'

The next day Bosley Crowther put his finger on what was wrong with the film in his review in *The New York Times*. 'It is a shame that a film made as beautifully and that has as much atmosphere in it as this one unquestionably has should be short on dramatic substance and emotional urgency. But that is what is missing from *Behold a Pale Horse.*'

Judith Crist, in the *New York Herald Tribune,* said it was 'a beautifully photographed, well-directed film and a disappointing one. Not all the dramatic clips of the Spanish Civil War nor the veritable babel of accents can lend refreshment, significance or depth to the story. Nor do the protagonists, Gregory Peck, looking appropriately baggy-eyed, paunchy and unkempt, Anthony Quinn, looking appropriately Neanderthal and well-groomed, Omar Sharif looking appropriately liquid-eyed and dedicated.'

But there was praise from Kate Cameron, who awarded the film four stars in her review in the *New York Daily News,* writing that the film 'compels attention from its opening scene to its fadeout, as it unfolds an absorbing drama. Peck's characterization tops his prize-winning performance in *To Kill a Mockingbird.*'

As Peck had feared, the film meant little to the American public and it was a sad failure.

16

Public Service

PECK'S INVOLVEMENT IN THE American Cancer Society's fund-raising activities in California allowed him less time than usual for filming, but in 1964 he did make *Mirage*, a Hitchcockian thriller directed by Edward Dmytryk. Peck played an amnesiac trying to learn why he is the target of assassins.

Peck began to have doubts about the film, which, he felt, suffered from a rather pedestrian old-fashioned cinematic approach. 'The story was basically a shell game,' he said, 'and it should have been treated more as a ballet of cinematic suspense.'

Peck suggested casting Walter Matthau as a detective after seeing him in a play. After *Mirage*, Matthau's career really took off. As Peck put it, 'I think my main contribution to the film was that I hired Walter Matthau and virtually launched him on his screen career.'

The film opened in May 1965. '*Mirage* pieces together a compelling puzzle that exists in a man's mind,' wrote Kathleen Carroll in the *Daily News*. 'The mystery remains elusive to the very end. Gregory Peck is everybody's affable, straightforward guy and the character he plays, at his understated best, immediately arouses sympathy.'

The *New Yorker* magazine said, 'It's the genuine article, dating back in spirit to the Upper Middle Hitchcock, or Intricate Puzzlement, period of movie thrillers, and I salute it with respect and relief. It kept me close to the edge of my seat up to the moment of denouement.'

In the summer of 1965, Peck went to Washington to witness the signing by President Johnson of the Arts and Humanities Act of 1965. He stood just a few feet away from the president, who had personally invited him, in the White House Rose Garden. The ceremony formally made the United States government an official patron of the arts for the first time in history.

The president sent the Pecks a photograph of the guests, on which he personally wrote, 'To Véronique and Gregory Peck – who added such beauty and talent to this dinner at the White House – with warm appreciation – Lady Bird Johnson, Lyndon B. Johnson.'

Thereafter, Peck became a charter member of the National Arts Council with the responsibility of helping to strengthen regional theatre throughout the country. To do this he visited theatres in twenty-six cities, accompanied by Véronique. President Johnson was so impressed with his dedication to public service that they became lifelong friends, and when a documentary was made called *A President's Country,* Johnson asked Peck to narrate it.

Peck was also involved in setting up the American Film Institute, which obtained a grant from the Arts Council. The AFI set up an archive, helped to obtain grants for non-commercial films and gave young would-be directors their first chance to make films.

In 1965 Peck agreed to co-produce *The Martian Chronicles,* based on the Ray Bradbury book, with Alan J. Pakula and Robert Mulligan. For several months they tried to come up with a workable script, but in the end the project was shelved.

Stanley Donen wanted Peck to star in a film originally called *Crisscross.* He was to play an Oxford professor who is asked by Middle Eastern oil magnates to decipher a hieroglyphic, only to find himself and the lovely Sophia Loren on the run from assassins. Before Peck formally accepted the film, he wrote a long Selznickesque letter to Donen outlining his thoughts and suggestions for improving the script and, in particular, his character. 'I would like to see all of his dialogue gone through and that he be given a consistently urbane style of speech,' he wrote.

Donen arranged the rewrite, and after Peck went through it, he cabled Donen formally to accept the film, saying, 'Delighted with new personality and overall dialogue on my character.'

At some point the film became *Cipher,* a title Peck disliked as much as he did the original. His suggestion of *Arabesque* was accepted by Stanley Donen; it was a trendy one-word title, both meaningless and intriguing, much like Donen's *Charade.*

Relations between Peck and Loren were mixed. As they

prepared to do a scene in which he had to hide fully clothed in a shower with naked Sophia, he gallantly told her, 'Don't be embarrassed. It's all strictly professional.'

To which she replied, 'Who's embarrassed?' and slipped off her robe. 'What makes you think I would be embarrassed?' she giggled.

But things were not so cordial when they filmed a chase scene in which he had to drag her along behind him as they are pursued by killers. His old ankle injury prevented him running too fast for too long, and she kept overtaking him. After several useless takes, Peck, out of puff and patience, told her, 'Will you *please* slow down? *I'm* supposed to be rescuing you.'

'You'll have to run faster if you want to rescue me,' she replied.

They did the scene again, and as she began to overtake him he pulled her back. She told Donen, 'Make him run faster.'

'I can't run faster,' said Peck.

'Well, try!'

Donen had to order her firmly to run slower. She was not happy. But the scene was completed.

Towards the end of 1965 he was asked if he would stand again as California Chairman for the American Cancer Society during the next year. This time he accepted without reservation, mainly because his stepmother, Harriet, had developed cancer and he now wanted to spend less time making films and more time doing charity work. In his inaugural speech he spoke about Humphrey Bogart. 'He died gallantly but we would rather have him around living and performing. Bogart, Cooper, Charles Laughton, Thomas Mitchell and recently the great Buster Keaton were all victims of cancer.' He said that he and the society could best help 'by raising funds for cancer research, to be helping to educate the public of the importance of early detection, to keep our friends around a little longer. At least some of my friends – and yours – might have been saved.'

To help raise awareness on behalf of the cancer society, Peck took a little girl, Julie Alice Dillard, herself a cancer victim who appeared on the society's posters, to meet President Johnson at the White House. He told friends that his work for the society was 'the most rewarding work I've ever done'.

Peck met with cancer specialists, went into cancer wards to

speak to patients, and even went into the operating theatre to watch tumours being removed. He addressed countless organizations, especially women's groups, and narrated a 30-minute film called *Investment in Life*. During his term as president the society raised $50 million.

In 1966 he found time to serve as chairman of the Motion Picture and Television Relief Fund Building and Endowment Campaign, promoting the care and housing of the film industry's older citizens. His fiftieth birthday was devoted to cancer research as he flew to Atlanta, Georgia, to have breakfast with 1,200 people, then to New Orleans for lunch with some six hundred, and on to Houston, Texas, for dinner with a thousand.

When he heard that the Philippines government wanted to start their own cancer research society, he and Véronique flew there to speak at a function for Filipino high society. He urged them to establish their own Cancer Society and build a clinic to provide free examinations. But those who attended proved to be more interested in socializing than donating or helping to raise money, and nothing was ever accomplished.

Back in the United States, Greg visited his stepmother, who was now hospitalized. One day he and his half-brother David arrived to be told they should go in one at a time. Greg went in first and as he held Harriet's hand, she told him, 'You've got to get them to make me die. I'm so sick and in such agony.'

'I'll try,' he told her.

A young doctor came in and began connecting her to various tubes. 'What are you doing?' Peck asked him.

'This will help her to feel better,' replied the doctor.

Feeling that Harriet's agony was simply being fruitlessly extended, Greg went to see her doctor and told him, 'She doesn't want to live. She can't go through any more.'

Within a few hours the doctor called Harriet's family, including Peck, to tell them that she had died.

In 1966 Peck appeared on television with Burt Lancaster and Gene Kelly to promote the Democratic Party. They said that they would each be happy to play a governor in a film, but that didn't mean they thought any of them would be any good as a real governor. The Republican candidate for governor of California was Ronald Reagan.

It was put to Peck that he should seriously consider going into politics and that he might even consider aiming for the White House. It was a time when many of Hollywood's more distinguished citizens were being wooed by the political parties. Peck stated, 'I am far from indifferent to the idea of public service. Like many men of my age who have enjoyed some success, I am interested in being of service in as many ways as I can in helping solve public problems.' But he was not, he maintained, interested in becoming either governor, senator or president.

Arabesque opened in May 1966 at the Radio City Music Hall to good reviews. *The New York Times* declared 'about 10 minutes after *Arabesque* gets underway, you'll lose track of its plot completely, and that's as it should be. Sophia Loren is not called upon to act but to Dior! A Yank exchange professor is played with Good Guy affability by Gregory Peck. A climax scene should make the chase buffs swoon.'

Wanda Hale gave the film four stars in the *New York Daily News*, saying the film was 'the spoofingest spoof yet on espionage adventure, with a handsome pair you'd least expect to take part in the wild, wonderful nonsense. The dignified Peck and the elegant Loren let themselves go on a mad, mirthful spree.' Richard Schickel wrote in *Life*, 'This is only commercial film-making at its mindless, marvellous best.'

Peck found time to travel to London to promote the film, and there was amused to find a small company, Gregory & Co, which prompted him to stand outside with Cecilia, then eight, and pose for the camera.

In 1967 Peck entered a horse he had purchased called Different Class in the Grand National. It came in third, a good result thanks to the work of trainer Peter Cazalet who was the Queen Mother's own horse trainer.

In June 1967 Peck, who had been serving on the Board of Governors of the Academy of Motion Picture Arts and Sciences, was voted in as president of the Academy. It is an office of considerable prestige in Hollywood, indicating the high regard in which colleagues in the film industry held him. In his acceptance speech, he said, 'I don't believe in amateur politics. I respect my own profession and that of politics. I can only repeat what I've said on previous occasions when political figures or columnists had thrown my name in the ring – that I'll never run for public office. No one could persuade me to change my mind. I hope to make more films, good ones. That is my profession.'

He began to transform the American Academy, enhancing its educational programme by giving grants to the AFI and providing 'internships' for trainee film makers to work with established directors. He also worked to end the reputation the Academy had as a tool of the studios by discouraging the extensive advertising that attempted to buy votes for Oscar nominees. 'We are not the studios,' he said. 'The Academy is not synonymous with the industry. The studios may cash in on our awards, but that is not why we are here.'

He worked hard persuading the new breed of young stars, including Dustin Hoffman and Barbra Streisand, to present awards at the upcoming Oscars. Four days before the ceremony, Dr Martin Luther King was murdered. The funeral was set for 8 April 1968. Louis Armstrong, Sidney Poitier, Sammy Davis Jr., Diahann Carroll and Rod Steiger, all of whom were to appear on the show, said they would not take part unless the ceremony was cancelled until after the funeral. Up to that time, nothing had ever stopped the Oscars. But Gregory Peck agreed that it should be postponed by two days. He said:

What Dr. King would like to have happened is for the whites of this country to grasp the concept that we need the talents, energies and pent-up imaginations of our minority group artists – perhaps even more than they need us. Call it self-enlightened interest, but I feel this country will never be whole until we have achieved total and full equality of opportunity for everyone. Films should celebrate the dignity of man, regardless of race, creed or color.

When the ceremony was held, Peck opened the show by pointing out that two of the Best Picture nominees – *In the Heat of the Night* and *Guess Who's Coming to Dinner* – were about racial tensions. He said, 'We must unite in compassion if we are to survive.'

That evening he received the Jean Hersholt Humanitarian Award. That same year he was given the Screen Actors' Award 'for his outstanding achievement in fostering the finest ideals in the acting profession'.

As busy as he was, he also found time to work with Véronique on the Inner City Cultural Center, which worked to establish the performing arts in black communities. He donated $100,000 and Véronique organized a benefit, which earned $55,000 for the cause.

His son Stephen, then twenty-one, was commissioned as a lieutenant in the Marine Corps in 1967 and went to Vietnam, where he served with distinction. It was a war Peck did not believe in, but he said, 'Despite my opposition to the war I was very proud of what he did in Vietnam.'

In 1968 Peck was back at Aintree to watch Different Class in the Grand National. Peter Cazalet stood with him, peering through the fog; the National was the one big race that had so far eluded the trainer. Different Class was running in second place when he went down in a terrible fall that involved fourteen horses. He did, however, survive to race another day, and even came first in lesser races. A few years later Different Class became sick with heart trouble and died. Shortly after that Peter Cazalet died. Peck felt that without Cazalet, who had become a good friend as well as a much valued trainer, he could not pursue his dream to win the National.

Five years earlier he had said he would probably retire in 1968. But now he was working hard, going from film to film; it was to prove one of the most disastrous periods of his career. He reluctantly joined Carl Foreman in an attempt to bring together an all-star cast and repeat the success of *The Guns of Navarone*, with a $14.5 million Cinerama western epic, *Mackenna's Gold*; since *How the West Was Won* Cinerama had developed a simpler yet still effective single-lens system. The movie told of a search for lost gold by greedy men, including outlaws and so-called gentlemen from Hadleyburg, and led reluctantly by Peck as Marshal Mackenna, the only man with any idea where to find it.

Foreman had written the film as a commentary on men and their motives, a commentary on the greed and selfishness of modern society. To him the gentlemen from Hadleyburg were related to the cowardly townspeople in *High Noon*, but in this case they were getting involved only for self-interest, not to help the marshal.

Steve McQueen had turned the role down, so Foreman, deciding that there was plenty of mileage in trying to reunite as many of the principals from *The Guns of Navarone* as possible, went to Peck.

181

Initially he wasn't interested. He eventually accepted it because, he said, he was grateful for *The Guns of Navarone*, but he insisted on script changes. Peck said, 'I guess it's more like *Duel in the Sun* than any other western I've done. It's almost a western fantasy – a quest for a storied mother lode.'

From *Navarone*, Foreman assigned J. Lee Thompson to direct, but bringing together the original cast proved impossible. Only Anthony Quayle was willing and available. Anthony Quinn turned down the role of the Mexican bandit, which went instead to Omar Sharif. He proved to be totally miscast. The roles of most of the cast were hardly more than cameos, including those of Edward G. Robinson, Raymond Massey, Eli Wallach and Telly Savalas.

'I'm always put off by the so-called all-star cast,' Peck has said 'I can smell a rat. They aim to buy their way into public favour by overpaying stars and featuring important players in small roles.' Nevertheless, it was a cast he much admired, especially Eddie Robinson, who, said Peck, was 'a darling – funny, warm, actorish, a bit theatrical – relatively guileless, a bit like a grown-up child.'

Robinson visited the Pecks and saw a painting by Picasso of a satyr climbing through a window, while a sleeping beauty lay naked in the foreground. 'That's Picasso, all right,' said Robinson. 'He's got the balls!'

As they got into a deep discussion on art, Robinson told the Pecks about a visit he made to the home of Matisse near Nice. There he saw a drawing of a vase of flowers constructed out of no more than a dozen lines. 'You know, Greg,' he said, 'it's the same with acting. You throw everything away that isn't essential and just give them what is.'

Peck was visited on the set by another political friend, Robert Kennedy, who was in Arizona campaigning. A month later, Kennedy was killed.

By the time *Mackenna's Gold* was finished, Foreman said that he could see that something had gone awry. He might even have agreed with Vincent Canby of *The New York Times*, who thought it to be 'a Western of truly stunning absurdity, a thriving example of that old Hollywood maxim about how to succeed by failing big'.

Part of the problem was that Foreman decided not to show it in Cinerama after all and Thompson, who had filmed it especially for that format, with giddy point-of-view shots, told me that the film lost much of its impact. But the biggest problem was with the production values: there were too many close-ups of actors stand-

ing against back projection, too many lousy special effects, especially in the climactic earthquake scene. The film also needed a
director with a vision for the fantasy element of the film, rather
than the more conventional approach Thompson adopted.

In June 1968 Peck took Cecilia and Anthony to an early morning
memorial mass for Bobby Kennedy. Not long after, he took part in
a concert in aid of the Mental Retardation Fund set up by Bobby
Kennedy.

By now, Peck was getting careless in his choice of films. He did
another western called *The Stalking Moon* in 1968; it was a time
when the western genre was worn out. But Peck was attracted by
the prospect of working once again with Robert Mulligan and Alan
J. Pakula, and this tale of an ageing scout escorting a white woman
who's escaped from captivity with the Indians appealed to him so
much he decided to make it for his own production company.

Mulligan and Pakula said they saw the film as a symbolic repre-
sentation of 'the struggle between the white settlers and the
Apaches, for the land of the American Southwest'.

Pauline Kael, writing in the *New Yorker*, attacked the film for
being racist. 'For many years, big budget Westerns have generally
tried to be respectful and sympathetic towards Indians, and now
The Stalking Moon goes back to the most primitive movie image of
the vicious savage. It is an example of dehumanizing the enemy as
a way of justifying our own humanity. The role of the decent super-
man requires an actor like Gregory Peck – an actor of proved
authority – and Peck is very good in it. Movies can open us up to
complexities and I don't think we should applaud this kind of
infantile, primitive regression.'

But Vincent Canby wrote in *The New York Times* that it was 'clas-
sically pure and simple in outline. A beautiful movie – and one that
may be too tasteful for its own good'.

During the film's production in Nevada, Greg and his family
stayed in Johnny Carson's desert house outside Las Vegas. Over the
first three or four nights, Greg and Véronique saw every show on
the Vegas Strip. They also played the tables and tried not to stay up
too late.

Peck was going to star in *Ice Station Zebra* for John Sturges at
Columbia, but MGM finally took over production and gave the

part to Rock Hudson. In autumn 1968, Peck did *The Chairman* for J. Lee Thompson, playing a top scientist who has a detonator implanted in his skull and is sent by Western intelligence into Communist China. Since very few pictures up to that time had dealt with life behind the Bamboo Curtain, Peck immersed himself in research and with producer Mort Abrahams and director Thompson viewed hours of newsreel footage depicting contemporary Chinese culture under the Communist regime.

They began filming in Hong Kong, the nearest they could get to Communist China, but delays in shooting led to disruptions, and the authorities asked the film company to leave the country with little but the opening scenes shot. Interiors were shot at Pinewood Studios in England and the remaining exteriors on the hillsides of Scotland, doubling for China. Somehow the film's excitement got lost somewhere between Hong Kong and Scotland, as Howard Thompson in *The New York Times* noted, when he said 'It begins so brilliantly it makes provocative entertainment for the first half, hits a snag, begins to fall apart and comes in for a tame, wobbly ending.'

Kevin Thomas of the *Los Angeles Times* said it was 'the kind of Hollywood hokum that can yield lots of fun and excitement if you're willing to go along with it. And because of the convincing charm of its star Gregory Peck it's not hard to do, for no one is more skilled or experienced on making getting out of tight spots believable.'

One day a cousin of Greg's from Ireland he had not met before arrived on the set at Pinewood. They sat up until three in the morning in his dressing room knocking back a bottle of Scotch between them while Peck waited to be called for a night shot of him crawling up tiled roofs and jumping over a 30-foot drop. Thompson needed Peck in close-up and was willing to shoot a double doing the actual jump in long. But Peck, slightly Scotched, insisted, 'No, I'll do it myself.'

'We can use a stunt man,' Thompson argued.

'I'll do it myself,' Peck persisted, and did the jump. Thompson, relieved his star survived the jump, decided not to go for any retakes.

Peck went straight into *Marooned*, which attempted to follow the trend in outer-space films kicked off by *2001: A Space Odyssey*. It attempted to give the public science fiction that had its roots in fact – or at least distinct possibilities. Three astronauts, played by James Franciscus, Richard Crenna and Gene Hackman, find themselves unable to return to earth. *Marooned* ended up becoming more factual than even producer M.J. Frankovich and director John Sturges had envisaged when, after production was complete, Apollo 13 was launched and very nearly failed to come back.

The film retained an air of authenticity up to the moment David Janssen comes to the rescue in another spacecraft, at which point the film lost all credibility. In 1968, no one believed such a rescue was possible. Of course, the events surrounding the accident prone Mir Space Station and the arrival of the space shuttle to retrieve the British astronaut, Michael Foale, in 1997, today gives the viewer a somewhat different perspective.

Peck played the NASA chief who directs the rescue from Earth. He was offered the part by Sturges and Columbia as compensation for losing *Ice Station Zebra*. Peck was required simply to play his typical dependable, honest and dignified self and the part offered little to excite him. He said, 'Technical people, engineers and those who are in total control don't make interesting parts. You can't show the inner emotion that the man feels because he has to be supremely efficient. The actors who played the astronauts had the interesting roles.'

'If you are enthralled by all the maneuvers of space shots, *Marooned* is for you,' wrote Frances Herridge in the *New York Post*. 'Moviegoers who like action will have to be patient in the first half, where the script stays with strict realism. But the second half drains every bit of drama out of the situation, with contrivances, unfortunately, that get more and more corny. Even when the script rings false, the actors don't. Peck is coolly himself as the unemotional Chief.'

Howard Thompson of *The New York Times* called it 'a handsome, professional and future-minded drama, admirably intelligent all the way, with a good cast headed by Gregory Peck.'

On 21 December 1968, the entire company stopped work on the film to watch the launch of Apollo 8, which went on to make the first manned voyage around the moon. 'We were very interested in the launch, of course,' said John Sturges, 'because it gave us the chance to study the whole mission while we were in production and learn from it to our benefit.'

*

In December 1968, Greg and Véronique were guests at a party at the Plaza Hotel in New York to say goodbye to the outgoing president. While dancing with Véronique, Johnson told her, 'We both have something in common.'

'I'm honoured, Mr President, to know that I have something in common with you,' said Véronique. 'What is it?'

'We both love Gregory.' Then he revealed, 'If I had decided to run for another term, I was going to offer him the post of ambassador to Ireland.' He then surprised her by telling her that he was going to give Greg the Medal of Freedom, the highest award a civilian can earn in America.

It became one of the president's last duties to present Peck with the medal at a special ceremony on 20 January 1969, where he read out the following citation:

> To Gregory Peck – an actor who has brought new dignity to the acting profession. Gregory Peck has enriched the lives of millions. He has given his energies, his talents and his devotion to causes which have improved the lives of people. He is a humanitarian to whom Americans are deeply indebted.

The Stalking Moon opened on 20 January 1969 at Loew's Tower East in New York, and failed to do well. Peck's film career may have been suffering, but he could not have worried too much at the time, having been awarded his country's highest civilian honour.

17

The Full-time Producer

IN 1969 PECK BEGAN revitalizing the Oscars show, making some drastic changes that departed from tradition. He dispensed with the services of the regular M.C., Bob Hope, in favour of a dozen hosts, including Ingrid Bergman, Frank Sinatra, Jane Fonda and Sidney Poitier. He also changed the venue from the Santa Monica auditorium to the Dorothy Chandler Pavilion at the Los Angeles Music Center. He brought in Broadway choreographer Gower Champion to produce some dazzling musical and dance routines. He tried to discourage the usual lobbying by studios to acquire votes, and issued a statement which went out with the mailshot to voters – and which has gone out ever since. This read:

This year, as in the past, you will be importuned by advertisements, promotional gifts and other lobbying tactics, in an attempt to solicit your vote. Each year, these crude and excessive solicitations embarrass the Academy, embarrass you and demean the significance of the Academy Award of Merit for outstanding achievement. All attempts by the Academy to discourage such promotions and advertisements have been in vain.

We call upon each Academy member to disregard these attempts to influence your vote and we urge you to register your displeasure with those who, in an unrestrained and ambitious manner, attempt to do so. Excellence in film making is the ONLY valid criterion for casting a vote for an Academy Award, and it is for your judgement of that excellence that the Academy has asked you to vote. No extraneous factors should be allowed to color your consideration of excellence. The Academy, the film industry and the world must trust your judgement.

One of the Best Actor nominees was *Charly* star Cliff Robertson, who was in the Philippines at the time of the ceremony, making *Too Late the Hero* for director Robert Aldrich. Peck begged Aldrich to allow Robertson back to Los Angeles for the Oscars, but Aldrich refused. In the event, Robertson won.

Michael Caine recalled how Robertson, knowing photographers would be waiting for him when he flew back to America, had a Filipino carve him an accurate replica of the Oscar to hold up. 'We got off the plane,' said Caine, 'and suddenly, through the crowd of photographers we saw Gregory Peck heading towards Cliff with the real Oscar. Cliff surreptitiously slipped me the wooden fake and Peck presented him with the real one.'

In 1969 Jack Benny asked Peck to appear in a television special, *Jack Benny's New Look*, to join him and George Burns in a re-enactment of an old vaudeville act called Goldie, Fields and Glide. Peck had no hesitation in accepting, and spent hours learning to do a soft-shoe shuffle with the two great comedians. He learned to sing 'The Shadow of Your Smile' so well that Jack Benny told him, 'Stop working at it. The worse you are, the funnier you'll be. Just sing funny!'

Peck loved the whole experience, and after the recording, he thanked Jack Benny and said, 'Any time you need a song and dance man just think of me.' They became great friends and often had dinner together. When Benny turned eighty, Greg and Véronique sent him a telegram which read: 'DEAR JACK. BIG DEAL.'

Mackenna's Gold opened in Philadelphia in March 1969 and later in New York in June, presented in 70 mm and stunning stereophonic sound. But it was hammered by the critics and largely avoided by the public. A week later *The Chairman* opened to poor business. When it opened in the United Kingdom, it was entitled *The Most Dangerous Man in the World*.

Marooned was given a big lift-off on 10 November 1969 at the Warner Theater in Washington. Among the guests were NASA officials who awarded the film with a commendation for its accuracy in portraying the US space programme. But the film failed to win big audiences in America. By the time it was released in Britain, the Apollo 13 crisis was in full swing, and the film ironically benefited and did good business. But overall, 1969 had not been a good year for Peck.

I have done several pictures that I probably shouldn't have done.
Things like *Mackenna's Gold*, like *Marooned*. They weren't very good.
The public didn't go to see them and the notices weren't all that
great. So I'll call them bad pictures. I knew they weren't worth much
when I read the scripts. But as soon as I started work on them,
damned if I didn't start believing in them. It just goes to prove you
can't be an actor and Pauline Kael at the same time.

What Peck did want to do, though, was make a film about the
American Civil War in which he could play Lincoln. He said, 'We
are what we are today because of the Civil War. It is in our blood,
whether we know it or not. It should be an epic film, the American
War and Peace, complete with full-scale battles. That would be a film
to remember – and be remembered by.' Playing the legendary
president became an ambition of his after he read all the available
material on the man.

In search of a commercial hit, he did *I Walk the Line* in 1969, a
contemporary tale of a Tennessee sheriff who forsakes his wife and
his job for the love of the daughter of a criminal. The screenplay,
by Alvin Sargent, was based on a book by Madison Jones, *An Exile*,
director John Frankenheimer gave his film the working title,
September Country.

Frankenheimer actually wanted Gene Hackman to play the
sheriff, but Columbia wanted a major star as insurance (Hackman
had not at that point achieved stardom in *The French Connection*)
and they insisted on Gregory Peck. Tuesday Weld was cast as the
girl he falls for.

Frankenheimer said

> For me, the film's story was that of a sensitive man who finds himself
> in the wrong environment and what can happen to him. It's how
> society can destroy an individual. It was brave of Gregory Peck to
> play the part because he was playing an older man who falls in love
> with a young girl for all the wrong reasons, and then decides to
> throw his whole life away to take her away with him. It's a very
> personal, small film about freedom of choice – even if the choice is
> not always a good one.

Peck liked the film while in production and thought the first
edit had merit. But he was dismayed when it was re-cut. 'The

189

picture I made was a much better picture than the one that showed up on the screen,' he said. 'It suffered, I feel, from some rather insensitive cutting and also the addition of the songs by Johnny Cash.' His argument about the Cash songs was that they gave the film too much of a 'country' feel, which would alienate urban audiences and those who just didn't like country-and-western music.

A scene was omitted in which the sheriff went swimming through the flooded rooms of his childhood home. Peck had clashed with Frankenheimer over this when the director tried to persuade Peck to do the scene nude. 'I make my living with my brains, not my behind,' Peck told him. 'I'll wear a diving suit.' The scene was shot, with Peck in a diving suit, but Frankenheimer felt that the effect was lost. 'What would be more natural,' he reasoned, 'than for the sheriff to just take off his clothes and dive in? It was also a way of showing the man's mental process. Instead he brings along his diving suit!' Peck felt that the omission of the scene 'reduced my character to a clichéd middle-age man with a lust for a young girl'.

For the 1970 Oscars show, his last as President of the American Academy, Peck tried to inject younger blood. 'But it's impossible to reach them,' he said. 'People like Dennis Hopper and Peter Fonda belong to the Academy, but they won't get involved.'

When Maggie Smith was the surprise win for Best Actress, in *The Prime of Miss Jean Brodie*, Peck said, 'This is great. Now you can see it's not rigged.'

I Walk the Line opened on 18 November 1970 to mixed reviews. Archer Winstein of the *New York Post* called it 'a tragedy of such simple components that the power and beauty of the performances come through unimpeded by any complexity or oddity. This situation enables John Frankenheimer to utilize fully his very considerable artistry. Gregory Peck gives a performance of unexpected depth.'

But according to Howard Thompson of *The New York Times*, the film was 'a minor drama that ends up chasing its own tail and falling to pieces quite literally in the middle of the road. It was admirable of Peck to try such a role in a hillbilly context after his usual expensive showcases. He performs with laconic restraint but he emerges a dull knucklehead who rates little sympathy.'

Against his better judgement, Peck returned to the Wild West in

Shoot Out, possibly Peck's worst ever film. It was produced by Hal Wallis and directed by Henry Hathaway – the team behind *True Grit* – in autumn of 1970 and featured Peck as Clay Lomax, a rough, ageing but somewhat endearing character – shades of John Wayne's Rooster Cogburn – just released from jail, and set on tracking and killing the former friend who betrayed him. En route he finds himself saddled with a six-year-old girl, and the comparisons with *True Grit* – the old cowboy and the girl on the trail of desperadoes – simply showed up the film's lack of originality with stark clarity.

Peck said, 'It was a trivial Western. I should never have made it. It was a mistake.' Charles Champlin of the *Los Angeles Times* agreed: 'Peck strides through this low-budget Universal Western like a giant through corn stubble, acting out the charade with craft and intensity and that riveting command of the screen which defines a star.'

Roger Greenspin wrote in *The New York Times*, 'It seems a lot to expect a seven-year-old girl to hold together a whole feature film full of inept adults, but that is what somebody must have expected of Dawn Lyn.'

Adding to his public service works was a position on the board of the Motion Picture Television Relief Fund, which ran the Country House and Hospital in Woodlands Hill, where veterans of the industry could retire and enjoy good health care. The Fund needed an immediate injection of half a million dollars. Peck personally produced the 50th Anniversary Gala of the Fund at the Los Angeles Music Center in June 1971. All the invited celebrities readily agreed to take part. Princess Grace flew in from Monte Carlo and was introduced on stage by Cary Grant. Frank Sinatra had announced the benefit would be his last performance before retirement, which resulted in the show being a sell-out.

Also taking part were James Stewart, David Niven, David Frost, Natalie Wood, Jack Benny, Jack Lemmon, Mitzi Gaynor, Rosalind Russell and Pearl Bailey. Two performances were put on in one night, with artists moving straight from the Dorothy Chandler Pavilion over to the Ahmanson Theater. The amount raised that night was $850,000.

Peck also served as a director of Los Angeles Public Broadcasting System affiliate station KCET-TV, of the Center

Theater Group of Los Angeles, of the Salk Institute for medical research and of Capitol Industries, Inc. His public service record was beginning to seem more impressive than his current movie record. *Shoot Out* opened in several New York cinemas at once on 13 October 1971, and died at the box office. That indignity was almost the last straw for Peck, who admitted he had picked some bad films, saying, 'But they were the best that were offered. I didn't do them only for the money. It just took a while for me to rid myself of the habit of getting up early in the morning and going to the studio.'

Apart from playing Lincoln, he had one other ambition, to play General Douglas MacArthur. He tried to persuade Universal to do it, but after all those years as a bankable star, Peck was suddenly a leading man in a succession of flops, and they rejected the idea as too risky.

He decided to forget about acting and go in search of his Irish roots in the Emerald Isle. There he visited the Ashe family farm in County Kerry. The Doc's cousin, Thomas Ashe, was still alive but very old. His son-in-law Tom Curran announced, 'It's Gregory Peck come to see you.'

The old man, looking at Greg, growled, 'The hell you say!'

'It's Gregory Peck, the *film star*,' explained Tom.

It took some time for Thomas Ashe to understand that this was his cousin's son, but he then drifted off into the past and believed he was talking to Doc Peck himself.

In 1973, Peck met President Nixon for the first time at a cocktail party being thrown by John Wayne at the American Film Institute. Nixon told Peck, 'You were so good in *Friendly Persuasion*. It's my favourite picture, which we show regularly at the White House.'

Peck simply replied, 'Thank you very much for coming, Mr President.'

In 1973 he made his first film for two years, another western, *Billy Two Hats*. He played a failed Scottish outlaw who has a penchant for quoting from the Bible and who dreams of returning to his native Scotland. He teams up with a mixed-race Indian, played by Desi Arnez, Jr., and the ensuing screen story concentrated more on character study and racial bigotry than it did on action.

There were rumours of a romance between Peck and Audrey Hepburn when they made *Roman Holiday* (1953). Hepburn admitted she had a crush on him, but she went on to marry Mel Ferrer, and Greg married Veronique

In his Captain Ahab make-up which made him almost unrecognizable, Peck engages in intense discussion with director John Huston during the filming of *Moby Dick* (1956)

In between takes on the Shepperton Studios set of *The Guns of Navarone* (1961) director J. Lee Thompson (*left*) prepares Peck for a moment leading up to the blowing up of the big guns

A dramatic moment from *The Guns of Navarone* (1961), although Peck joked that the real plot of the film was 'David Niven really loves Tony Quayle (*right*) and Gregory Peck loves Anthony Quinn (*left*). Tony Quayle breaks a leg and is sent off to hospital. Tony Quinn falls in love with Irene Papas, and David Niven and Peck catch each other on the rebound and live happily ever after'

During a break in filming *The Guns of Navarone*, Greg and Veronique go to the races with their close friends, the Nivens

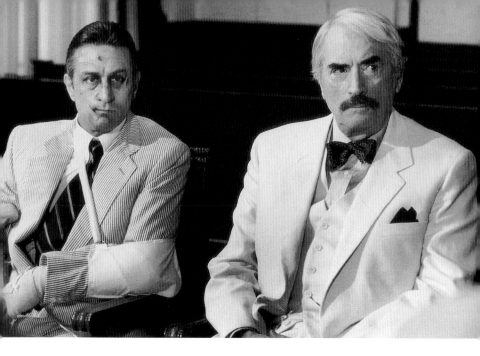

In Martin Scorsese's 1991 remake of Peck's own 1962 production *Cape Fear,* Greg appeared as attorney for Robert De Niro who recreated the role of the killer originally played by Robert Mitchum almost thirty years earlier

Professional gambler Peck gets into a clinch with river boat singer Debbie Reynolds in the all-star Cinerama epic *How the West Was Won* (1962), a film he disliked intensely, making him vow never to appear in another all-star picture

As the small-town lawyer defending a black man (played by Brock Peters) charged with rape in *To Kill a Mockingbird* (1962), Peck received the Best Actor Oscar after four previous nominations had failed to bring him the coveted gold statuette

An injury to his left ankle in 1948 prevented Peck from running far or fast, so when he had to run with Sophia Loren from the bad guys in *Arabesque* (1966) she kept overtaking him in take after take until the director ordered her to run slower

On the set of the western adventure *Mackenna's Gold* (1968) with producer Carl Foreman (*left*) and director J. Lee Thompson (*right*). It was a failed attempt to repeat the success of their previous joint effort *The Guns of Navarone*

Peck and Lee Remick had the devil of a time playing parents to their satanic screen son, Damien, in the blockbusting horror film *The Omen* (1976) which relaunched Peck's acting career after a three-year hiatus

Peck had long wanted to portray General Douglas MacArthur and finally got to do so in *MacArthur* (1977) which, despite Greg's own personal efforts to save it in the editing stage, was flawed by the cuts which served to shorten the film and make it less controversial

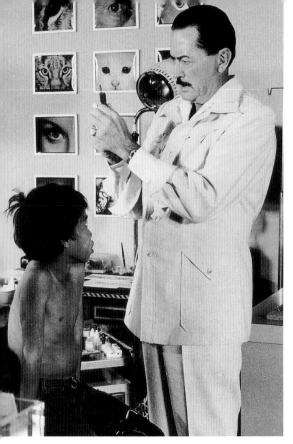

In a startling change of
screen image, Peck played
the evil, real-life Nazi Dr Josef
Mengele in the fictitious *The
Boys from Brazil* (1979),
creating clones to resurrect
the Third Reich

Jane Fonda starred in and
produced *Old Gringo* (1989),
with handsome Jimmy Smits
(*right*) as a dashing Mexican
Revolutionary, and Peck as
real-life elderly American
writer Ambrose Bierce – the
old gringo of the title – who
disappeared without a trace
in northern Mexico

Peck worked with a Scots dialect expert and grew a full beard before flying out to Israel where the film was shot just outside the city of Ashkelon, in 1973.

'It was a little picture that didn't amount to much,' said Peck. 'The story was weak, the plot was diffuse, but there were moments – scenes that were fluid, that were well done and lifelike and genuine. It has some lovely scenery, but basically the screenplay was flawed and not completely thought out or well constructed. But I liked the character and I liked doing it. We thought it was an interesting little Western anecdote to tell, but we must have been wrong. But you write those things off when that happens, and you think, "Well, we did our best." '

When it opened in England in April 1974, it was well received by the *Observer*'s Russell Davies who wrote, '*Billy Two Hats* is quite a nice little Western. Considering what an extraordinary melange of experiences and rawness, bogusness and authenticity the picture is, it comes off surprisingly well.'

In America the film was panned by Judith Crist in *New York* magazine as 'an international mishmash of a Western that is as gloomy and pretentious as it is perfectly awful'.

In 1974, the U.S.A. Film Festival held its first 'Great American Actor Retrospective,' which was conceived to honour actors and actresses 'whose large, varied and distinguished bodies of work have exhibited the genius of American film'. The first recipient was to be Gregory Peck, who attended the festival in Dallas. He was allowed to choose six of his own films himself; they were *Yellow Sky*, *Twelve O'Clock High*, *Roman Holiday*, *The Gunfighter*, *Captain Horatio Hornblower* and *To Kill a Mockingbird*. Introducing them to a large and enthusiastic audience, he explained he had chosen what he felt represented a cross-section of his work, and added, 'I think I've inadvertently selected a sort of cross-section of the work of some of the great American directors.'

During the festival Peck told the audience, 'I was in an Italian studio in Rome and walking by the dubbing room when I heard the sound of my own voice, so I opened the door and peeked in. There was an Italian actor standing in front of a screen doing me in Italian. They'd played it in English first, then cut out my voice and he'd match lips with the Italian dialogue.'

He said that the Italian actor was delighted to meet him and kept asking him, 'Are you in good health? Do you stay in good shape? You exercise?'

'What is all this interest in my health?' asked Peck.

'Well,' said the Italian actor, 'I've dubbed your voice in twenty-four movies and I've raised five children doing your voice and I hope I'm going to go on doing it for a long time.'

Peck laughed and promised the Italian actor that he would do his best to stay in good health. 'In fact,' Peck told him, 'I am inspired to take better care of myself than ever before, knowing that another family depends so much on me!'

Peck may have been in good health but his oldest son, Jonathan, had an enlarged heart, high blood pressure and arteriosclerosis. He had been to Africa with the Peace Corps and had been a news writer for CBS. His father noticed how red his eyes often seemed to be and that, despite his former athletic prowess, he tired quickly when they played tennis together. On top of all this, Jonathan was deeply depressed. Being the eldest son of Gregory Peck had not been easy for him, especially because he looked so much like him.

What Greg didn't know, though, was that Jonathan had fallen in love with a young divorcee with two children and wanted her to move into his Santa Barbara house. But she had only just come through the trauma of her divorce and had no desire to be tied down in a relationship so soon.

Jonathan fell in love with another girl, a student at Berkeley. She committed suicide and her death deeply affected Jonathan. Greg took him on a fishing trip to the Sierras which, thought Greg, had helped lift his son's spirits. But Jonathan was embroiled in some inner torment that he could never explain to his father.

When Jonathan landed a job as a correspondent at a Santa Maria television station, delivering three filmed news stories a day, he sank into a further depression. Often news was slow in the small town a hundred miles north of Santa Barbara, and it became a chore just to try to find something to report. Greg told him, 'Just tell them there isn't any news.'

'I can't do that,' replied Jonathan. 'I *have* to deliver three stories a day.'

When there was news, he had to operate the camera, do the interviewing, provide a commentary and edit it. He often had to stay up all night, even on the slow days. The station's small budget couldn't stretch to providing him with an assistant. He also worried that he would be accused of wasting film on worthless stories, so Greg sent him a dozen cans of film which the station didn't have to pay for.

Greg told him if he quit his job, he would help his son financially. But Jonathan didn't want to be a quitter. His father, however, was quitting acting. He said in 1974:

> I get offered quite a few scripts, but to be quite honest about it, I haven't had an outstanding script offered to me for a couple of years. And to go on doing a succession of *Billy Two Hats* would be embarrassing. I don't like it when pictures go out and get lost and no one goes to see them, because you put just as much effort into them as the films everyone goes to see. You spend all those days and nights shooting it, you get up early and learn your lines and study your character. And you work just as hard or harder on a bad script as you do on a good one. And at this point in my life, it's embarrassing to have a picture go out and get lost like that. So I'm just not going to do any more of those. I'll retire first. I'll go to the south of France or take up charity work rather than do a series of mediocre pictures.

With Véronique and the children, he stayed in Cap Ferrat for the next five months. He read, cycled, swam and socialized with old friends like the Nivens and the Rainiers. He'd earned himself a fortune and knew he never needed to work again. But boredom set in and he began thinking about producing films. Véronique agreed that being a full-time producer would be a good move for him.

He set about producing a comedy Western called *Billy Boy*, which would star Walter Matthau and be directed by Milos Forman. He raised the money from various backers, but when Matthau's agent demanded a bigger fee for his client, the backers got cold feet, pulled out, and the project was cancelled.

Peck had better luck with *The Dove*. He had read in *National Geographic* magazine the story of a sixteen-year-old boy who sailed around the world single-handed in a 23-foot sloop. He decided to turn it into a film.

Before leaving California to produce *The Dove*, Greg gave Jonathan money for sessions with an analyst. Then he flew to

London to work at EMI-Elstree Studios. Charles Jarrott directed
The Dove in Fiji with unknown James Bottoms as the lone yachts-
man, and Deborah Raffin as the girlfriend who waits for him at
each port of call. It was a film about endurance, courage, and
sexual innocence – something that was quite out of fashion in films
in 1974.

Peck had to remain at Elstree where he was busy setting up
other projects and keeping an eye on the budget, which started
out at £1.3 million. When it rose to £2.2 million, he persuaded
Paramount to put up the additional funds.

He remained in London, living in Chelsea, while the film was
edited and scored, and then released. It did disappointing business
on both sides of the Atlantic. But it did well in Japan, Australia and
New Zealand and succeeded in making a small profit.

It was while he was still in London in 1974 that he got caught up
in political controversy once more. He saw on the BBC news that
President Nixon had drawn up a so-called 'Enemies List' of 500
people who were blacklisted by the White House, many of whom
had spoken out against the Vietnam War. These included Jane
Fonda, Paul Newman – and Gregory Peck. He was outraged that
the president had personally endorsed the blacklisting and that
liberals in Hollywood were not to be tolerated. As a consequence,
three films he should have produced were cancelled by the
financier, a giant corporation which had contributed generously to
Nixon's election campaign. Eight months' work went down the
drain for Peck, and he was unable to recoup his lost money.

He returned to America and, as a result of Nixon's 'Enemies
List,' began setting up a film production of *The Trial of the
Catonsville Nine*, based on a successful play that had been staged in
New York and Los Angeles. It related the trial of Father Daniel
Berrigan and eight others who were charged for dodging the draft
during the Vietnam War. Peck personally put up $200,000 of his
own money, which constituted a third of the tiny budget. The rest
of the finance came from like-minded friends. 'In the old
Hollywood days,' said Peck, 'we would have spent that on a trailer.'

The original stage cast repeated their roles for the film, which
was shot in just eight days. He said, 'We were not only killing
50,000 American boys, but God knows how many Vietnamese
women and children and old people were killed too. We destroyed
the countryside, the whole country in the process of making it free;

that was our concept of freedom. It was a civil war in which we should never have been involved. Making the film was my way of trying to influence public opinion to get it all stopped.'

He took the finished film from studio to studio, trying to find someone to pay for its distribution. Robert Evans, then a production executive at Paramount, told Peck that the film needed to be made and should be seen. So did Frank Yablans, Paramount's president, but he was only prepared to spend a minimum amount to get several prints produced. The film was shown in New York, Boston, Washington and Los Angeles, but without serious money behind it, it didn't stand much of a chance. It quickly disappeared.

18

Satanic Salvation

FOR SOME TIME, JACK BENNY had been trying to persuade Véronique to appear with him in a television sketch, but she always turned him down. Towards the end of 1974 she finally gave in when he suggested a sketch, packed full of typical Benny one-liners, in which she and Greg would invite him to dinner. Not many weeks before the show was scheduled, Benny was struck down by cancer. Insisting he would still do the show in December, he arranged for a photocall with the Pecks, but at the last moment he was too ill to attend, so they posed with a blown-up photograph of him. The show never happened. A few days later, on 26 December, he died; Peck was a pallbearer at his funeral.

Benny had given Peck a gift, a money-clip with an inscription that read: 'To Greg with love from Jack.' Shortly after Benny's death, the money-clip was stolen, so Jack's widow, Mary, replaced it. Although it was not the original, Peck treasured it. 'I like to think of Jack every day,' he said, 'and I do.'

In the early summer of 1975 the Pecks returned to Cap Ferrat, and there he received a telephone call telling him that his son Jonathan had been found dead with a gun near his body. The conclusion was that he had committed suicide. Greg blamed himself for not being there when his son must have needed him the most in his final hours. Peck said, 'If only he could have picked up the phone and said, "Things are just bearing down so much on me tonight, I can't stand it," I would have said, "I'll be right there. We'll go off to Tahiti or somewhere." My regret that I'll live with for the rest of my life is that I was in France instead of in California.'

He caught the first flight to Los Angeles, leaving Véronique behind to close down the house, and went straight to see Greta. A couple of days later Véronique and the children arrived for the funeral. Never at any other time in his life had Peck had to face such a tragedy that threatened to bring him down completely, and Véronique was afraid that it might break him completely. She said that ultimately he surmounted the tragedy because of 'all of us together, feeling for the other and somehow doing the right thing instinctively'. She told Michael Freedland that the fact Greg did survive the ordeal was 'a great expression of his love for her, for Anthony and Cecilia'. Peck decided the best therapy for him now was to throw himself into work.

But he felt he could not bring himself to go through all he had in getting films like *The Trial of the Catonsville Nine* and *The Dove* to the screen. As he approached the age of sixty, he felt he did not want to waste endless months, or even years, trying to get films made when most projects didn't see the light of day, and those that did were commercially disappointing.

He was saved by *The Omen*.

The idea for the story of a young boy who is the devil incarnate came from a Los Angeles advertising executive, Robert L. Munger, who pitched it to producer Harvey Bernhard.

Bernhard raised some development money and assigned David Seltzer to write the screenplay, which went under the working title of *The Anti-Christ*. The script that developed told of Robert Thorn, an American diplomat in Italy, whose baby son dies at birth. Thorn accepts a substitute child without telling his wife, Katherine, and their boy, Damien, grows literally into a little demon. In essence, the film jumped on the devil-movie bandwagon begun by the success of *The Exorcist* a couple of years before.

Publicity pointed to the film's inspiration springing from a verse in the so-called 'Book of Revelations', leading many to suppose the Bible itself provided the prophecy that inspired the film.

> When the Jews return to Zion
> And a comet rips the sky
> And the Holy Roman Empire rises
> Then you and I must die.
> From the eternal sea he rises

200

Creating armies on either shore,
Turning man against his brother
'Til man exists no more.

In fact no such verse can be found anywhere in the Bible; nor
can the 'Book of Revelations'; the correct title is the 'Revelation of
John'. Seltzer later said that the film had no religious pretensions
at all and was 'pure escapism. I wanted to see if I could write something really outlandish and really commercial.'

Seltzer's finished screenplay went to Warner Brothers, which
took a seven-month option on it. Just days before their option was
due to expire, director Richard Donner came across the script and
took it to Alan Ladd Jr., who was chief of production at Twentieth
Century-Fox. On the day Warner's option expired, Fox bought the
script for Donner to direct.

They needed a major star and offered it to Charlton Heston. He
considered it, then backed out. Then someone thought of sending
the script to Gregory Peck, who saw through its many faults to
recognize the seeds of a good, and commercially successful film.

The script read like a good pulp thriller. It had some loopholes,
though. I always thought that Robert Thorn, as an ambassador,
would be too intelligent to just accept a substitute child without
question and without asking to see the body of his own dead son, or
researching the background of the substitute child. And I am not at
all sure that a man of his social standing would have deceived his
wife even out of deep, abiding concern for her and wanting to spare
her the pain of knowing about her own baby's death. But I could see
that it was a sort of roller coaster thrill ride for the audience.

Harvey Bernhard and Richard Donner have conceded that the
screenplay was not watertight, but as Donner pointed out, 'Even
the best Hitchcock movies had holes.' He was also unhappy with
that part of the script which had demons appearing on screen. He
felt that a more restrained approach would make the film more
believable, and Seltzer consequently agreed and amended the
script to Donner's satisfaction.

Donner worked on a rewrite of the script with Seltzer to create
a rhythm of thrills and lulls that would keep the audience on the
edge of their seats. The structure incorporated moments

201

purposely devised to give the viewers a false sense of security, only to shock them again.

Part of Donner's plan was to try and perplex the audience by making it seem possible that Robert Thorn might simply be having a nervous breakdown and that the horrors engulfing him are more to do with his obsessions and growing madness. This aspect of the film never worked because the publicity made it all too clear that Thorn was dealing with the Devil himself.

Peck knew that this film would be perceived as his 'comeback' and he wanted to ensure that Richard Donner was the right man to direct it. He asked George Chasin to check out Donner's television work for him to view, but before seeing any of it, Peck was invited by Donner to a meeting. They agreed on the changes that needed to be made to the script. Peck telephoned Chasin and told him, 'Forget the TV special. I like Dick.'

Fox set a budget of $2.5 million, and Donner prepared an eleven-week shooting schedule. He worked extensively on pre-production, formulating back-up plans for the days when the unpredictable British weather would force out changes in the schedule. Then it was discovered that a European film called *The AntiChristo* was on release, so a working title of *The Birthmark* was substituted, in reference to the three sixes that supposedly appear on the bodies of the Devil's servants.

In October 1975 Peck flew from Los Angeles to London to start filming. Across the Atlantic a bolt of lightning knocked out one of the plane's engines. Eight hours later another plane, this time with David Seltzer on board, was also struck by lightning. Those involved with the film joked that there must be a jinx on them all.

Then an IRA bomb exploded at the London Hilton, where Bernhard and Donner were staying. On the first day of shooting, one of the film crew barely escaped injury in a head-on car collision. The idea of the jinx suddenly seemed less funny. Some scenes were shot in Israel, where a private jet was hired to collect Peck from the location. He cancelled it at the last minute and it was rented by five Japanese businessmen. The plane crashed, killing them all.

Despite the mishaps that seemed to have developed into a full-blown curse, Peck enjoyed making the film, and especially liked working with Lee Remick, who was, like Peck, American insurance. 'She was a wonderful screen partner,' Peck said of her.

Towards the end of filming, the screen-devil bandwagon was rolling merrily along. Alan Ladd Jr. told a reporter, 'Almost every movie company has five or six devil movies in the works.' In fact, Fox and Harvey Bernhard announced they would be making two sequels.

After eleven weeks, Donner brought the film in on schedule but slightly over budget, at $2.8 million. Immediately after the film wrapped on Christmas Eve, Peck flew to Los Angeles and was home in time for dinner with Véronique and the children. Meanwhile, the film's special effects man, John Richardson, and his female assistant went to the Netherlands to work on *A Bridge Too Far*. Their car was hit by a truck; Richardson received head injuries, but his assistant was killed.

Fox knew that the film needed a massive promotional campaign; unlike *The Exorcist*, it was not based on a bestselling book. So David Seltzer needed to write one; the novelization went on to sell 3.5 million copies. Some 1,300 trailers were produced to show in cinemas across the United States and sneak previews were shown to a total of 700,000 people, who gave it rave reviews by word of mouth.

The publicity campaign should have cost a staggering $2.8 million, doubling the cost of the film, but in the end it rose to $6 million. Therefore *The Omen* (as it had been renamed) had to be a big, big hit.

When it opened on 25 June 1976, the critics were divided. The *New York Post*'s Frank Rich called it, 'a very cagey, though far from airtight horror movie. Given the script's drawbacks, there's no denying that director Richard Donner has gotten everything out of the material that he possibly can. Peck is a more prepossessing diplomat than many appointed by recent Washington administrations, and Miss Remick continues to be about the loveliest woman on earth.'

Kathleen Carroll of the *New York Daily News* thought it 'truly a rare find: the horror movie that displays real thought and intelligence. Peck gives one of the peak performances of his career.' Rich Eder of *The New York Times* called *The Omen* 'a dreadfully silly film, which is not to say that it is totally bad. Its horrors are not horrible, its terrors are not terrifying, its violence is ludicrous – which may be an advantage – but it does move along.'

The American National Council of Churches published an article that said, 'This is a must-see film. If nothing else it will provoke parishioners into reading the Bible.' By contrast, the US Catholic Conference took exception to the film, as they had to *The Exorcist*, describing it as 'one of the most distasteful ever put out by a major studio'.

Church ministers denounced the film, while stories began to spread about the so-called *Omen* jinx. Vatican radio proclaimed, 'The religious institutions are anything but enthusiastic about this type of interest in the devil. Nothing and nobody prevents movies from dealing with Satan. But in front of such a serious theme tackled for reasons and towards ends absolutely consumeristic and economical, the proverbial tail of the devil comes to one's mind.'

Donner responded by saying how surprised he was that the Church would object to a film that served in some measure to inform people about the Devil's work, saying that the Church 'must admit that the Devil can be alive and well on planet earth,' he said, 'and if so, isn't it important to gather our religious strength to ward off this evil? The best way to have that is to have an informed public. *The Omen* is certainly not a film about the Devil winning, but a warning of his presence.'

The film went on to break every existing record for an opening weekend of any previous Twentieth Century-Fox film, amassing $4.3 million in just three days. Its final total was more than $100 million, making it Gregory Peck's most successful film of all time, and one of the year's biggest hits, competing only with Universal's *Midway* as the most successful film of 1976.

19

Back to War

NOTHING SUCCEEDS IN HOLLYWOOD like success. Producing partners Richard D. Zanuck and David Brown, along with
producer Frank McCarthy, had announced their hopes to make
MacArthur in 1972, after the enormous success of *Patton* in 1970.
McCarthy had produced the latter for Twentieth Century-Fox,
where Zanuck and Brown had been employed as executives. Now,
flushed by Universal's success with *Midway*, that studio gave the go-
ahead for Peck's dream movie, *MacArthur*, and because of the
success of *The Omen*, he was asked to play the famed general.

Peck immersed himself in everything ever written about
MacArthur, met many people who had known him, and surprised
himself by growing fond of the man he had thought a fascinating
but dislikable character. He was in agreement with Frank
McCarthy: it was absolutely vital to present the general as a
complex human being, to get under the skin of the man himself,
but avoid trying for an impersonation of him. Peck rejected a
complex makeup job that made him look a lot like MacArthur but
hid many of the actor's own facial expressions; instead he opted
for an effective and subtle cosmetic similitude, which included
parting his hair on the right side, and shaving the crown of his
head to give him a small bald patch.

Before filming, Peck met with Laurence Olivier, who happened
to be something of an authority on MacArthur (he played the part
himself a year later in *Inchon*). Olivier asked Peck, 'How's your
breath control?'

'Why?' replied Peck.

Olivier explained that MacArthur had the ability to deliver long
passages of speech without pausing for breath. 'You will need the

breath to carry through to the end of each phrase,' Olivier advised him. Peck went away and practised.

The film attempted to portray the last twenty years of the general's life, beginning with his withdrawal from the Philippines in 1942 to his final farewell at West Point. Peck stood before 4,000 West Point cadets and gave the famous 'Duty-honour-country' speech, afterwards saying that he had found the moment so awesome 'my hackles rose'.

As he was preparing to enact this scene, Peck was asked if he had gone so far into the part that he had begun to dream he was MacArthur. Peck replied, 'No, but I did have the typical actor's dream that I got up in front of four thousand people and couldn't remember a word.'

One moment was destined to become a classic out-take: Peck stepped off a landing craft into the sea, found it was five feet deep instead of just knee deep, lost his footing and disappeared under the surface, while his hat floated on the surface. He saw the funny side of it and re-emerged laughing.

As an actor who tended to take his role home with him, Peck even took his MacArthur persona house hunting with Véronique. She was keen to show him a property she had found on North Carolwood Drive. During his lunch, wearing his military tunic and braided hat and carrying a swagger stick, he arrived at the house and inspected it in the way MacArthur might have inspected the Philippine beaches.

'Right,' he said to Véronique, pointing his swagger stick at her, 'buy it!'

He did, however, leave his MacArthur persona at the studio when he presented the prestigious Scopus Award – given by important Jewish organizations – to Frank Sinatra.

He had promised not to do any of his infamous memo writing on this film, but he succumbed and wrote to McCarthy, 'I have tried to keep my word and not bombard you with memos. This has taken a great deal of self-control, since I am a graduate of the David O. Selznick school of memo writing.' He told McCarthy that he had discovered in a book by Courtney Whitney, who had been one of MacArthur's aides, aspects of the character that were missing from the screenplay and which he hoped they could add. He made numerous other suggestions, some of which were implemented, some ignored.

Zanuck and Brown made an attempt to stop the memos by writing to him, 'Our aim and that of the studio is to make this a *great* motion picture. Should you ever find that this is for some reason significantly less than what you and we expected and hoped it would be, you will find us *totally* supportive.' Their letter did not staunch the flow of communications, however, as Peck became increasingly dissatisfied with the way the film was being made. Meetings were held to discuss his grievances, as he pleaded with them to shoot the whole of MacArthur's Congressional speech, arguing that 'the worst that can happen is that the audience will shuffle or cough a little. The best is that they will be aroused to the point of applauding. The present cutting insures that they will not'.

Peck later said, 'I always hoped that the picture would be a historical drama that would illuminate the era. I hoped that because of the drama of the confrontation between MacArthur and President Truman, young people might become interested and reappraise their thinking.'

He was also disappointed to find that Universal were penny-pinching by trying to shoot battle scenes in California that should have been filmed in the Pacific Islands and then editing them into archive material.

As filming approached its final days, Peck tried desperately to score some points by phoning Zanuck and Brown. They sent him a telegram:

YOUR FEELINGS REGARDING MACARTHUR AS EXPRESSED YESTERDAY ON THE PHONE ARE TREMENDOUSLY APPRECIATED BY US. YOUR DEDICATION AND CREATIVE CONTRIBUTION TO THIS FILM HAVE BEEN OF ENORMOUS BENEFIT TO US ALL. WE WILL ALWAYS BE DEEPLY GRATEFUL.

The film wrapped and Universal, Zanuck, Brown and McCarthy agreed, if not with complete accord, that the film was too long at three hours. Various versions were shown at sneak previews. At one point the film ran to 144 minutes, and finally 128 minutes. Peck objected to some of the scenes ending up on the cutting-room floor.

'It was important to have both MacArthur and Truman represented fairly,' he said. 'These events are twenty-six years in the past. I thought we could let MacArthur have his full due. Some of his strongest diatribes were removed from the picture – diatribes against the Joint Chiefs of Staff, China, the British, against anyone opposing his retaking all of Korea.' He complained in a letter to the producers and the director that the film gave the impression that Truman was 100 per cent right and that 'by defusing MacArthur, we may be being too clever by half, too proper and "balanced". We may be cheating the audience of the chance to cheer, take sides and argue.' He said that if the picture went out in a version that lacked passion 'God forbid, then it will fail.'

When he heard that a scene had been cut in which MacArthur informs Russian representatives in Tokyo that he will not permit the Soviets to control any of Japan, he said that had he known the scene was going to be omitted 'I would never have undertaken to play the part'. The scene was restored.

He concluded that 'the film was made by the wrong studio' and criticized Universal for failing to make pictures with any real content. 'The executives at Universal are creatures of the MCA Conglomerate,' he said, 'who enjoy scanning stock reports and counting grosses.'

Comparisons with *Patton* were inevitable. The *New York Daily News*'s Kathleen Carroll said the film 'misfires almost completely. As played by the ramrod-straight, ever-dignified Gregory Peck, he is a regal, imposing figure, but Peck's unbending performance gives no hint of MacArthur's inner complexity or his deeper conviction.'

Jack Kroll of *Newsweek* said that *MacArthur*

> doesn't have the flair and panache of *Patton* but in many ways it cuts deeper and churns up more food for thought. This prosaic, limited, naggingly honest film finally achieves a strangely touching quality, thanks mainly to Gregory Peck, whose voice and bearing evoke exactly the "transcendent sincerity and essential rectitude" that historian Trumbull Higgins found in one of the most enigmatic heroes in American history. *MacArthur* is hardly a brilliant film, but it has a certain dogged integrity, and the figure of MacArthur as hero and bogeyman remains a crucial one.

Vincent Canby, writing in *The New York Times* thought 'Gregory Peck is remarkably good. He makes the character disgracefully appealing, even when he is being his most outrageous. He displays a wit that gives an edge to the performance and humanity to a character who it might well have been impossible to be around. His speeches are so cannily handled by the film and Mr. Peck that one is constantly finding oneself at equal distances between the sneer and cheer.'

Richard Schickel of *Time* wrote, 'One must regretfully conclude that Gregory Peck is not the ideal choice to play MacArthur. While he tried hard to adopt the grand MacArthur manner he just cannot manage it. The fire, the touch of lunacy, is not there, though Peck does it nicely when he portrays the aged general, flames banked, the mood autumnal.'

Peck was delighted that a number of his peers, including James Stewart and Jack Lemmon, called to congratulate him, and one director he preferred not to name told him, 'The picture is not worthy of your performance.'

In 1978 Peck starred with Laurence Olivier in *The Boys From Brazil.* Sir Lew Grade had acquired the rights to the book by Ira Levin for $250,000, and set aside a budget of $6 million. Director Franklin J. Schaffner offered Peck the most atypical role of his career – that of Josef Mengele, who carried out horrifying experiments on prisoners in the Nazi death camps and then escaped to South America. Levin's book, on which the screenplay was based, was a fictional account of Mengele's discovery of a method of cloning replicas of Hitler, produced from samples of the Führer's own blood, and his plan to establish a Fourth Reich. The boys from Brazil of the title are the young Hitler clones.

Peck was initially reluctant to take a role that was in such stark contrast to his screen persona. But he was drawn to the opportunity of reminding the world of the horrors of Nazism, especially those instigated by Dr Mengele. Franklin J. Schaffner further convinced Peck that it was an acting challenge he could not pass up. 'It was a plum role,' Peck conceded, and one that offered him a rare opportunity to stretch his acting muscles. 'The man was a human rattlesnake, and I personally loathe everything Mengele represents, but perhaps in bringing such an evil creature to the minds of people, the horror of all that he and the Third Reich did will not be forgotten.'

The film was shot in Lisbon and Vienna, where Greg was accompanied by Véronique and Cecilia, then eighteen, who worked on set as an assistant unit photographer, and Anthony, twenty-three, who became an assistant director on the set. Cecilia went on to become a successful photographer whose work was published in various important magazines, while Anthony attended the Juilliard Institute in New York to study drama. Peck took great pride in seeing him take part in his student plays, and boasted that Anthony was 'superb in comedy' and that when he played a blind Vietnam veteran 'he got better notices than any I ever had'.

Laurence Olivier's role was that of Ezra Lieberman, a character based on Jewish Nazi-hunter Simon Wiesenthal, who devoted his life to tracking down Nazi war criminals. James Mason played Colonel Siebert, security chief for the Nazi underground.

'One of my lifetime ambitions was to work with Laurence Olivier,' said Peck. 'He was just beautiful – a darling. He was gallant, funny, easy to be with and not at all intimidating to me or the others. And I was thrilled as well to play a scene with James Mason, whom I've always admired.'

In an attempt to completely hide his own personality and create a totally antipathetic visual effect, Peck insisted on a thorough makeover, having his hair blackened and growing a moustache that was also dyed black to harden his features. But most of the transformation in his malevolent performance came about purely through the nuances of his performance. He even took to carrying a picture of Mengele around with him.

He took the character home at the end of each day's shooting, which would not have been a pleasant prospect for Véronique were it not for the fact that he did so with some humour. He barked orders for his dinner and clicked his heels, and would cut into a joint of meat with sadistic relish.

Véronique said that waking up every morning next to him during the making of that film 'was a shock,' and she noted that 'all the women who have seen him are terribly upset at his appearances'.

After sharing an elevator in Lisbon with an American couple, Peck heard the woman say to her husband, 'Did you see that weird creep in the elevator?' Greg was delighted at the comment.

While Peck portrayed Mengele for the screen in this fictitious story, the real Mengele was living under presidential protection in Paraguay in a sumptuous villa near San Antonio, with a yacht, helicopters and motorcades at his disposal. Peck noted, 'He manages to live in far more luxury than movie stars in Hollywood. But I wouldn't say he lived comfortably. I think we'd welcome him showing up and trying to sue us for libel.'

Peck was looking younger than his sixty-two years, and kept in shape by exercising three days a week under the guidance of a Japanese American, Kim Lee. When he was at home, he kept trim doing the gardening that he loved, growing his own vegetables and cultivating an assortment of colourful plants and flowers. The two gardeners he employed found it hard to do their jobs when he was about.

Some scenes had to be shot back in the United States at Lancaster, Pennsylvania, where Peck, Schaffner and Olivier were awarded honorary degrees at Franklin and Marshal College. Peck took the opportunity to address the budding actors on campus, telling them, 'Train your voices. Have a decent respect for breath control. Learn to move with precision and purpose. Fence, dance, exercise, do gymnastics. *You* are the only instruments you will ever have with which to express your talents and imaginations.'

The film was just a little too heavy-handed and typical of the expensive output coming from Lew Grade, whose name had started to become synonymous with the costly disasters of the late 1970s. A film on a less grand scale might have been more effective. By the end of the production, the budget had almost doubled.

The film opened on 5 October 1978 at the Ziegfeld Theater in New York. Jack Kroll of *Newsweek* wrote, 'Peck throws his characteristic decorum to the dogs and plays Mengele as a monstrous, ranting genius of moral idiocy. Olivier's ironic, subtle acting as usual has a thousand nuances.'

Time's Richard Schickel found it 'all pretty silly stuff. But the peculiarity of this film is the expensive sobriety with which it has been mounted. There is the fascination of watching Gregory Peck, Mr. Integrity himself, playing Mengele. He seems to be enjoying his change of face and pace. But no more than that.'

Pauline Kael had nothing good to say about it in the *New Yorker*. 'When veteran American actors are cast too strongly against type, they look ridiculous. Who could accept John Wayne or James Stewart – or Gregory Peck – as a Nazi sadist?'

In 1978 Carey Peck decided to run for Congress. Greg didn't really understand Carey's love of politics, saying, 'It's a very tough job and a tough life, but an exciting challenge.'

He even tried to talk his son out of it, but Carey told him that he wanted a measure of his own power so that he could bring about change. 'You've got to win an elective office to make changes and improve things,' he told his father. That, said Peck, was when he understood what every father had to realize – that his son was his own man. Peck maintained that he never wanted power of his own; that was one reason why he had never directed a film. 'My son is a different breed of cat,' he said.

As Carey embarked on the campaign trail, Greg went with him, raising funds for his campaign and managing to get people like Walter Matthau and George Burns to contribute.

A few months later, Peck made one of his rare television appearances, on a George Burns special called *George Burns' 100th Birthday*, even though the comedian was still a sprightly 82.

At the end of 1968 Frank Sinatra, who had collected the Scopus Award from Peck, now returned the compliment. Dinah Shore also received an award, but as the two recipients posed with Sinatra for the photographers before the presentation, Sinatra lost his temper for reasons never explained, and after letting lose a tirade at the cameramen he stormed out, leaving Peck, Véronique and Shore looking decidedly bemused.

Sinatra returned to present the awards, and introduced Dinah Shore by saying, 'Outside of Jack Daniels, nothing finer has ever come out of Tennessee.' Upon accepting the award, she sang in Hebrew and then said, 'This award would have meant more to my father than all my previous ones put together. He was a dedicated student of the Talmud.'

Then Sinatra presented Peck with his award and said, 'Who but Gregory Peck could go from *Gentleman's Agreement* to *The Boys from Brazil?*' The irony was not lost on Peck, who pointed out, 'I filmed the biblical film *David and Bathsheba* in Arizona some years ago. Much later I shot *Billy Two Hats* in Israel – it was a Western set in Arizona!'

In early spring 1979, Peck presented Laurence Olivier with the Filmex Award for his 'extraordinary contribution to film making'. In his short speech before handing over the award, Peck said that Olivier was 'an inspiration to actors the world over. He has given to audiences for fifty years a robust *joie de vivre* and noble sensitivity. And we're all the better off because of him.'

Olivier was greeted with a standing ovation from the audience, which included many Hollywood luminaries, among them Paul Newman and Joanne Woodward, who were making their first public appearance since the tragic death of their son, Scott. Behind closed doors, Peck had some words of empathy, sympathy and sincere consolation for them.

Peck was sporting a moustache when he and Véronique were among the guests of honour to see White House veteran Harvey Silbert receive the 1979 Scopus Award. Frank Sinatra was also there; it was only in recent years he and Peck had become firm friends.

The moustache was for his role in *The Sea Wolves*, produced by Euan Lloyd and directed by Andrew V. McLaglen early in 1980. It was based on a true incident but not made public until the 1978 publication of the book *The Boarding Party* by James Leasor. It was the tale of a group of ageing members of the Calcutta Light Horse, which had last seen action during the Boer War of 1900. The veterans silenced a German spy ship, the *Ehrenfels*, docked in the neutral port at Goa, then a Portuguese colony on the Indian Ocean, where it had been transmitting information on Allied shipping to the U-boats. Because of the Official Secrets Act, the story of the CLH's extraordinary mission was withheld from the public for thirty-five years.

Peck played Lieutenant-Colonel Lewis Pugh, whose job was to supervise clandestine operations against the enemy in India. Peck, then sixty-three, said, 'It's not too late for new adventures. If the Civil War epic materializes, that would be fine. Meanwhile, I'm a gardener who goes off now and then for a few months to make a movie somewhere.'

He left his garden this time to be happily reunited on screen with David Niven, seventy, who played chief of the Calcutta Horse. Among his team was Trevor Howard, sixty-four. In fact, most of the cast were over sixty, except for 52-year-old Roger Moore who played an SOE operative in the style of his James Bond persona. One London critic dubbed it, 'Golden Oldies Go To War.'

Moore told me that the film was really a follow-up to *The Wild Geese*, which he had starred in the year before – with Richard Burton and Richard Harris – for Lloyd and McLaglen. He said, 'Because there seemed to be an awful sort of sameness about it all with this bunch of ageing guerrillas, Lloyd and McLaglen went off

213

on a different track by approaching Gregory Peck, who then wondered if there might be a job in it for David Niven.' In fact, said Niven, 'It was a bit like *The Wild Geese Take off from Navarone*! It's nice to be back working with Gregory Peck again after all these years.'

Peck was apprehensive about his British accent when surrounded by so many true Brits. Roger Moore told me, 'I told Greg that if Laurence Olivier can get away with playing MacArthur in *Inchon!*, then he could certainly get away with playing a British lieutenant. I thought his British accent was very convincing.'

Filming took place in New Delhi and the Indian port of Goa (which had been restored to India since its independence). 'The heat was extreme,' said Moore, 'sometimes reaching 140 degrees.'

Peck recalled, 'David was as chipper as always on Goa. He didn't much like his part, but he made it a lot better than it was. He had begun to take long fast walks every day, late in the afternoon after work.' Niven had discovered that his arm and leg muscles ached, and he felt that a healthy dose of exercise would cure it. His voice also mysteriously began to slur. The sad truth was that he was suffering the first effects of motor neurone disease.

The film opened on 5 June 1981 at several cinemas in New York. It was dedicated to the memory of Earl Mountbatten, who was himself an honorary commander of the Calcutta Light Horse. David Denby, in the *New Yorker*, said it was 'a dear, silly old action movie ... a sweet epitaph for a movie genre that has been put out to pasture'. Vincent Canby of *The New York Times* wrote, 'if the film sounds like a geriatric *Guns of Navarone*, that's more or less the way it plays'. 'Its most notable distinction,' wrote Archer Winstein in the *New York Post*, 'is the roster of famous old movie stars assembled from both England and America.' Ian Christie of the *Daily Express* said, 'It's fun and thrills – yes, it really is! ... a splendid piece of entertainment and a worthy tribute to the men who pulled off the bizarre operation.'

20

A Lifetime's Work Goes on

IN 1981 PECK WAS SEDUCED into making his first television commercial. It was for Dodge cars. But it was not a completely unconditional surrender to commerce. Frank Sinatra, a volunteer spokesman for Chrysler, had taken Peck on a tour of the Chrysler plant in Detroit, and when Peck learned that the company's troubles could result in the loss of 600,000 jobs, he did the commercial and donated his fee to the Motion Picture and TV Fund.

He also made his first television movie, *The Scarlet and the Black*, shot in Rome in 1981. It was the true story of an Irish Vatican priest who hid Allied soldiers from the Nazis and helped them escape. The film was based on the book *The Scarlet Pimpernel of the Vatican* by J.P. Gallagher. Peck was excellent as the priest, complete with an authentic-sounding Irish accent, and Christopher Plummer was suitably menacing as the German officer with whom Peck plays a deadly cat-and-mouse game. For a television movie, the casting was first-class, with Sir John Gielgud as Pope Pius XII. Unfortunately, the lacklustre direction by Jerry London meant that the film never looked or felt like anything more than a television movie. Even the presence of Peck, who accepted the role because there was little else of quality being offered to him, failed to enliven the proceedings.

Peck finally got to play Abraham Lincoln, but it was hardly in the Civil War epic, the American *War and Peace* he had envisaged. Instead it was a brief cameo in a television mini-series, *The Blue and the Grey*. At sixty-five, he was really too old to play Lincoln, but it was clearly his last chance to do so. After that, Peck went back to being a gardener for the next six years.

By 1983 it was known that David Niven was dying from the

muscle-wasting disease he had first noticed in Goa. Peck was a regular visitor to Niven's retreat in Cap Ferrat, and after Niven passed away on 27 July 1983, Peck and Peter Ustinov led a memorial service for him in Hollywood.

Greg had befriended most American presidents since the early 1960s, and in 1983 he joined President Ronald Reagan – whose governorship of California he had openly opposed – for a state dinner at the White House. Around then, Reagan had nominated Judge Robert Bork to the Supreme Court, a move that alarmed Peck, who said, 'I came to the conclusion that having that guy on the Supreme Court would be the beginning of turning back civil rights – and I felt it was time to step up and bat.'

And he hit a few rounds by appearing on television to oppose the nomination. Reagan was outraged, especially when the judge lost, and had Peck's name removed from all future White House functions. Peck said, 'I don't think it was my TV spots that defeated him. What gave the spots so much importance was when Martin Fitzwater [White House Press Secretary] said publicly that President Reagan regarded me as a "former friend".'

By this time Peck was itching to do some more big-screen acting, and he bought all the rights to the 1936 classic film *Dodsworth* to remake, playing the Walter Huston part himself. But he failed to get the studios interested in investing, and he hung his hopes on *Judgement Day* which seemed all set to go in 1985 until the production company failed to fulfil Peck's contractual stipulation that William Friedkin direct it. He sued the company for $2.5 million plus $10 million punitive damages.

In 1986 Peck joined his old friend Audrey Hepburn and an assortment of other actors, including Laurence Olivier and Charlton Heston, to appear in a biographical documentary, *Directed by William Wyler*. Peck was seventy years old, and although in good health, not able to handle his drink as well as he had back on the set of *The Guns of Navarone* in 1960. Kirk Douglas recalled a dinner at '21' in New York in 1986 with the Pecks and the Sinatras. 'I was sitting between Barbara Sinatra and Greg Peck,' said Douglas, 'and during the meal, Barbara suddenly didn't feel well, and went home. Shortly after that, Greg disappeared. The next day he said he thought he had had too much to drink. I was the same age as Greg and was feeling fine; I stayed.'

That same year Californians were asked to vote on Proposition 65, which, if passed, would force the governor to list and eliminate all chemicals causing toxic contamination through the state. Jane Fonda and her political activist husband Tom Hayden formed Network with Whoopi Goldberg, Rob Lowe and Michael J. Fox, among other younger stars, to fight for the Yes vote. They were up against formidable opposition from the oil and chemical companies, but Fonda and Hayden got on the phone to call, among many, Gregory Peck to join Network's fight. He did, and other stars followed as they rode the campaign bus for three days throughout California, finally winning the vote.

When a TV remake of *Inherit the Wind* was set up Peck was mooted as first choice to play the part of the atheist defence lawyer played by Spencer Tracy in the 1960 cinema version, with Kirk Douglas as the religious prosecutor which Fredric March had portrayed. But somehow the part eluded him and it was instead played by Jason Robards.

Peck finally made his return to the cinema screen in 1987 in *Amazing Grace and Chuck*. He found himself in the seat of American government, having previously been there as Lincoln. Now he was simply 'Mr President' of 1987, and a more wholesome and distinguished president America could not have hoped for. This was, of course, still the era of the ageing American president, the relative youth of J.F. Kennedy having been an anomaly. Since then the also relatively youthful Bill Clinton has changed the face of Hollywood's US presidents to look like Michael Douglas (*The American President*) and Bill Pullman (*Independence Day*). Director Mike Newell explained why he wanted to cast Peck as the president:

> We all know what the President looks like, but our character had to be a sort of an idealised, all-American President. He's seen as a "good guy", and these days Presidents are all too often seen in the opposite light. In the film, he's a mixture of all the good things about the President. He's the sort of man you are convinced would do things for all the right reasons – and who better to portray him than Greg Peck. He has something that is very difficult to achieve. As soon as you enter the area of politics and people with titles that really exist, then you step away from pure fiction into a very awkward mixture of documentary and fiction.

The film told the wistful tale of Chuck, a schoolboy baseball champion, who goes on an outing to an American nuclear missile base, and horrified at the thought of nuclear war, protests by refusing to speak or play baseball. When Boston basketball superstar Amazing Grace Smith (played by real-life basketball superstar Alex English) gives up his own career to join the lad in protest, other sporting personalities both sides of the Iron Curtain follow suit until, finally, the president of the United States summons the boy to the White House.

Peck felt that *Amazing Grace and Chuck* was something special to lure him back in front of the cameras.

> The story intrigued me. It's a contemporary subject which slots squarely into 1987, very much about things which people everywhere can identify with today. Nuclear disarmament is a universal theme. This is essentially a modern fable of small-town America, the sort that Frank Capra used to make so brilliantly. The script says, 'If only this could really happen, then the world would be a wonderful place.' That's the way Capra's pictures were. The little people overcoming the rich, the powerful and the corrupt. I love the theme of this movie and that's why I had to be a part of it.

The problem was, Newell is not Capra, and *Amazing Grace and Chuck* was not *Mr. Smith Goes to Washington*. It was, said *Variety*, 'destined to go down in history as the camp classic of the anti-nuke genre. As amazingly bad as it is audacious, the film will live forever in the hearts of connoisseurs of Hollywood's most memorably outrageous moments.' *Variety* did, however, think that Peck was 'impressive'. But the film was a box-office flop and was retitled *Silent Voice* for release in the UK, where it fared no better.

Peck was more careful about his next choice of film, *Old Gringo*, which Jane Fonda produced in 1988. It told the true story of Ambrose Bierce, the elderly American writer who disappeared without a trace in northern Mexico at the time of the Revolution. Burt Lancaster was originally cast as Bierce for a fee of $1.5 million. Columbia was, however, unable to get insurance to cover him, after recent heart surgery, so he had to be dropped. Peck got the role and the fee. Lancaster sued Columbia, and Fonda, who was friendly with both Lancaster and Peck, stayed out of the legal wrangling. She said, 'I have an idea for another film I'll do with Burt.' But that film never materialized.

Meanwhile she found working with Peck 'a delight' and said that his acting 'looks seamless, almost effortless'. She played schoolteacher Harriet Winslow, who finds her emotions torn between Bierce and a young Mexican general played by Jimmy Smits. She described the film, shot in Mexico at a cost of $25 million, as 'the biggest film I've ever done and one of the most difficult'. It had taken her eight years to get the film made, and by the time shooting was under way, she was little less than an emotional wreck, due in part to her disintegrating marriage.

When she and Peck shared a screen kiss, they rehearsed the scene endlessly for days, working out how to choreograph it with a fanatical zeal. When writer Ron Rosenbaum asked Peck what it was like to work with someone so enthusiastic, he replied, 'Well, it's a benevolent fanaticism.' Neither she nor director Luis Puenzo were satisfied with the result which perfectionist Fonda felt was due to her own shortcomings, not Peck's. She recalled that they were supposed to finish the scene on a Saturday but knew they would have to pick up on it again on the Monday. That weekend, she said, she had a nervous breakdown. But she pulled herself together enough by Monday to carry on.

Peck was in some awe of Jane who, at fifty, looked and seemed at least ten years younger. He said, 'I'd look around at all the hundreds of people on the set in Mexico, and then look at Jane and think to myself, My God, this girl is the reason we are all here. It all rests on her slender shoulders.'

Old Gringo should have been Columbia's big blockbuster for Christmas 1988, but because of post-production difficulties it was held over till 1989. *Variety* said, 'As the embittered, sardonic journalist Ambrose Bierce, Gregory Peck has found a role that suits him to a T. He portrays the world-weary Bierce with relish and wit. The paternalistic figure in a nebulous love triangle with Fonda and Smits, Peck exudes a sympathetic mien despite his crusty exterior. His best moments come long before the denouement, and the film's wittiest lines are his alone.'

Kim Newman wrote in *Empire*,

Because this is A Fonda Film, her character unfortunately tends to get the most time, which is a shame since she's the least interesting of the three leads. Gregory Peck gives an Oscar-worthy performance, charming his way towards a heroic death and imparting the collected wisdom of years of misanthropy to many things. Like the character, you get the impression that the actor is doing many things – heroically riding a horse, striding through battles, playing a love scene, being a movie star – for the last time. Always an underrated actor, it's a pleasure to see Peck, like Bierce, taking one last shot and hitting dead centre.

Because of a corporate upheaval at Columbia, *Old Gringo* didn't get the attention it deserved. 'After the many years Jane Fonda put in to get it made,' said Peck, 'it's a pity to see it destroyed in 48 hours. It made less than $2 million at the box office, a disastrous return for the $25 million romantic extravaganza. People didn't go right away – it should have been given more time to get going, but by the time people wanted to go, it wasn't playing anymore.'

In 1990 Peck co-starred with Danny De Vito in *Other People's Money*. Although he was billed above the title with De Vito, Peck's was really just a supporting role in a film tailored for De Vito. The latter played Larry Garfield, a fiscal cowboy who makes a profit from other people's money, even though the other people tend to end up financially destroyed. It's no wonder they call him Larry the Liquidator. In a sense he was a small, fat, funny version of Michael Douglas in *Wall Street*.

The film was adapted from an off-Broadway hit and directed by Norman Jewison. Peck played Andrew Jorgensen, a fatherly businessman loved by everyone including animals and children. His leggy lawyer, Katie Sullivan, played by Penelope Ann Miller, has the task of trying to stop Larry getting at Jorgensen's money. The film should have been a biting satire through 'the script's generous helping of funny lines,' as noted by *Empire*'s Kim Newman. She added that De Vito's delivery 'works less well than it used to because De Vito is no longer interested in seeming less than completely loveable'. She also felt that all the supporting characters were 'shoved in to the background where they won't upstage De Vito'.

David Aldridge said in *Film Review*, 'Neither they [De Vito and Miller], nor guesting veterans Gregory Peck and Piper Laurie, are especially served by a seen-it-all-before storyline, nor by direction that's on the staid side. Still three-star stuff, though.'

Part of the problem seems to have been a certain amount of re-editing. Peck complained in the *Washington Post* that the film had been changed after being test-shown. 'It absolutely takes the back-bone out of everything. You get pictures that aren't going to make anybody mad, certainly not challenge anybody's intelligence. They've tried to turn motion picture-making into an industry like making shoes and sausage.'

When Martin Scorsese approached Peck with an idea to remake *Cape Fear*, the veteran was intrigued. Scorsese had the idea of turning Bowden, the part Peck had played in the original, from being an unimpeachable prosecutor into a defence counsel who withholds vital evidence. The ex-con Mitchum had played would be even more sadistic and the film far more horrific. Scorsese cast Nick Nolte in Peck's role, and Robert De Niro in Mitchum's. Then Scorsese offered Peck and Mitchum cameo spots in the film. Ordinarily, Peck would have balked at that idea, but he admired Scorsese and liked the idea of playing De Niro's older defence attorney.

The film, released in 1992, was a huge hit, but it repelled many critics. Kenneth Turan asked in the *Los Angeles Times*, 'Have our lives become so hollow that this kind of unapologetic bludgeoning of our sensibilities passes for jolly weekend entertainment?'

Dave Kerr of the *Chicago Tribune* reasoned, 'A slasher film by Scorsese is still a slasher film.'

'What's puzzling at this stage in his career,' said Hal Hinson of the *Washington Post*, 'is the way Scorsese could have set his sights so low.'

Empire's Matt Mueller noted, 'Scorsese runs the risk of alienating elements of the audience who are looking for an easily identifiable hero – both Nolte and (Jessica) Lange, unlike Gregory Peck and Polly Bergen in the original, being far from sympathetic.' But, said Mueller, the film itself was 'stylish, harrowing and brilliantly compelling'.

After completing *Cape Fear* Peck next enjoyed the rare pleasure of working with his daughter Cecilia who accepted an unusual challenge from her father; to put down her camera for a while and take up acting so they could play father and daughter, Gardner and Maggie Church, in a TV production, *The Portrait*.

It was a story that turned the tables on the oft-told tale of offspring who fail to live up to their parents' expectations. This was of a daughter's disappointment in the way her elderly and highly respected parents have turned out. Cecilia played Maggie, an artist who leaves her pad in New York to return to her retired parents' suburban house so she can complete an unfinished portrait of them for her up-coming one-woman show, only to find they are in the process of packing, having sold the house. Amid the confusion of packed boxes, she tries to get them to sit, but, like two children who can't remain still, they clown around while Maggie scolds them for spoiling her attempts to paint them. Gardner is a professor and a poet who should, she feels, behave with dignity, while her mother Fanny, played by Lauren Bacall, seems to only encourage his silliness with her own brand of childish humour.

Maggie eventually loses her patience and decides to give up and move back to New York but Gardner persuades her to stay, admitting that he and Fanny are not the perfect parents she'd like them to be, saying, 'That's who we are. I'm sorry that we don't live up to your expectations. We can't. But for your own well-being, accept us with our flaws and stop longing for us to change. My dear, we won't. We can't.' And therein lies the theme of this touching, funny story which Greg co-produced and which reunited him with Lauren Bacall who played his wife Fanny.

Had it been made for cinema, allowing it the time, care and attention theatrical films demand, it may well have become a classic to compare with *On Golden Pond* which explored similar themes for Henry and Jane Fonda. Nevertheless, as TV movies go, it remains an engaging entertainment which presents Peck with one of his most touching performances ever.

In December 1992, Peck went to visit Audrey Hepburn at the Cedars-Sinai Medical Center where she had undergone an operation to remove a colon tumour. The disease had spread too far for doctors to save her, and she was given just weeks to live. Peck visited her often, just to sit with her and hold her hand, as did Elizabeth Taylor and other friends. She had spent her last years working tirelessly for UNICEF, the United Nations children's charity, and had personally persuaded stars like Peck, Roger Moore and Sophia Loren to aid her in her cause.

Audrey had been romantically involved with actor Robert

Wolders since 1980; they had fallen in love following the death of his wife Merle Oberon, a close friend of Audrey's, in 1979. She was able to spend her last weeks at home with Wolders, and was tended by two nurses, paid for by Gregory Peck.

She died on 20 January 1993. Peck was among the mourners at her funeral, as was Mel Ferrer, divorced from her since 1968 but still deeply fond of her; he stood at the graveside with Sean, the son Audrey had given him. After her death, Peck said, 'Audrey thought of films as fairy tales and being in them part of a fairy-tale existence. I think that's why she was never tripped by her fame.'

As he approached eighty, Peck seemed to be in retirement. He was still happy with Véronique, and his children had done well. Cecilia was a successful photographer. Stephen had majored in public speaking, theatre and communications at Northwestern University. Carey had majored in the school of foreign science at Georgetown University. Anthony had become an actor, appearing in films such as *Die Hard* and *In the Line of Fire*.

Gregory Peck had not made a film since Scorsese's *Cape Fear*, and it looked like he might never do so again. Then Anthony, deciding to try his hand at screenwriting, delivered a screenplay, *Dr. Dermott*, written with his father in mind for the title role of an elderly university professor who reviews his life's disappointments. Anthony admitted his inspiration for the film was Ingmar Bergman's *Wild Strawberries*. In November 1997, it was announced that Martin Scorsese would direct it and that, at eighty-one, Peck would make his first film in six years.

First, however, Peck did a cameo in a TV production of *Moby Dick* as Father Mapple. He'd played Starbuck on the stage, Ahab in the film, and now the bible thumper on TV. He was back in the public eye on Monday 23 March, 1998, when he joined a tremendous line-up of all the surviving stars who had ever won an Academy Award for either a leading performance or supporting performance on stage at the Oscars show.

Despite previous talk of retirement amid dissatisfactions about the dumbing-down of Hollywood, his enthusiasm for his job had never gone away for good. He has said, 'Acting is the best profession there is; loving the job you do, meeting talented people and getting well paid for it. No matter how long I work at it, there are things to learn, doors to open, new roads to travel. I'm glad it's a life's work and one that's never finished within a lifetime.'

Filmography

d – director
p – producer
s – screenplay
n – novel
ph – photography
c – cast

Days of Glory, 1944, RKO. *d* Jacques Tourneur, *p* and *s* Casey Robinson, *ph* Tony Gaudio, *c* Tamara Toumanova, Gregory Peck, Alan Reed, Maria Palmer, Lowell Gilmore, Hugo Haas.

The Keys of the Kingdom, 1944, Twentieth Century-Fox. *d* John M. Stahl, *p* Joseph L. Mankiewicz, *s* Joseph L. Mankiewicz, Nunnally Johnson, *n* A.J. Cronin, *ph* Arthur Miller, *c* Gregory Peck, Thomas Mitchell, Vincent Price, Rose Stradner, Roddy McDowall, Edmund Gwenn.

The Valley of Decision, 1945, MGM. *d* Tay Garnett, *p* Edwin H. Knopf, *s* John Meehan, Sonya Levien, *n* Marcia Davenport, *ph* Joseph Ruttenberg, *c* Greer Garson, Gregory Peck, Lionel Barrymore, Donald Crisp, Preston Foster, Gladys Cooper.

Spellbound, 1945, David O. Selznick. *d* Alfred Hitchcock, *s* Ben Hecht, Angus MacPhail, *n* *The House of Dr Edwardes* by Francis Beeding, *ph* Georges Barnes, *c* Ingrid Bergman, Gregory Peck, Leo G. Carroll, Michael Chekhov, Rhonda Fleming, John Emery.

The Yearling, 1946, MGM. *d* Clarence Brown, *p* Sidney Franklin, *s* Paul Osborn, *n* Marjorie Kinnan, *ph* Charles Rosher, Leonard

Smith, *c* Gregory Peck, Jane Wyman, Claude Jarman Jr., Chill Wills, Clem Bevans, Margaret Wycherly, Henry Travers.

Duel in the Sun, 1946, David O. Selznick. *d* King Vidor, *s* David O. Selznick, Oliver H.P. Garrett, *n* Niven Busch, *ph* Lee Armes, *c* Jennifer Jones, Gregory Peck, Joseph Cotten, Lionel Barrymore, Lillian Gish, Walter Huston, Herbert Marshall.

The Macomber Affair, 1947, Benedict Bogeaus. *d* Zoltan Korda, *p* Casey Robinson, *s* Casey Robinson, *story The Short Life of Francis Macomber* by Ernest Hemingway, *ph* Karl Struss, *c* Gregory Peck, Joan Bennett, Robert Preston, Reginald Denny, Carl Harbord, Jean Gillie.

Gentleman's Agreement, 1947, Twentieth Century-Fox. *d* Elia Kazan, *p* Darryl F. Zanuck, *s* Moss Hart, *n* Laura Z. Hobson, *ph* Arthur Miller, *c* Gregory Peck, Dorothy McGuire, John Garfield, Celeste Holm, Anne Revere, Dean Stockwell.

The Paradine Case, 1947, David O. Selznick. *d* Alfred Hitchcock, *s* David O. Selznick, *n* Robert Hichens, *ph* Lee Garmes, *c* Gregory Peck, Alida Valli, Ann Todd, Louis Jourdan, Charles Laughton, Charles Coburn.

Yellow Sky, 1948, Twentieth Century-Fox. *d* William Wellman, *p* and *s* Lamar Trotti, *ph* Joe MacDonald, *c* Gregory Peck, Anne Baxter, Richard Widmark, Robert Arthur, John Russell, Henry Morgan.

The Great Sinner, 1949, MGM. *d* Robert Siodmak, *p* Gottfried Reinhardt, *s* Ladislas Fodor, Christopher Isherwood, *ph* George Folsey, *c* Gregory Peck, Walter Huston, Ava Gardner, Agnes Moorehead, Ethel Barrymore, Melvyn Douglas.

Twelve O'Clock High, 1949, Twentieth Century-Fox. *d* Henry King, *p* Darryl F. Zanuck, *s* Sy Bartlett, Beirne Lay Jr., *ph* Leon Shamroy, *c* Gregory Peck, Hugh Marlowe, Gary Merrill, Millard Mitchell, Dean Jagger, Robert Arthur.

The Gunfighter, 1950, Twentieth Century-Fox. *d* Henry King, *p*

Nunnally Johnson, *s* William Bowers, William Sellers, *ph* Arthur Miller, *c* Gregory Peck, Helen Westcott, Millard Mitchell, Jean Parker, Karl Malden, Skip Homeier, Mae Marsh.

Only the Valiant, 1950, Warner Brothers. *d* Gordon Douglas, *p* William Cagney, *s* Edmund H. North, Harry Brown, *ph* Lionel Lindon, *c* Gregory Peck, Ward Bond, Gig Young, Barbara Payton, Lon Chaney Jr., Neville Brand.

David and Bathsheba, 1951, Twentieth Century-Fox. *d* Henry King, *p* Darryl F. Zanuck, *s* Philip Dunne, *ph* Leon Shamroy, *c* Gregory Peck, Susan Hayward, James Robertson Justice, Raymond Massey, Kieron Moore.

Captain Horatio Hornblower, 1951, Warner Brothers. *d* and *p* Raoul Walsh, *s* Ivan Goff, Ben Roberts, Aeneas Mackenzie, *novels* C.S. Forester, *ph* Guy Green, *c* Gregory Peck, Virginia Mayo, Robert Beatty, James Robertson Justice, Terence Morgan, Moultrie Kelsall.

The World In His Arms, 1952, Universal. *d* Raoul Walsh, *p* Aaron Rosenberg, *s* Borden Chase, *ph* Russell Metty, *c* Gregory Peck, Anthony Quinn, Ann Blyth, John McIntire, Andrea King, Carl Esmond, Eugenie Leontovitch.

The Snows of Kilimanjaro, 1952, Twentieth Century-Fox. *d* Henry King, *p* Darryl F. Zanuck, *s* Casey Robinson, *story* Ernest Hemingway, *ph* Leon Shamroy, *c* Gregory Peck, Susan Hayward, Ava Gardner, Hildegard Neff, Leo G. Carroll, Torin Thatcher, Marcel Dalio.

Roman Holiday, 1953, Paramount. *d* and *p* William Wyler, *s* Ian McLellan Hunter, John Dighton, *ph* Franz Planer, *c* Gregory Peck, Audrey Hepburn, Eddie Albert, Harley Power, Harcourt Williams.

Night People, 1954, Twentieth Century-Fox. *d*, *p* and *s* Nunnally Johnson, *ph* Charles G. Clarke, *c* Gregory Peck, Broderick Crawford, Anita Bjork, Walter Abel, Rita Gam, Buddy Ebsen.

The Million Pound Note (U.S. Title *Man With a Million*), 1954, GFD/Group Films. *d* Ronald Neame, *p* John Bryan, *s* Jill Cragie, *story* Mark Twain, *ph* Geoffrey Unsworth, *c* Gregory Peck, Jane Griffiths, Ronald Squire, Joyce Grenfell, A.E. Matthews, Reginald Beckwith.

The Purple Plain, 1954, GFD/Two Cities. *d* Robert Parrish, *p* John Bryan, *s* Eric Ambler, *n* H.E. Bates, *ph* Geoffrey Unsworth, *c* Gregory Peck, Maurice Denham, Win Min Than, Lyndon Brook, Brenda de Banzie, Bernard Lee.

The Man in the Gray Flannel Suit, 1956, Twentieth Century-Fox. *d* and *s* Nunnally Johnson, *n* Sloan Wilson, *ph* Charles G. Clarke, *c* Gregory Peck, Fredric March, Jennifer Jones, Ann Harding, Arthur O'Connell, Henry Daniell.

Moby Dick, 1956, Warner/Moulin. *d* and *p* John Huston, *s* Ray Bradbury, John Huston, *n* Herman Melville, *ph* Oswald Morris, *c* Gregory Peck, Richard Basehart, Frederich Ledebur, Leo Genn, Orson Welles, Harry Andrews.

Designing Woman, 1957, MGM. *d* Vincente Minnelli, *p* Dore Schary, *s* George Wells, *ph* John Alton, *c* Gregory Peck, Lauren Bacall, Dolores Grey, Sam Levene, Tom Helmore, Mickey Shaughnessy.

The Bravados, 1958, Twentieth Century-Fox. *d* Henry King, *p* Herbert B. Swoope, *s* Philip Yordan, *n* Frank O'Rourke, *ph* Leon Shamroy, *c* Gregory Peck, Stephen Boyd, Joan Collins, Albert Salmi, Henry Silva, Lee Van Cleef.

The Big Country, 1958, UA/ Anthony/Worldwide. *d* William Wyler, *p* William Wyler, Gregory Peck, *s* James R. Webb, Sy Bartlett, Robert Wilder, *n* Donald Hamilton, *ph* Franz Planer, *c* Gregory Peck, Jean Simmons, Charlton Heston, Carroll Baker, Burl Ives, Charles Bickford, Chuck Connors.

Pork Chop Hill, 1959, UA/Melville/Milestone. *d* Lewis Milestone, *s* James R. Webb, *ph* Sam Leavitt, *c* Gregory Peck, Harry Guardino, George Peppard, Woody Strode, James Edwards, George Shibata, Rip Torn.

Beloved Infidel, 1959, Twentieth Century-Fox/Company of Artists. *d* Henry King, *p* Jerry Wald, *s* Sy Bartlett, *book* Sheilah Graham, *ph* Leon Shamroy, *c* Gregory Peck, Deborah Kerr, Eddie Albert, Philip Ober, Herbert Rudley, Karin Booth.

On the Beach, 1959, UA/ Stanley Kramer. *d* Stanley Kramer, *s* John Paxton, James Lee Barrett, *n* Nevil Shute, *ph* Giuseppe Rotunno, Daniel Fapp, *c* Gregory Peck, Ava Gardner, Fred Astaire, Anthony Perkins, Donna Anderson, John Tate.

The Guns of Navarone, 1961, Columbia/Open Road/Carl Foreman. *d* J. Lee Thompson, *p* Cecil F. Ford, *s* Carl Foreman, *n* Alistair Maclean, *ph* Oswald Morris, *c* Gregory Peck, David Niven, Stanley Baker, Anthony Quinn, Anthony Quayle, James Darren, Gia Scala, Irene Papas.

Cape Fear, 1962, Universal/Melville-Talbot. *d* J. Lee Thompson, *p* Sy Bartlett, *s* James R. Webb, *n* *The Executioners* by John D. MacDonald, *ph* Sam Leavitt, *c* Gregory Peck, Robert Mitchum, Polly Bergen, Martin Balsam, Lori Martin, Jack Kruschen, Telly Savalas.

How the West Was Won, 1962, MGM/Cinerama. *d* Henry Hathaway, John Ford, George Marshall, *p* Bernard Smith, *s* James R. Webb, *ph* William Daniels, Milton Krasner, Charles Lang Jr., Joseph La Shelle, *c* Carroll Baker, Lee J. Cobb, Henry Fonda, Carolyn Jones, Karl Malden, Gregory Peck, George Peppard, Robert Preston, Debbie Reynolds, James Stewart, Eli Wallach, John Wayne, Richard Widmark.

To Kill a Mockingbird, 1962, Universal. *d* Robert Mulligan, *p* Alan J. Pakula, *s* Horton Foote, *n* Harper Lee, *ph* Russell Harlan, *c* Gregory Peck, Mary Badham, Philip Alford, John Megna, Frank Overton, Rosemary Murphy, Ruth White, Brock Peters.

Captain Newman MD, 1963, Universal-Brentwood-Reynard. *d* David Miller, *p* Robert Arthur, *s* Richard L. Breen, Phoebe and Henry Ephron, *n* Leo Rosten, *ph* Russell Metty, *c* Gregory Peck, Tony Curtis, Angie Dickinson, Eddie Albert, Bobby Darin, James Gregory.

Behold a Pale Horse, 1964, Columbia/Highland/Brentwood. *d* Fred Zinnemann, *p* Fred Zinnemann, Alexander Trauner, *s* J.P. Miller, *n* *Killing a Mouse on Sunday* by Emeric Pressburger, *ph* Jean Badal, *c* Gregory Peck, Omar Sharif, Anthony Quinn, Raymond Pellegrin, Paolo Stoppa.

Mirage, 1965, Universal. *d* Edward Dmytryk, *p* Harry Keller, *s* Peter Stone, *n* Walter Ericson, *ph* Joe MacDonald, *c* Gregory Peck, Diane Baker, Walter Abel, Walter Matthau, Leif Erickson, Kevin McCarthy.

Arabesque, 1966, Universal. *d* and *p* Stanley Donen, *s* Julian Mitchell, Stanley Price, Pierre Marton, *n* *The Cipher* by Gordon Votler, *ph* Christopher Challis, *c* Gregory Peck, Sophia Loren, Alan Badel, Kieron Moore, Carl Duering.

Mackenna's Gold, 1968, Columbia/Highroad. *d* J. Lee Thompson, *p* Carl Foreman, Dimitri Tiomkin, *s* Carl Foreman, *n* Will Henry, *ph* Joseph MacDonald, *c* Gregory Peck, Omar Sharif, Telly Savalas, Camilla Sparv, Edward G. Robinson, Raymond Massey, Anthony Quayle, Lee J. Cobb, Julie Newmar, Eli Wallach.

The Stalking Moon, 1968, National General. *d* Robert Mulligan, *p* Alan J. Pakula, *s* Alvin Sargent, *n* Theodore V. Olsen, *ph* Charles Lang, *c* Gregory Peck, Eva Marie Saint, Robert Forster, Frank Silvera.

The Chairman (UK title *The Most Dangerous Man in the World*), 1969, Twentieth Century-Fox/APJAC. *d* J. Lee Thompson, *p* Mort Abrahams, *s* Ben Maddow, *n* Jay Richard Kennedy, *ph* Ted Moore, *c* Gregory Peck, Anne Heywood, Arthur Hill, Conrad Yama, Francisca Tu, Keye Luke.

Marooned, 1969, Columbia/Frankovich-Sturges. *d* John Sturges, *p* Frank Capra Jr., *s* Mayo Simon, *n* Martin Caidin, *ph* Daniel Fapp, *c* Gregory Peck, Richard Crenna, David Janssen, James Franciscus, Gene Hackman, Lee Grant.

I Walk the Line, 1969, Columbia/Frankenheimer/Lewis/Halcyon/Atticus. *d* John Frankenheimer, *p* Harold D. Cohen, *s* Alvin

Sargent, *n An Exile* by Madison Jones, *ph* David M. Walsh, *c* Gregory Peck, Tuesday Weld, Estelle Parsons, Ralph Meeker, Lonny Chapman.

Billy Two Hats, 1973, UA/ Algonquin. *d* Ted Kotcheff, *p* Norman Jewison, Patrick Palmer, Mitchell Lifton, *s* Alan Sharp, *ph* Brian West, *c* Gregory Peck, Desi Arnez Jr., Jack Warden, Sian Barbara Allen, David Huddleston.

The Omen, 1976, Twentieth Century-Fox. *d* Richard Donner, *p* Harvey Bernhard, *s* David Seltzer, *ph* Gil Taylor, *c* Gregory Peck, Lee Remick, David Warner, Billie Whitelaw, Leo McKern, Patrick Troughton.

MacArthur, 1977, Universal/Richard D. Zanuck. David Brown, *d* Joseph Sargent, *s* Hal Barwood, Matthew Robbins, *ph* Mario Tosi, *c* Gregory Peck, Dan O'Herlihy, Ed Flanders, Ward Costello, Marj Dusay, Ivan Bonar.

The Boys From Brazil, 1979, ITC/Producer Circle. *d* Franklin Schaffner, *p* Martin Richards, Stanley O'Toole, *s* Heywood Gould, *n* Ira Levin, *ph* Henri Decae, *c* Gregory Peck, Laurence Olivier, James Mason, Lilli Palmer, Uta Hagan, Steven Buttenberg, Denholm Elliott, Rosemary Harris.

The Sea Wolves, 1980, Richmond-Lorimar-Varius. *d* Andrew V. McLaglen, *p* Euan Lloyd, *s* Reginald Rose, *n Boarding Party* by James Leasor, *ph* Tony Imi, *c* Gregory Peck, Roger Moore, David Niven, Trevor Howard, Barbara Kellerman, Patrick MacNee.

Amazing Grace and Chuck, 1987, Tri-Star/Rastar. *d* Mike Newell, *p* and *s* David Field, *ph* Robert Elswit, *c* Jamie Lee Curtis, Alex English, Gregory Peck, William L. Peterson, Joshua Zuehike.

Old Gringo, 1989, Columbia Tri-Star. *d* Luis Puenzo, *p* Lois Bonfiglio, Jane Fonda, *s* Aida Bortnik, Luis Puenzo, *ph* Felix Monti, *c* Jane Fonda, Gregory Peck, Jimmy Smits, Patricia Conteras, Jenny Gago, Gabriela Roel, Sergio Calderon.

Other People's Money, 1991, Warner Brothers/Yorktown. *d*

Norman Jewison, *p* Norman Jewison, Ric Kidney, *s* Alvin Sargent, *play* Jerry Sterner, *c* Danny De Vito, Gregory Peck, Penelope Ann Miller, Piper Laurie, Dean Jones.

Cape Fear, 1991, Universal/Amblin/Cappa. *d* Martin Scorsese, *p* Barbara de Fina, *s* Wesley Strick, *n* *The Executioners* by John D. MacDonald, *ph* Freddie Francis, *c* Robert De Niro, Nick Nolte, Jessica Lange, Joe Don Baker, Juliette Lewis, Gregory Peck, Robert Mitchum.

Bibliography and Sources

As well as interviews with Gregory Peck, I have also drawn from those I've conducted with David Niven, J. Lee Thompson, Ava Gardner, Anthony Quinn, Joan Collins, Lee Van Cleef, Carl Foreman, Anthony Quayle, Carroll Baker, Jean Simmons, Charlton Heston, Joseph Cotten, Ingrid Bergman, Harvey Bernhard, Richard Donner, David Brown, John Huston, Deborah Kerr, Louis Jourdan, John Frankenheimer, Roger Moore, Andrew McLaglen, John Sturges, Audrey Hepburn, Diane Baker, Walter Matthau and George Peppard.

BOOKS

Anderson, Christopher, *Citizen Jane*, Virgin Books, 1993.

Bergman, Ingrid, with Alan Burgess, *My Story*, Michael Joseph Ltd, 1980.

Davidson, Bill, *Jane Fonda*, Sidgwick & Jackson, 1990.

Douglas, Kirk, *The Ragman's Son*, Simon & Schuster Ltd, 1988.

Eels, George, *Robert Mitchum*, Robson Books, 1984.

Freedland, Michael, *Gregory Peck*, W.H. Allen, 1980.

Gardner, Ava, *My Story*, Transworld Publishers, 1990.

Geist, Kenneth, L., *Pictures Will Talk*, Frederick Muller Ltd, 1978.

Griggs, John, *The Films of Gregory Peck*, LSP Books, 1980.

Holden, Anthony, *The Oscars*, Little, Brown and Company, 1993.

Madsen, Axel, *William Wyler*, W.H. Allen, 1974.

Morley, Sheridan, *The Other Side of the Moon*, Weidenfeld & Nicolson, 1985.

Niven, David, *The Moon's a Balloon*, Hamish Hamilton Ltd, 1971.

Nolan, William F., *John Huston: King Rebel*, Sherbourne Press, 1965.

Quirk, Lawrence, J., *The Passionate Life of Bette Davis*, Robson Books (UK), William Morrow & Co. Inc (US), 1990.

Spoto, Donald, *The Dark Side of Genius: The Life of Alfred Hitchcock*, Plexus Publishing Ltd, 1994.

Thomson, David, *Showman: The Life of David O. Selznick*, Andre Deutsch Ltd (UK), Alfred A. Knopf, Inc (US), 1993.

Woodward, Ian, *Audrey Hepburn*, Virgin Publishing Ltd, 1993.

Index